Politeness in the History of English

The concept of politeness permeates all aspects of modern life and society. However, to what extent has this phenomenon changed over time? This book traces the elusive concept of politeness from its beginnings in the Middle Ages up to the present day. Detailed case studies of mostly literary texts provide insights into historically specific ways of being polite, from discernment politeness in Old English to recent examples, such as non-imposition politeness. Readers will gain a better understanding of both the folk notion of politeness and specific scholarly definitions, and how these can be applied to historical data. The long diachrony provides a novel perspective both on the concept of politeness and on the history of the English language in its social context, making this essential reading for politeness specialists, cultural historians and historical linguists alike. Politeness emerges as a multifaceted phenomenon that is both culture-specific and history-specific.

ANDREAS H. JUCKER is Professor of English Linguistics, University of Zurich.

Politeness in the History of English

From the Middle Ages to the Present Day

Andreas H. Jucker

University of Zurich

CAMBRIDGE
UNIVERSITY PRESS

University Printing House, Cambridge CB2 8BS, United Kingdom

One Liberty Plaza, 20th Floor, New York, NY 10006, USA

477 Williamstown Road, Port Melbourne, VIC 3207, Australia

314–321, 3rd Floor, Plot 3, Splendor Forum, Jasola District Centre, New Delhi – 110025, India

79 Anson Road, #06–04/06, Singapore 079906

Cambridge University Press is part of the University of Cambridge.

It furthers the University's mission by disseminating knowledge in the pursuit of education, learning, and research at the highest international levels of excellence.

www.cambridge.org
Information on this title: www.cambridge.org/9781108499620
DOI: 10.1017/9781108589147

First published 2020

Printed in the United Kingdom by TJ International Ltd, Padstow Cornwall

A catalogue record for this publication is available from the British Library.

ISBN 978-1-108-49962-0 Hardback

Cambridge University Press has no responsibility for the persistence or accuracy of URLs for external or third-party internet websites referred to in this publication and does not guarantee that any content on such websites is, or will remain, accurate or appropriate.

Contents

Figures

Tables

Preface

This book makes a bold attempt to trace the elusive concept of politeness in the history of the English language from the Middle Ages to the present day. Needless to say, this volume is only one of many different possible histories of politeness in the English language. It could be visualised as a photo album with many different pictures of an extended road trip. It contains pictures taken along the way, both close-ups of interesting details and long-shot panoramas of entire sceneries. The close-ups may be more or less typical for the place at which they were taken but they do not reveal the full picture, while the long shots provide a more comprehensive picture of the scenery but do not provide the details. The album includes pictures taken at popular points where many other people travelling along the same road have stopped before to take a picture, but it also includes pictures that are more personal at locations that have so far not been detected by many. On several occasions, it includes pictures that others have taken, possibly with older cameras (i.e. older theoretical frameworks). They can reveal interesting details even if they are in monochrome rather than the full range of colours. On some stretches of the journey, the album follows a leisurely pace with many pictures. At other places it just cruises on for long stretches with only cursory glances at the changing scenery. Many others have travelled along some parts of this road before me and have published their travel impressions, and indeed my own account is indebted to many of them. But so far, I believe, nobody has published an account of the entire journey from the earliest beginnings of the English language up to the present day.

My own excursions into the history of politeness started almost fifteen years ago when I became interested in the use of the address terms *ye* and *thou* in Middle English and later in Early Modern English. My interest expanded to other aspects of politeness and to other periods in the history of English until it became feasible to try to fill in some of the remaining gaps and to combine the earlier studies with more recent work in order to sketch out a long diachrony of politeness.

This book integrates extracts of previously published work. All the chapters that contain earlier work specify its origins. In two cases, the previously published work was co-authored and I am very grateful to my co-authors, Larssyn Staley (Chapter 2) and Irma Taavitsainen (Chapter 4 and Chapter 7), for granting me permission to reuse some of that work in this context. I also thank all the editors and publishers of my previously published work to allow me to reuse extracts from those publications.

The cover illustration of this book depicts a scene from the eighteenth century. The original is a hand-coloured mezzotint entitled 'The polite maccaroni presenting a nosegay to Miss Blossom' and was published in 1772 in London. It was meant as a satire on a dandy who imitated continental fashions. As such, it illustrates the concerns of this book in multiple ways. The eighteenth century was the time when politeness became an ideology (see Chapters 7 and 8) and an issue of social class, here vividly represented in the difference between the flamboyant dress of the upper-class couple and the plain dress of the street vendor. While aristocratic polite society claimed 'politeness' as their preserve that distinguished them from the lesser classes, the rising middle class insisted on moral behaviour that was superior to the hollow surface of etiquette and politeness. Thus, the image represents politeness in a particularly important historical and social context together with its ambivalent character between desirable behaviour and butt of satire.

Over the years, many people have helped me to shape my thinking about politeness in the history of English, and I wish to thank all of them from the bottom of my heart, even if they are too numerous to be mentioned individually here. Most of them can easily be found in the list of references at the end of this book. Two people, however, deserve a particular word of thanks: Magdalena Leitner and Mirjam Schmalz. They have read the entire manuscript in painstaking detail and have saved me from numerous blunders and infelicities. All remaining errors, needless to say, are my own.

1 Exploring Politeness in the History of English

1.1 Introduction[1]

The British have a reputation for being excessively polite. A caricature version of this is available as a picture postcard on which two pictures illustrate allegedly incorrect and correct polite behaviour in a British context (Ford and Legon 2003; see also Wierzbicka 2006: 31). In the picture illustrating the 'incorrect' behaviour, a man who is drowning shouts 'Help!' but gets no more than a haughty shrug and a turned shoulder from a passer-by and his dog. In the adjacent picture, illustrating the 'correct' behaviour, the drowning man politely exclaims, 'Excuse me, Sir. I'm terribly sorry to bother you, but I wonder if you would mind helping me a moment, as long as it's no trouble, of course.' In response, the passer-by immediately comes to the rescue with a life belt, and even his dog changes appearance, puts on a friendly face and wags its tail.

To the extent that we appreciate the humour of this cartoon, it appears that it contains at least a grain of truth. We recognise a type of behaviour that we stereotypically associate with present-day English in a British context. However, it is clear that the cartoon presents a version of British politeness that is both simplified and exaggerated. It reduces politeness to an excessive endeavour not to impose on a stranger in a public context even in an emergency. It is an elaborate apology for imposing on the passer-by and disturbing him in his walk with the dog. This has come to be known as negative politeness (Brown and Levinson 1987), and Stewart (2005: 128) comments that 'in certain circumstances at least, British English tends towards negative politeness and favours off-record strategies in carrying out certain face-threatening acts' (Stewart 2005: 128). But to what extent is this really typical of British English – is it something that goes back to earlier periods of English, or is it a type of politeness that has developed only recently?

According to the *Oxford English Dictionary*, the noun *politeness* with the meaning 'courtesy, good manners, behaviour that is respectful or considerate of others' is first attested in the English language in 1655 (*OED* 3rd ed.,

---

[1] Some passages of this chapter are taken from Jucker (2008, 2012a and 2016).

politeness, n. 3a). The adjective *polite* with the meaning 'refined, elegant, scholarly; exhibiting good or restrained taste' is somewhat older and goes back to about 1500 (OED 3rd ed., polite, adj. and n. 2a). It is a borrowing from Latin *polītus*, the past participle of *polīre* 'to smooth, to polish'. Are we, therefore, to assume that polite behaviour and politeness did not exist prior to this, or – if such behaviour did exist – that there was no need to talk about it? This is, of course, unlikely but a more precise answer depends very much on what we mean by 'polite behaviour' and 'politeness'. The OED definitions give a first indication of how the terms are being used in English, but we should not assume without further investigation that the behaviour described as polite in the sixteenth and seventeenth century is the same as the behaviour that we might want to describe with these terms in present-day English. And how exactly did an English person in the seventeenth century show his or her good manners? Was non-imposition as important then as the cartoon makes us believe it is today? Politeness is an elusive concept that defies any attempts at an easy and quick definition, and non-imposition politeness of the type presented in the above-mentioned caricature is, in fact, a very recent phenomenon, as I will show in Chapter 9.

But, the term 'politeness' is not only an everyday word of the English language with more or less closely related terms in other languages, such as *Höflichkeit* in German, *politesse* in French, *beleefdheid* in Dutch and so on; it is also an established technical term in scholarly work in linguistics and in particular in pragmatics. As with other terms, this dual existence is not unproblematic. Basically, technical terms are nothing more than conventional expressions for abstract concepts; they are arbitrary labels that abbreviate lengthy descriptions of specific objects of investigation. The object of investigation may not always be very clearly delimited, and different researchers may not always agree about the use of specific terms, but the problems are exacerbated if the same term also has a life as an everyday expression. Everyday expressions are by their very nature fuzzy and subject to multiple variations, such as historical, dialectal, social and even personal differences. Such terms, therefore, usually have a much wider application than technical terms, and uncertainty often arises if the two are allowed to be confused, which is the case if a technical definition is refused simply on the grounds that the term means 'something else' in everyday language. It is, of course, unhelpful if a technical term is used to refer to something entirely different from that which the everyday meaning of the expression suggests. However, a technical term is not an everyday expression, and therefore it has a more specific denotation. Thus, it has become standard practice in politeness research to distinguish clearly between the technical term 'politeness' and the everyday notion 'politeness' (see Section 1.2).

The opposite of politeness is impoliteness or rudeness, and together these notions have received a lot of attention from researchers in pragmatics. More recent research regularly focuses on the whole spectrum from politeness to impoliteness including a wide spectrum of behaviour between these two poles. This more comprehensive field of study is often referred to as 'interpersonal pragmatics' (see, for instance, Locher and Graham 2010) or as '(im)politeness research' (see, for instance, Culpeper, Haugh and Kádár 2017). However, in this book I would like to focus more on the polite end of the spectrum in order to make the task somewhat more manageable. And even the focus on politeness will not allow a comprehensive account of its development across the entire history of the English language but only one that highlights some particularly noteworthy moments.

A truly comprehensive history of politeness in English does not yet appear to be possible. There are many excellent general histories of the English language, such as, for instance, the six-volume *Cambridge History of the English Language*[2] or the volumes by Baugh and Cable (2002), Mugglestone (2006), van Kemenade and Los (2006) or van Gelderen (2014), but they all focus on the language system, the phonology, morphology and syntax of the English language and its vocabulary. Issues of actual language use (i.e. the pragmatic level) are hardly mentioned at all, and even less is said about the level of politeness and impoliteness. The field of historical pragmatics is still relatively young, and despite a growing body of work on general questions and on specific problems in the history of individual languages, there are no large-scale overviews of the development of the pragmatic level of individual languages, and the following pages can offer no more than a first step in this direction by highlighting a range of selected aspects.

1.2   Epistemological Status of Politeness

First of all, it is necessary to distinguish more systematically between politeness as an everyday word and politeness as a technical term. It has become standard to call the everyday notion of the term *politeness* 'first-order politeness' or 'politeness$_1$', and the technical term 'second-order politeness' or 'politeness$_2$', and the same distinction applies to the term *impoliteness* (see in particular Watts 2003: 4; but also Watts et al. 1992: 3; Kasper 2003). Watts has the following to say about the two terms:

A theory of politeness$_2$ should concern itself with the discursive struggle over politeness$_1$, i.e. over the ways in which (im)polite behaviour is evaluated and commented on by lay members and not with ways in which social scientists lift the term

---

[2] Hogg (1992); Blake (1992); Lass (1999); Romaine (1998); Burchfield (1994); Algeo (2001).

'(im)politeness' out of the realm of everyday discourse and elevate it to the status of a theoretical concept in what is frequently called Politeness Theory. (2003: 9)

Kasper (2003: 2) also states that 'first order politeness phenomena constitute the empirical input to politeness theories'. Thus, the object of study is, in effect, according to Watts or Kasper, the term *politeness*, or its equivalent in other languages, and how it is used by native speakers of each language. What are the phenomena that are described by this term, and how are they evaluated?

Examples (1) to (3) are three extracts from the *British National Corpus*, in which the term *polite* is used:

(1)   He laughed loudly at things that weren't funny and littered his English with expletives to appear more at home in the language. The chief, smug, supercilious and opinionated, was undaunted by our indifference. The English, he said, were a strange people. They liked to pretend that they were fair-minded and *polite*, but he himself had found that they were not *polite*. (BYU-BNC FEM 1531)

(2)   His voice was sharp, yet as intimate as if he had known her for a long time. There was to be no paddling around in the shallow waters for this man, Ruth thought. And with the thought came a tiny prick of fear. 'I'm not being coy,' she protested. 'I was trying to be *polite*. I'm not very good at *polite* conversation.' (BYU-BNC CB5)

(3)   Marion: Tea or coffee?
       Lucy: Whatever you're making.
       Cathi: Whatever you want.
       Lucy: Tea please. I don't drink coffee, I was just being *polite*. (BYU-BNC KPN)

In extract (1), a speaker comments on 'the English', who, according to him, consider themselves fair-minded and polite but, in his opinion, are not. Thus, the epithet politeness is indiscriminately applied, or not applied, to an entire nation but the extract does not give enough information on why the speaker finds the English to be lacking in politeness. In extract (2), the speaker admits to not being good at 'polite conversation'. Her attempt at being polite in conversation, she fears, may have come across as 'coy'. And in (3), Lucy describes her reluctance to specify her preference as being polite. Apparently, she did not want to put Marion to the trouble of preparing tea just for her, but when the offer is made again, she states her preference with what looks like an apology for not having been more specific in the first place.

A careful analysis of the terms *polite* and *politeness* in such contexts give us an ethnographic view of how speakers of English talk about politeness. It tells us much about the semantics of the words *polite* and *politeness* and thus about speakers' perception of what it means to be polite; or, in Kasper's terms, 'the semantics of the lexical entry "politeness" thus sheds light on social members' perception and classification of politeness' (2003: 2). In a historical context, such analyses of the relevant politeness vocabulary are particularly important. We do not have direct access to native speaker intuitions, and we cannot use experimental methods (see Chapter 2).

Politeness$_2$, on the other hand, is related to politeness research. Brown and Levinson's (1987) classical view of politeness may serve as an example. They define politeness as a redress to a face threat. Politeness is used strategically to achieve specific interactional goals. Speakers behave in a rational and purposeful way, and because the face of both interlocutors is constantly at risk in the interaction, both of them engage in face work in order to maintain each other's face. Speakers cannot enhance their own face directly because it is what others see in the speaker. Therefore, it is generally in each speaker's interest to maintain the face of their interlocutors in order to enhance their own face in others' eyes.

The notion of face comes in two different kinds (Brown and Levinson 1987: 61). Positive face relates to the wish of every person to be liked and appreciated by other people, while negative face relates to the wish of every person to be free in their own actions and to maintain their own territory. Face threats are seen as being threats to either one or the other of these two kinds of face, and face work, too, is seen as relating to one or the other. Positive politeness strategies, therefore, show the speaker's approval of the addressee, while negative politeness strategies give the addressee the option of self-determination, at least nominally if not in reality.

Brown and Levinson (1987: 13) have proposed a distinction between positive and negative face as universals, but this claim can easily be misunderstood as an ethnocentric projection. However, Brown and Levinson clearly envisage a great deal of cultural variation. In particular, they envisage much cultural variation in what constitutes a face threat and in the members of a society who have special roles in enhancing, maintaining or threatening the face of others. In addition, the balance between positive and negative face is also very likely to be culture-specific.

The cartoon mentioned at the beginning of this chapter highlights negative politeness. It is the type of politeness that signals non-imposition, and – at least on the surface – gives the addressee as many opportunities as possible to comply with the request or not. According to Watts, politeness theory should not concern itself with such second-order notions of politeness because they are artificially created and do not always coincide with the everyday notion of politeness. However, technical terms have the advantage over present-day concepts that they can be given more precise definitions and thus serve as useful labels for clearly delimited sets of phenomena.

Terkourafi (2011) argues that the distinction between politeness$_1$ and politeness$_2$ cannot be maintained because the two ultimately depend on each other. However, she appears to be using the terms in a slightly different sense. She uses the term politeness$_1$ for the rules found in the prescriptive norms stipulated, for instance, in courtesy manuals. Such rules perform an important gatekeeping and social regulatory role for the preservation of social order. They typically emanate from the higher social classes, who use them to keep the lower social classes at a safe distance. Such a definition of first-order politeness is more specific than the general understanding, according to which first-order politeness applies more broadly to the everyday notion of the term *politeness*. Second-order politeness, according to Terkourafi, consists of the descriptive and, therefore, theoretical accounts of how politeness is actually used. On this basis, she argues that the prescriptive norms in the politeness manuals (i.e. first-order politeness) generally follow and reflect the descriptive norms (i.e. second-order politeness) because the ruling classes stipulate their understanding of appropriate behaviour as rules for future behaviour. Thus, 'prescriptive norms historically follow and reflect descriptive ones, while at the same time constraining future practices and so feeding back into the descriptive norms that gave rise to them in the first place' (Terkourafi 2011: 176). However, the study of first-order politeness on the basis of how the term *politeness* and other politeness-related vocabulary items are used in everyday discourse is not as clearly related to prescriptive norms as the study of courtesy books or politeness manuals. Second-order politeness, as described by Watts and others, generally has a descriptive basis but it is criticised because it does not cover the same range of phenomena as first-order politeness.

Eelen (2001: 32) distinguishes a third level of description, which he calls 'politeness-in-action'. In fact, he splits politeness$_1$ into an action-related side and a conceptual side. The action-related side is concerned with actually behaving in a particular way in interaction. The conceptual side, on the other hand, refers to 'the commonsense ideologies of politeness: to the way politeness is used as a concept, to opinions about what politeness is all about' (Eelen 2001: 32). He concedes that Watts et al. (1992) were concerned with the conceptual side of the everyday notion of politeness. Intuitively it is clear what Eelen has in mind. He makes a distinction between the thing itself and people's perception of the thing. However, we do not even have to invoke the philosophical question of whether things have a reality outside of their perception by humans. Even if politeness-in-action exists without being perceived, it does not have any useful status for the scholar. Scholars can either observe how people talk about behaviour for which they choose to use terms like *polite, impolite, rude, civil* and so on (politeness$_1$ studies), or they may study a range of phenomena for which they introduce a technical term (such as 'politeness', i.e. politeness$_2$). But they cannot study behaviour of a particular kind unless they specify what particular kind of behaviour they want to study.

Watts summarises the criticism levelled against Brown and Levinson's (1987) politeness theory as follows:

Between 1978 and 1987 and immediately after the reprint in 1987 opposition was raised against Brown and Levinson's conceptualisation of politeness as the realisation of face threat mitigation. Their approach did not seem to account for ways in which politeness had been understood in the English-speaking world prior to the late twentieth century, nor did it seem to account for ways in which related lexemes in other languages were used to refer to equivalent aspects of social behaviour. (Watts 2005: xi)

Thus, Brown and Levinson are criticised for delineating and defining a concept for the purpose of their research because it does not conform to the everyday notion with the same name. They chose to focus on one specific aspect and, therefore, ignore others.

However, it is often useful for scholars to define their objects of investigation as precisely as possible and to give them names in order to talk about them. Even if these names look like normal words of a particular language, however, they are only technical terms with a more or less well-defined denotation while words in everyday language generally have fuzzy denotational boundaries.

Watts (2005: xiii) describes politeness as 'a slippery, ultimately indefinable quality of interaction which is subject to change through time and across cultural space. There is, in other words, no stable referent indexed by the lexeme *polite*'. This is indeed true for politeness$_1$, which makes it a fascinating task to trace exactly these historical and cultural changes and differences. How is the term used in everyday language in the course of time and across different social groups? But the slippery quality of the everyday notion does not mean that scholars cannot provide a more or less precise definition of what kind of concept they are investigating on a particular occasion. If they use the term 'politeness' for this concept, it will probably be related in some way to the everyday notion, but it is inappropriate to expect the technical term to have the same denotational boundaries as the fuzzy everyday term. In their introduction to the volume *Politeness in Language*, Watts et al. state that one of the main aims of the papers collected in this volume is to 'question more profoundly what polite linguistic behaviour actually is' (1992: 2; see also Watts 2005: xv). This is a fundamentally essentialist way of proceeding. It starts with a term and tries to find the 'real' or 'true' concept for it. But scholarly work has to move in the other direction. It must describe interesting phenomena or concepts and then provide a label for them. The act of labelling itself is fairly trivial. It is not empirically interesting. Its one and only purpose is to make it easier to refer to the concept that has been described.

Once this has been accepted, it does not make sense to blame researchers for using different terminologies or for not agreeing on 'what politeness actually *is*' (Watts 2005: xv). Every researcher is free to focus on objects of his or her choice and to use any label that seems convenient for the purpose. Obviously, such disagreements make it more difficult to compare different approaches. But the comparison has to use the underlying concepts that the different researchers have set out to describe and not the arbitrary labels that they have chosen to use for their purpose (see Janicki 1989, 1990). Watts acknowledges that it is impossible to delimit politeness$_1$ with any kind of precision but he nevertheless maintains that it is politeness$_1$ which should be the 'rockbed of a postmodernist approach to the study of linguistic politeness' (2005: xxi).

   The distinction between politeness$_1$ and politeness$_2$ is related to the distinction between emic and etic approaches to politeness (Spencer-Oatey and Franklin 2009: 16). Sometimes the two sets of terms are even used more or less synonymously. The terms emic and etic originate with Pike (1954) and are derived from phonetics and phonemics, where phonetics studies the properties of sound production, transmission and reception, while phonemics studies the inventories and regularities of the specific sounds that are used by speakers of a particular language. In the words of Triandis: 'Emics, roughly speaking, are ideas, behaviours, items, and concepts that are culture-specific. Etics, roughly speaking, are ideas, behaviours, items, and concepts that are culture general – i.e. universal' (1994: 67–8; quoted after Spencer-Oatey and Franklin 2009: 16). Spencer-Oatey and Franklin (2009: 16) stress that these approaches are not contradictory but rather complementary. In order to describe the particular sounds of a language and their relation to each other, we need the terminology provided by the study of articulation in general. In order to describe the sounds of English (phonemics), it is necessary to use terms relating to place of articulation and so on (phonetics). Figure 1.1 plots the relationship of the distinction between emic and etic approaches and the distinction between first- and second-order concepts.

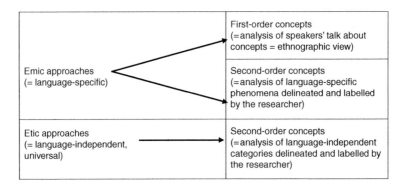

Figure 1.1 Relationship between emic/etic and first-order/second-order distinction

An etic approach is always language-independent and, therefore, relies on second-order concepts that have been delimited by the researchers. Emic approaches, on the other hand, can either use second-order concepts if they focus on language-specific phenomena that have been delineated and labelled by the researcher, or they can use first-order concepts if they focus on the everyday terms that are being used by specific language users. Such an approach can be called 'ethnographic' because it analyses the actual interactions in specific cultures or societies or it can be called 'metapragmatic' because it analyses how speakers talk on a metalevel about their use of language (see Blum-Kulka 1992).

A historical study of politeness must necessarily adopt an emic approach. The object of investigation is politeness in a particular culture and across a particular period of time. But this still leaves open the possibility of studying (im)politeness$_1$ or (im)politeness$_2$. In the former case, the scholar sets out to study politeness-related terms, such as *politeness, courtesy, tact* and *civility*, or terms such as *impoliteness, rudeness* and *incivility* (with all their diachronic spelling variants). In the latter case, the scholar defines a particular aspect of verbal behaviour or a particular communicative task (e.g. in the areas of face mitigation, maintenance and enhancement), and tries to locate linguistic patterns and expressions that are being used to carry out this task.

In this book, I will use both approaches. In the following chapters, I will regularly rely on an analysis of the available politeness vocabulary for a given time period, and I will consider the discourse on politeness in different time periods. Such discourses can be found both in fictional texts in which an author presents characters that comment on appropriate behaviour or in conduct literature, in which the author provides advice to readers on how they should behave and talk in certain situations. But I will also apply some of the standard second-order conceptualisations of politeness to selected data from periods throughout the history of English in order to find out whether these specific forms (e.g. non-imposition politeness) existed at specific points in the history of English or to find out when in the history of English they started to develop. Our knowledge of the different politeness cultures in the history of English is still patchy, and it seems advisable to combine different perspectives in order to gain a broader understanding of the development of politeness over the course of time.

1.3 Three Waves of Politeness Research

Politeness research has undergone considerable changes since the publication of the pioneering study by Brown and Levinson in 1978 and its republication in 1987. Grainger (2011) and Culpeper (2011b) describe the development of politeness research since then in terms of three waves (see also Culpeper and Hardaker 2017). The metaphor of the wave is a useful one because it is a reminder that there can be no clear-cut boundaries between the three sets of approaches, and in fact any characterisation that serves to distinguish the three waves is bound to exaggerate differences that in reality are subtler.

The first wave was initiated and shaped by publications such as Lakoff (1973), Leech (1983) and, most prominently, Brown and Levinson (1987). It is characterised by a reliance on a technical definition of what politeness is (i.e. it is a second-order or politeness$_2$ approach). In such approaches linguistic forms are mapped to specific politeness functions. Indirect requests, such as, 'Could you pass the salt, please?', for instance, are analysed as instances of negative politeness. The earliest approaches focused exclusively on polite behaviour. Impolite behaviour came to be analysed only later (e.g. Culpeper 1996) and was seen as the flip side of politeness. This type of approach very much focuses on the speakers and their attempt to strategically maintain their own and their addressee's face.

The second wave consisted mainly of a rejection of the first wave (see in particular Eelen 2001; Watts 2003; Locher and Watts 2005; and, for an overview, Mills 2011). The main point of criticism was generally that Brown and Levinson's model assigned specific politeness values to individual linguistic expressions. Instead, the critics argued that politeness values are not static, and specific linguistic expressions do not have fixed politeness values. Such values are always discursively negotiated, and the analytical focus shifts from the speaker to the interaction between the speaker and the addressee. Such approaches have come to be known as discursive or postmodern politeness approaches. Locher and Watts describe the task of the discursive politeness analyst as follows:

We consider it important to take native speaker assessments of politeness seriously and to make them the basis of a discursive, data-driven, bottom-up approach to politeness. The discursive dispute over such terms in instances of social practice should represent the locus of attention for politeness research. By discursive dispute we do not mean real instances of disagreement amongst members of a community of practice over the terms 'polite', 'impolite', etc. but rather the discursive structuring and reproduction of forms of behavior and their potential assessments . . . by individual participants. (Locher and Watts 2005: 16)

In literary contexts, too, passages can be found in which politeness issues are discussed explicitly, as for instance in Shakespeare's *King Henry VI, Part 3*, in which King Henry reflects on the semantic values of address terms (see Busse 2006: 210).

(4)   Richard: Good day, my lord. What, at your book so hard?
         King Henry: Ay, my good lord – my lord, I should say rather.
                      'Tis sin to flatter; 'good' was little better:
                      'Good Gloucester' and 'good devil' were alike,
                      And both preposterous; therefore not 'good lord.'
                      (3H6 5.6.1–5, King Henry VI, Part 3; quoted after Busse
                      2006: 210)

King Henry has been captured by Richard and his followers. In this exchange, which takes place in the tower, the king uses the conventional term of address, 'my good lord', but then corrects himself and leaves out the adjective *good* which, according to him, does not apply to Richard. Thus, King Henry negotiates the value of the address term between the conventional form and the residual semantic meanings of its constituent parts.

The third wave, finally, consists of a consolidation between the first and the second wave. It recognises that linguistic forms generally have default values, but these default values must always be contextually verified. Name-calling and swearing, for instance, are intrinsically impolite because such forms are conventionally associated with impolite contexts. In a paper that basically uses a first-wave approach, Culpeper (1996: 352) recounts an anecdote in which the term 'silly bugger' was used as a friendly reproach and calls this 'mock impoliteness', a term that in itself suggests a discrepancy between the intrinsic and conventional force of 'silly bugger' and its friendly and jocular use on this particular occasion. In later work, this discrepancy is taken more seriously. The analysis depends crucially both on the situationally negotiated value and its default, conventional value. Jucker (2012b), for instance, shows how the surface politeness of characters in Ben Jonson's play *Volpone, or The Fox* contrasts with the underlying motives of deception and intrigue (see Chapter 5). Culpeper and Hardaker propose the solution of 'conventionalised expressions or routinised formulae' (2017: 210). Specific expressions have empirically verifiable meanings that are either polite or impolite, but these meanings are not completely stable. In actual conversational contexts they are often challenged. Figure 1.2 gives an overview of the main features of the three waves.

It is difficult to find purist proponents of either the first wave or the second wave. First-wave researchers recognised that in particular contexts, individual linguistic elements could have politeness values that differed from the usual ones, and second-wave researchers generally accepted that not everything is discursively negotiated at all times. However, politeness theory has moved forward by concomitant shifts in perspective. It was important for the theoretical perspective, for instance, to move from a focus on the speakers and their politeness strategies to the discursive interaction between interactants, and it was equally important, in the third wave, to redress the

First Wave
- Mainly based on Brown and Levinson (1978, 1987)
- Clear focus either on politeness or – in slightly later work – on its flip side, impoliteness (Culpeper 1996)
- Based on strategies to mitigate face-threatening acts (FTAs)
- Focus on speaker strategies
- Relatively clear mapping of specific linguistic forms to specific politeness (or impoliteness) functions
- Politeness (or impoliteness) seen as technical terms, i.e. politeness$_2$ (or impoliteness$_2$)

Second Wave
- Based on a rejection of first-wave approaches (Eelen 2001; Locher and Watts 2005)
- Usually called discursive or postmodern approaches
- Focuses on a broad spectrum of social interaction between polite and impolite and the unmarked space between the two (politic behaviour) (Watts 2003)
- Based on the everyday use of terms such as *politeness* or *impoliteness*, i.e. politeness$_1$ and impoliteness$_1$
- Shift of focus to the addressee
- Based on the conviction that linguistic elements do not have inherent meanings; meanings are always negotiated between speaker and addressee
- Increase of publications on impoliteness (Bousfield 2008; Locher and Bousfield 2008; Culpeper 2011a)

Third Wave
- Relational, frame-based and interactional
- Encompass both speaker and addressee perspectives
- 'Pay attention to context yet accommodate more stable meanings arising from particular linguistic forms' (Culpeper and Hardaker 2017: 208)
- Based on formulae that tend to have specific politeness or impoliteness effects

Figure 1.2 Three waves of politeness research (loosely based on Culpeper and Hardaker 2017: 206–8)

balance somewhat and focus on the interaction between inherent im/politeness values and their discursive negotiations in specific contexts. Or, as Mills puts it,

Politeness can be seen as a set of enregistered forms, whose meaning is not completely fixed, but yet which have a certain degree of conventionalisation; politeness can thus be seen as a set of resources which individuals can draw on and modify in interaction. (2017: 2)

This book starts very clearly from a third-wave perspective. Linguistic expressions have conventional default values, but such values are often renegotiated in actual contexts. 'Polite' words are used to insult, 'impolite' words are used in friendly banter and so on and so forth. And in order to understand how speech communities interact politely or less politely, it is necessary to look both at conventionalised meanings and at the ways in which they are used in actual situations. In some of the case studies in this book, the focus will be more on the conventionalised meanings, as for instance in the considerations of the politeness vocabulary at a given point in the history of English. The terms that are used by a speech community to refer to polite behaviour give us an insight into priorities and value judgements. Which aspects of 'polite' behaviour in a broad sense were deemed sufficiently important to be lexicalised? Such questions allow for some generalisations across time periods even if it is clear that generalisations hide and ignore untypical uses of these terms, as for instance in the case of irony, sarcasm, friendly banter or other contextual re-evaluations. Other case studies will adopt a more discursive approach and study short extracts of interactions. With these case studies we get closer to the actual discourse of what is polite or impolite and how interactants use and discuss certain terms. But such microscopic pictures do not lend themselves easily to generalisations across time periods. The data for these discursive case studies are often taken from fictional sources. They do not provide direct evidence for non-fictional language use, but they are interesting in themselves. They show us how specific authors chose to represent such interactions at given points in the history of the English language.

1.4   Types of Politeness and Outline of the Book

This book sets out to discover and highlight different forms and manifestations of politeness in the history of the English language. It does not start from a preconceived idea of what exactly politeness is. On the contrary, it starts from an investigation of how people talked about politeness in a very broad sense. Thus, the starting point is a search for first-order conceptualisations of politeness in the form of lexical items within a broad semantic field of expressions of politeness or in the form of extracts from the available sources that provide evidence for the discursive negotiations of what exactly people considered to be adequate forms of interpersonal behaviour.

Such searches must necessarily be selective. They depend on the available material and my own limitations of familiarity with specific sources. Today, researchers have vast corpora of texts available for almost every period in the history of English, and corpora are useful tools for generalisations across substantial periods in the development of the language. But generalisations are always risky. They tend to rely unduly on inherent meanings of specific search terms because the frequency of occurrence of a particular term generally tells us little about its actual usage in specific contexts. Such limitations can to some extent be minimised through more complex search techniques, such as collocational searches. A specific term is not traced on its own but together with the terms in whose company it tends to occur, which gives us insights into the different shades of meaning of the original term. Moreover, searches can be combined with sample analyses of specific extracts in which researchers can apply their philological understanding of the text to a precise understanding of how a specific term is being used in a specific context. In the following chapters, I will combine both the wide-angle perspective of large corpora, with its inherent risk of overgeneralisation, and the close-up perspective of selected texts, with its risk of not being sufficiently representative or typical of the period in which it occurs.

These investigations of the changing conceptualisations of politeness must, of course, always be seen against the background of the changing cultural and socio-historical context. But first, Chapter 2 will give an outline of different research methods that are available for historical politeness research and an overview of the data problems that pertain to such investigations. Anglo-Saxon England will provide the starting point for our investigation in Chapter 3. It was a complex world of Germanic tribes, Scandinavian influences and early Christianisation. It was also a violent society with frequent wars and strict tribal organisation which was characterised by obedience and kin loyalty rather than by politeness in any modern sense. Terms such as *polite*, *courteous* or *civil* did not exist. Instead there were terms such as *þeáwfæstness* 'adherence to the rules of right conduct or method, discipline, obedience to rule', which are indicative of a what might be called 'discernment politeness'.[3] Christianisation contributed concepts such as *humilitas* and *caritas* (Kohnen 2008b). In Middle English, through the influence of French, a new concept of politeness manifested itself in the form of *curteisie* ('courtesy'). Chapter 3 presents detailed case studies of the concept of *curteisie* in Chaucer's *Canterbury Tales* and in the anonymous poem *Sir Gawain and the Green Knight*.

Chapter 4 is devoted to nominal and pronominal terms of address in Middle English. French was the source for the rise of the distinction between *ye* and *thou*. On the surface, it appears that the choice between *ye* and *thou* (and their

---

[3] *Anglo-Saxon Dictionary Online*: www.bosworthtoller.com/031592.

relevant case forms) is governed by considerations of deference and respect. However, the characters in Chaucer's *Canterbury Tales* or in *Sir Gawain and the Green Knight* use a retractable system that is highly responsive to the interactional status of the interactants. There are no default values for specific dyads of speakers. The interactants in a conversation have to decide on the appropriate pronoun on the fly. The decision is taken on the basis of the social status of the interactants, their relationship towards each other and – crucially – on the situational status, where the situational status depends on temporary considerations of power within the interaction. In a similar fashion, nominal terms of address are sensitive interpersonal devices that reflect the interactive behaviour between people and their social class distinctions. The chapter presents detailed case studies of the use of *ye* and *thou* in selected examples from the *Canterbury Tales* (the Wife of Bath's Tale, the Miller's Tale and the Friar's Tale) and in *Sir Gawain and the Green Knight*.

Chapter 5 is devoted to the Renaissance period and early modern England. In the fifteenth century, the Italian author Baldesar Castiglione published *Il Cortegiano*, a courtesy book dealing with questions of etiquette. It was soon translated into many languages, including English, and had a profound influence on English culture and English forms of politeness. Castiglione advocated a new kind of gentleman who should do all things with what he called *sprezzatura*, a kind of 'effortless mastery'. Examples can be found in Shakespeare's plays. The notion of *curteisie*, which characterised politeness in the Middle English period, was replaced by the notion of *civility* (see Bryson 1998).

Shakespeare's plays have also been analysed within the theoretical framework proposed by Brown and Levinson (1987), for instance by Brown and Gilman (1989) or Kopytko (1995), who trace forms of positive and negative politeness in a few selected plays by Shakespeare. These approaches are reviewed and critiqued in some detail, but the focus lies on an alternative approach: a third-wave discursive analysis of two plays by Ben Jonson, *Volpone, Or the Fox* and *Bartholomew Fair*, in which I show how the default politeness values of specific linguistic forms interact with the discursive contexts in which they occur. Name-calling and swearing, for instance, are generally impolite because of their long-standing and routine associations with impolite contexts, but in specific contexts (e.g. banter among good friends) they may come across as friendly. With increased use in such 'polite' contexts, swear words may ultimately lose their emotional charge and their inherent impoliteness.

Chapter 6 continues the investigation of terms of address in Early Modern English. The distinction between *ye* and *thou* still existed but its significance had already changed. The singular pronoun *thou* had acquired overtones of an insult in certain situations ('If thou thoust him some thrice, it won't be amiss', says one of Shakespeare's characters), and in fact within less than a century after Shakespeare, the distinction more or less disappeared and gave way to *you* as the only pronoun of address. The chapter reviews the extensive literature on terms of address in Shakespeare (both in their pronominal and nominal form), and provides a case study of terms of address in Shakespeare's *Romeo and Juliet*.

Two chapters are devoted to the eighteenth century, which has often been called the age of politeness. Politeness turned into an ideology in a society in which class distinctions increasingly became both more important and more permeable (Watts 1999). The higher social classes used politeness as a distinguishing criterion to keep the lower social classes at a distance, while the latter insisted on high moral standards rather than the hollow formalities of politeness. Chapter 7 focuses on two polite speech acts: compliments and thanks. They express the speaker's appreciation and gratitude towards the addressee and can, therefore, be described as polite inherently or by default, even if, on occasions, they may have entirely different values in ironic, sarcastic or otherwise marked uses. Their eighteenth-century functional profiles differ from their present-day counterparts. In particular, compliments have a much wider application including ceremonious compliments, compliments of introduction, compliments of greetings and even compliments of condolence. The investigation in this chapter is based on a combination of careful readings and corpus searches of selected handbooks, newspapers and novels.

Chapter 8 turns to some of the educational literature of the eighteenth century, in particular educational theatre and epistolary novels, in which issues of politeness and appropriate behaviour are discussed at great length. The eighteenth century saw a surge in new books that catered for the needs of the growing middle class to learn appropriate behaviour that might help to ascend further in the class hierarchy, such as dictionaries, grammar books, conduct manuals and even children's books. The case studies of this chapter are devoted to eighteenth-century drama in the form of plays by Richard Steele and George Lillo, which were explicitly intended to be educational (Jucker 2016), and to epistolary novels by Samuel Richardson and Fanny Burney.

Chapter 9 is devoted to the rise of non-imposition politeness in American English. Culpeper and Demmen (2011) maintain that non-imposition politeness, which has been claimed to be typical of politeness in Western cultures (see for instance Brown and Levinson 1987: 129–30), is relatively recent. Ability-oriented conventional indirect requests (*could you*, *can you*) are not attested before 1760, and there are very few before 1800. Culpeper and Demmen note an increase in the nineteenth century but the forms are still rare, and they surmise that a sharp rise must have occurred after 1900, and, therefore, later than the data they were investigating. However, a case study of a few selected non-imposition elements (*please, could you, can you* and *would you*) indicates that a sharp increase occurs only in the third quarter of the twentieth century (i.e. after 1950 and much later than previously assumed), and there is clear evidence that such forms of non-imposition politeness may already be receding.

The last chapter, finally, provides a summary and conclusion. It briefly reassesses the long diachrony of politeness as outlined in this book and explores the question as to when in the history of English politeness turned from being a characterisation of good character to a description of pleasing behaviour that may be used to disguise underlying motives of a less pleasing nature.

2   Research Methods and Data Problems

2.1   Introduction[1]

Since the beginnings of the study of politeness and – somewhat later – impoliteness, a wide range of approaches has been employed to provide new insights within this field of research. Back in the nineteen seventies, researchers still relied heavily on their native-speaker intuitions to theorise about issues of politeness (for instance, Lakoff 1973, 1975), but it did not take long for researchers to turn to more empirical modes of investigation (see Jucker and Staley 2017 for an overview). However, not all of these methods are equally suitable for tackling historical data. Experimental methods, such as questionnaires, discourse completion tasks and role plays, which all rely on native speaker participants, are out of the question. Diary studies, which involve the collection of relevant material in everyday situations, would equally require a time-travelling device. The politeness researcher interested in how people used language to be polite in the past must necessarily rely on material that records language use. For the very recent past, there are some audio recordings. The availability of such recordings is increasing steadily and offers exciting new research opportunities for the historical pragmaticist. Jucker and Landert (2015), for instance, investigate aspects of the turn-taking system in a popular BBC Radio 4 talk show programme for which audio recordings are available that go back to the 1950s, and Reber (2018) uses recordings of Prime Minister's Question time in the British House of Commons that go back to 1978 for her investigation of the use of quotations and reported speech in spoken interactions. But the time depth and the range of material that is available is, of course, severely limited. For a larger time depth and a wider range of material, the researcher is limited to written materials. However, even with written materials, a range of different methods offer themselves to the historical pragmaticist or – in particular – to the historical politeness researcher. They range from a focus on individual words and their meanings in specific

---

[1] This chapter integrates some passages from Jucker and Staley (2017) and from Jucker (2016). My thanks go to Larssyn Staley for graciously permitting me to reuse some of our co-authored material here.

contexts to the careful qualitative scrutiny of small sample texts, and from these small sample texts to large-scale quantitative investigations of huge corpora.

In this chapter, I am going to survey the most prominent and most useful methods of investigation that offer themselves to the politeness researcher interested in historical data. Which method is most suitable always depends on the specific research questions that are being asked and on the type of material that is available for any given period of time. In the following chapters, a range of different methods is going to be used to tackle individual questions about politeness in the history of English. A combination of methods is more likely to provide a broad and varied picture of politeness at various historical points than a reliance on one single method.

This chapter will also give a brief outline of the types of data that can be used for such analyses. The further back we go in the history of English, the more scarce these resources become in terms of both sheer quantity and the range of different types of writing. However, one type of data is particularly prominent throughout the entire period and it is also particularly useful for the investigation of patterns of polite and impolite language behaviour, and that is the various forms of fictional writing. It will be helpful, therefore, to justify in more detail the use of fictional language for the investigation of actual language use.

2.2   The Dimensions of Historical Politeness Research

The different methods of historical politeness research can be located on several different dimensions. First of all, it is useful to make a distinction between approaches that focus on the use of specific polite linguistic items and those that focus on elements that are used to talk about politeness. I will call this the 'use-mention distinction'[2] that distinguishes between various forms of polite interaction and the metadiscourse of politeness. The second dimension concerns the difference between quantitative studies that are generally based on corpus searches, on frequency measures and statistics, and qualitative studies that focus, usually, on small sets of data that can be searched and analysed manually. The difference between first-order politeness (or politeness$_1$) and second-order politeness (or politeness$_2$) (see Chapter 1) is interrelated with these dimensions but it is not co-extensive with either of them, as I will

---

[2] Sperber and Wilson (1981) use these terms, which derive from analytical philosophy, to talk about irony, which they analyse as a case of mention rather than use. A person who makes an ironic utterance, e.g. 'What a nice day', when it is actually pouring, does not use this utterance in the normal way, but quotes – or mentions – it to poke fun at someone who actually predicted a nice day or at a hypothetical person who might describe it as such. Here the terms are used in a slightly different way to distinguish between elements that are used to convey politeness and elements that are used to talk about politeness.

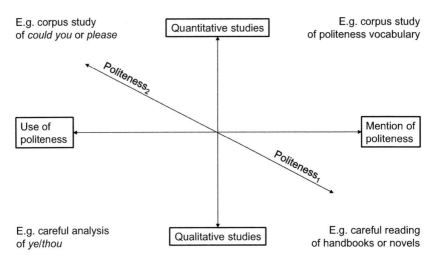

Figure 2.1 The dimensions of historical politeness research

describe in more detail below. Figure 2.1 gives an overview of these dimensions with relevant examples from the four corners of the field.

The following sections describe these dimensions in more detail and link them to the chapters to follow.

2.3   The Use of Politeness

Early studies of politeness regularly focused on specific linguistic elements which were claimed to be useful or even typical in polite interactions. This was the starting point for Lakoff (1973: 56), who claimed, for instance, that tag questions and compound requests convey politeness because of their non-imposing nature. Brown and Levinson (1987) focused in their classic study on the various linguistic strategies that mitigate face threats. They, too, identified indirect requests as somehow more polite than direct requests. In the meantime, these approaches have come under criticism because they imply that specific linguistic items are inherently polite or impolite (see Chapter 1). However, much research is still being carried out that focuses on specific elements and their potential, given the right context, to convey politeness. These can be small elements like *please* (Sato 2008; Murphy and De Felice 2018), speech acts such as complimenting and praising (Kampf and Danziger 2018) or apologising (Haugh and Chang 2019), or diagnostic elements for non-imposition, deference and solidarity politeness, such as *could you*, *Sir* and *mate* (Culpeper and Gillings 2018). Researchers are generally careful to point out that these elements are not invariably polite. In certain real-life contexts, their politeness values may be discursively negotiated or even completely reversed, as for instance in cases of irony or sarcasm.

Approaches to the use of politeness can be either mainly quantitative or mainly qualitative. Quantitative studies establish frequency figures of specific elements and on this basis provide statistical information on their distribution in the data under investigation, while qualitative studies provide more detailed analyses of richly contextualised instances of these elements. Quantitative studies rely more heavily on generalisations across contexts and on relatively invariant default politeness values of the elements under investigation. As a result, such studies depend on second-order definitions of politeness. Qualitative studies can pay more attention to the ambivalent and discursive nature of politeness elements. Their reliance on second-order definitions is, therefore, smaller.

In the context of historical politeness studies, it is probably fair to say that a majority of researchers focus on the use of politeness rather than on its mention. Brown and Gilman (1989) and Kopytko (1995), for instance, adopted the method proposed by Brown and Levinson (1987) for their investigation of plays by William Shakespeare. They, too, identified a broad range of linguistic strategies that are used to mitigate face threats and convey politeness. Brown and Gilman are careful to avoid quantification, but Kopytko provides elaborate statistics to assess the relative levels of positive and negative politeness in the different plays under analysis. This work will be reviewed in some detail in Chapter 5.

Lutzky and Demmen (2013) focus on *pray* and its role as a politeness marker in Early Modern English (see also Culpeper and Archer 2008). They adopt a quantitative approach and study its occurrence in the sociopragmatically annotated Drama Corpus which combines data from three Early Modern English corpora and contains material from 1500 to 1760. On this basis, they can provide statistical evidence for the diachronic development of the frequency of *pray* as well as its relative use by men and women and by different social classes.

From the thirteenth to the seventeenth century, English provided two different pronominal terms of address for a single addressee: *ye* and *thou* and their appropriate case forms. Like *pray*, they are small elements that affect the politeness level of the utterance in which they occur, and they have received a lot of attention from historical pragmaticists, from both quantitative and qualitative perspectives. Stein (2003), for instance, investigates the use of *ye* and *thou* in Shakespeare's *As You Like It* and *King Lear*. He is interested in the numerical patterns of *ye* and *thou* usage in different speaker dyads, and in the ways that the social hierarchy of the speakers, their relationship to each other and their gender influence these usages. Busse (2002a, 2003) developed a statistical measure to find correlations between the pronouns *ye* and *thou* and different types of nominal terms of address, such as titles of courtesy (e.g. *liege*, *lady*), terms of address indicating occupation (e.g. *lieutenant*, *parson*), terms of endearment (*love*, *chuck*) or terms of abuse (e.g. *knave*, *villain*). For each of these terms Busse looks at the pronominal terms of address that co-occur with them and establishes the specific ratio between *ye* and *thou* for this term. As a result, he can plot the *you*-fulness or *thou*-fulness, as he calls it, of each specific nominal term of address and of entire groups of such terms. It turns out that *liege* is one of the most *you*-ful ones. It almost invariably co-occurs with *you*. While *bully* is one of the most *thou*-ful terms, which almost invariably co-occurs with *thou* (Busse 2003: 204, 212). I have previously used a similar approach for a more detailed analysis of Shakespeare's *Romeo and Juliet* (Jucker 2012c; see also Chapter 6). Leitner (2013) uses a combined quantitative and qualitative approach to investigate *thou* and *you* in witness depositions of the late sixteenth and early seventeenth century in Late Middle Scottish and Early Modern Northern English. It turns out that in this data *thou* was still relatively frequent at a time when it was rapidly declining in depositions of a more southern origin. But it was only through a qualitative microanalysis that the details of pronoun usage, which depended not only on the rank of the depicted interactants but also on their emotions, could be discerned.

Other research on the *ye-thou* distinction in Middle and Early Modern English is more consistently qualitative. Hope (1994), for instance, looks at the deposition records of the ecclesiastical court of Durham and on the basis of a careful reading of relevant passages establishes how the usage of *thou* and *you* encode not only differentials of status but also emotional involvement, such as anger. Burnley (1983, 2003) also used a qualitative approach to establish the factors that influence pronominal choices in Chaucer's language. These factors include not only the relationship between the speaker and the addressee: their respective familiarity with each other, their age and their social status, but also the fictional genre in which the depicted interaction occurs – either courtly or non-courtly. In some of my earlier publications, I have also used a qualitative approach to develop a more dynamic system of pronoun choices in Chaucer's *Canterbury Tales* (2000a, 2006a, 2010 and 2011b; see also Chapter 4). On the basis of a careful reading and philological interpretations of selected tales, I argue that the choice depends not only on the factors highlighted by Burnley but also – and crucially – on the dynamics of the interaction. Characters often switch from *ye* to *thou* or vice versa because they gain or lose interactional power over a particular interactant, which affects the level of politeness or respect that they want to express with their choice of a particular pronoun of address.

A large range of speech acts has been investigated in historical contexts for their potential to express specific levels of politeness. Some are considered to be inherently face threatening and, therefore, in need of politeness work, in particular requests, which can be analysed as impositions on the addressee needing specific mitigating strategies. Kohnen (2011), for instance, has looked at the politeness levels of directive constructions in Old English. Busse (2002b) investigated the ways in which politeness strategies in requests changed in the history of English with a special focus on *pray* and *please* as courtesy markers. And Del Lungo Camiciotti (2008) analysed requests together with promises in commercial communication of the nineteenth century and highlighted the ambivalent nature of indirectness, which did not necessarily add to the politeness of specific requests. Culpeper and Demmen (2011), on the other hand, used a quantitative approach to trace selected conventional indirect requests, in particular ability-oriented requests involving *could you* and *can you*, in nineteenth-century English. In Chapter 9, I use a similar approach to trace elements of non-imposition politeness in American English throughout the nineteenth and twentieth century up to the present day. Other speech acts, at least in their default usages, can be seen to be polite in themselves, as for instance compliments. Taavitsainen and Jucker (2008; see also Chapter 7) looked at compliments in the eighteenth century by adopting a philological approach that is mainly based on reading relevant source texts and locating interesting specimens manually in the data or by using relevant lexical items for exploratory corpus searches.

There are also studies that focus on larger stretches of discourse and account for the emergent nature of politeness values by analysing the function of utterances in both their discourse and social context. Politeness values are seen as discursively constructed by the interactants in the given context. This constitutes a departure from research that analyses single utterances in isolation, in which politeness values have been seen as more or less inherent features of the linguistic form, towards a discursive approach that uses naturally occurring and contextualised discourse. Bargiela-Chiappini and Harris state that 'The preference for isolated speech acts should be replaced by (or at least be embedded in) the analysis of exchanges clearly located in the arena of social interaction (Meier 1995) where goals, interests, ends, motivations are played out' (2006: 17). In the context of present-day data, such approaches can be termed 'interactional'. They rely of transcriptions of spoken discourse. In the context of historical data, where researchers have to rely on written data, such approaches can be termed 'philological'.

Interactional research is often based on data sets, or what researchers sometimes refer to as small corpora, compiled by the researcher or research group. The spoken discourse compiled for such research is audio- or videorecorded and tends to be restricted to a specific genre, such as workplace discourse (cf. Holmes 1993), service encounters (cf. Placencia 2008; Kong 1998) or hospitality encounters (cf. Grainger et al. 2015). Placencia explains that delimiting the context to a specific genre 'allows communicative activities, such as requests, to be studied in the sequences in which they are embedded' (2008: 4). By collecting their own small corpora, researchers often gain access to more information about the interactants and the social context of the interaction than is generally available for larger corpora. The focus on naturally occurring goal-oriented discourse in preselected contexts allows researchers to see how specific types of interaction are negotiated and how they unfold. Having the surrounding social context – and, according to Placencia, the co-text – is essential 'for the interpretation of the rapport value of each utterance in relation to the preceding or following utterances' (2008: 4). Such an approach provides the researcher with the context necessary to base their analysis of politeness on how the discourse unfolds and is negotiated, including the interactants' reactions to a particular utterance.

Such approaches are particularly suitable for historical investigations. Important sources of written texts of the past are trial proceedings, witness depositions, letters and, in particular, fictional texts (see Kytö 2010). As Jucker and Kopaczyk (2017) have argued, fictional texts are written by and for specific people with a real communicative purpose. Moreover, both fictional and nonfictional texts may contain elements of the other. One must, as with all data, think critically about the type of data, the communicative context and the generalisations that can be made.

Fries (1999), for instance, provides a detailed analysis of Thomas Morley's *Introduction to Practicall Musicke*, published in 1597 and written in the form of a conversation between two pupils who wish to be instructed in the art of music making and a master, presumably the author himself. Fries focuses, in particular, on elements such as greetings, farewells, thanks and the use of *I pray you* and assesses their contribution to the overall politeness of the entire text.

In Leitner and Jucker (forthcoming), we used a discursive approach to analyse the politeness and impoliteness of the interaction in a sequence of letters in Middle Scots from the second half of the sixteenth century. The letters concern a dispute between the chief of a clan and one of his most trusted men about the latter's conflict with a different clan, and a discursive close reading of the letter sequence reveals how the correspondents carefully negotiated their own roles and positions in the clan networks in a balance between accusation, offence and good relationships. In Jucker (2012b and 2015; see also Chapter 5), I present a discursive reading of two plays by Ben Jonson: *Volpone, or The Fox*, first performed in London in 1606, and *Bartholomew Fair*, first performed in London in 1614. A careful analysis of selected extracts of *Volpone* reveals how the surface politeness of the language used by its upper-class Venetian characters stands in stark contrast to their underlying motives of intrigue and deception. In *Bartholomew Fair*, which provides a vivid picture of a London fair at the beginning of the seventeenth century with characters from a broad range of different social classes and backgrounds, the characters are much more open and engage in interactions that are often exceedingly impolite. In both plays, the discursive analysis not only dissects the use of politeness – and impoliteness – but also focuses on metadiscursive passages in which the characters talk about the politeness and appropriateness of each other's language. In this sense, the approaches in these case studies combine a qualitative analysis of both the use and the mention of politeness (see next section). In Jucker (2016; see also Chapter 8), this approach is extended to two plays from the eighteenth century: the sentimental comedy *The Conscious Lovers* by Richard Steele and the domestic tragedy *The London Merchant, or The Story of George Barnwell* by George Lillo, both first performed in London in the early eighteenth century. However, in these cases the analysis focuses not only on the interactions between the characters (i.e. the politeness on the intradiegetic level of the plays) but extends to the interaction of the playwright with theatre audiences (i.e. the extradiegetic level). The literary genres of these plays and, even more explicitly, their prefaces make it clear that it was an important aim for Steele and Lillo to both entertain and educate their audiences. They wanted not only their characters but also their plays to be polite.

2.4   The Mention of Politeness

Since the discursive turn and Watts's seminal 'Linguistic politeness and politic verbal behaviour: Reconsidering claims for universality' (1992), much research has advocated a first-order approach to politeness research (cf. Eelen 2001; Watts 2003; Locher and Watts 2005; see also Chapter 1). One such method is to investigate the way in which people comment on and discuss politeness, in other words the study of politeness metadiscourse. In its short history, research on politeness metadiscourse has relied on many sources of data: corpora (Culpeper 2009; Jucker et al. 2012; Jucker and Taavitsainen 2014), interviews (Spencer-Oatey 2011), online fora comments (Kleinke and Bös 2015), etiquette manuals (Young 2010; Terkourafi 2011) and other spoken data resources such as exploitative TV shows, tapped phone calls and documentaries (Culpeper 2010). The defining feature of research on politeness metadiscourse is its focus on speakers' discourse on discourse. For Kleinke and Bös, who investigate the metadiscourse of impoliteness, impoliteness metadiscourse utterances are 'those elements that provide an assessment regarding the appropriateness of participants' communicative behaviour and/ or feedback on the ongoing discussions' (2015: 58).

Similar research is found under the headings of 'impoliteness metadiscourse' (Culpeper 2010), 'metalanguage of politeness' (Culpeper 2009), 'metapragmatic (im)politeness comments' (Spencer-Oatey 2011), 'metacommunicative expressions' (Jucker and Taavitsainen 2014; Jucker et al. 2012) and 'metapragmatic comments/utterances' (Kleinke and Bös 2015). Despite the slight variations in terminology, all of this research takes a first-order perspective (at times in combination with a second-order perspective) and investigates language users' reference to the use of (im)polite language.

According to Busse and Hübler, metacommunicative expressions can 'range from full utterances (or even utterance sequences), with some lexeme(s) at their centre that denote(s) a communicative concept . . . to simply adverbials . . . or conjuncts' (2012: 3). In (im)politeness metadiscourse research, this has translated into the analysis of the use of terms synonymous for or related to (im)politeness as well as the analysis of the use of speech act verbs in a discursive rather than performative sense. Studies focusing on the use of semantically similar terms to comment on or question (im)politeness tend to start with a thesaurus or with terms discussed in previous research. Culpeper first compiled a list of terms, 'impolite, rude, opprobrious, scurrilous, aggressive, threatening, abusive, offensive, insulting, discourteous, ill-mannered' (2009: 64), obtained from various thesauri before investigating their use in the Oxford English Corpus (OEC), a two billion-word corpus of written English. His aim was to provide a 'contrast between what is happening in academia and what the "lay person" is doing' (Culpeper 2009: 71).

For historical investigations, vocabulary studies are particularly fruitful. Jucker et al. (2012), for instance, investigated how people talked about politeness in particular periods of the English language and what they considered polite and impolite. For this purpose, we begin with the relevant entries in the *Historical Thesaurus of the Oxford English Dictionary*. After investigating the semantic field of *courtesy* and *politeness,* we then proceeded to search for related terms in the Helsinki Corpus and investigated differences in the use of politeness metadiscourse in various periods, genres and prototypical text categories. Once texts with high frequencies of politeness metadiscourse were found, a closer reading was performed to see what could be gleaned from usage in specific texts about how politeness was perceived. In taking terms from thesauri as a starting point for larger corpus-based searches, scholars gain access to (im)politeness metadiscourse; however, with automated searches there is always the possibility that other terms – unknown to the researchers – have been used and therefore are not retrieved in the search. Nonetheless, this method provides valuable insights into how people comment on (im)politeness. Chapter 3 uses this method for a more focused analysis of the politeness vocabulary of the Old English period. It starts with relevant items from the *Thesaurus of Old English* and traces them in actual text passages in order to get a better understanding of the type of language and behaviour that they denoted. One item (*curteisie*, 'courtesy') is picked out for a more detailed study of how it was used in Middle English and in particular in the work of Geoffrey Chaucer (see Jucker 2010) and in the late fourteenth-century Middle English alliterative romance *Sir Gawain and the Green Knight* (see Jucker 2014). Chapter 5 singles out *sprezzatura*, meaning something like 'effortless mastery', as a key term in the metadiscourse of politeness and desirable behaviour. And Chapter 8 provides first a large-scale quantitative perspective of relevant politeness terms and how their relative frequency developed from the eighteenth century to the present day, before moving on to a more focused analysis of these vocabulary items in eighteenth-century epistolary novels. Thus, the analysis relies fundamentally on a combination of a large-scale quantitative with a microscale qualitative investigation of specific vocabulary items.

The above-mentioned studies on the metadiscourse of (im)politeness all start with terms related to or used to describe (im)politeness. Another approach is, however, to start with a speech act verb to search for and investigate how people comment on and evaluate said speech act. This approach is applied by Jucker and Taavitsainen (2014) in a diachronic investigation of compliments in American English using the Corpus of Historical American English (COHA) and the Corpus of Contemporary American English (COCA). We highlighted that speech act verbs can be used both performatively and discursively (see also Kohnen 2012) and that discursive uses (i.e. metapragmatic expression usage) often point back to the actual compliment (Jucker and Taavitsainen 2014: 261), which may or may not have used the performative verb. The distinction between performative and discursive uses is, however, not made in all metadiscursive studies. Kleinke and Bös, due to their combination of first-order and second-order approaches to politeness, do not make such a clear-cut distinction and posit that when combining politeness$_1$ and politeness$_2$ approaches it becomes clear that 'the majority of metapragmatic comments are rude themselves' (2015: 64).

First-order approaches to the vocabulary of politeness and impoliteness give researchers a different and insightful perspective on how participants in an interaction perceive relational aspects and politeness. These first-hand insights provide invaluable information to researchers embarking on cross-cultural politeness research and they are indispensable in any attempt to explore the concept of politeness in earlier periods. A focus on vocabulary items generally implies a focus on the conventionalised meanings of words irrespective of their actual usage in specific contexts in which these meanings can be used in ironic or other non-conventional ways. This is the reason why such studies are often combined with a closer reading of how these terms are used in specific contexts, which turns them into studies of the discourse of politeness.

2.5   Data Problems

As has been pointed out above, historical studies of politeness and impoliteness and historical pragmatics in general must necessarily rely on written data, with the exception of studies of the very recent past. This is a restriction that we must always bear in mind when we assess the available evidence for certain forms of politeness in the past. The evidence is seriously skewed and patchy. It provides insights into a very limited range of communicative practices: those that were carried out by means of written texts or were recorded and described in written texts. For the Old English period, the surviving evidence comes mainly from chronicles, charters, homilies and other religious texts. In the course of time the range of written genres diversified and multiplied. The evidence became richer, but in the context of all the spoken communication that was never recorded, the surviving evidence is still severely limited, and it is severely skewed the further back we go in history. Let us imagine that future linguists working in the year 2500 or so try to uncover the linguistic practices of English at the beginning of the twenty-first century. And let us assume that only written texts have come down to them but not actual speech recordings. Their evidence for language use would be very rich but it would not be comprehensive. It would cover a very broad range of genres from trivial everyday exchanges via today's social media and transcripts of television serials to newspapers and scholarly treatises. But it would not include any of our everyday casual or formal face-to-face encounters, despite the fact that for most of us, even for dedicated academics, the face-to-face spoken interactions constitute the majority, perhaps even the vast majority, of our daily language use. For earlier periods the skewing is much stronger. Literacy rates were low, and a large proportion of the population did not have access to and did not need written texts. Their linguistic practices might be reflected to some extent in a range of different texts, in factual or fictional accounts of everyday interactions in letters or in literary texts, for instance. But even if we make the best use of the different sources that we do have, the emerging picture will always be severely biased and incomplete.

In the early work in the field of historical pragmatics in the 1990s and 2000s, researchers regularly tried to justify their use of written data for pragmatic analyses by claims that drama texts or personal letters, for instance, are somehow particularly close to actual spoken language in an attempt to get as close as possible to what might be considered 'real' language use (see Culpeper and Kytö 2000; Jucker 2000b; Kytö 2010). In the meantime, attitudes have changed. We are no longer searching for patterns of 'real' language use but, somewhat more modestly, for patterns of language use in specific communicative contexts. This does not allow us to generalise our findings to 'language in general' but it opens up our perspective to all types of written texts as communicative events in their own right (see Jucker and Taavitsainen 2013: 25; Taavitsainen and Jucker 2015: 9).

Fictional language turns out to be particularly important in the search for different types of politeness in different historical periods. One reason for this is that it is readily available for more or less the entire history of the English language. The second, and perhaps even more important, reason is that fictional texts often describe everyday communicative interactions. They can be analysed on two different levels. On the extradiegetic level, they can be analysed as communicative acts between authors and their readers or, in the case of plays, between playwrights and theatre audiences. And on the intradiegetic level, they can be analysed as representations of (fictitious) interactions between (fictitious) characters, often with multiple levels of fictitious narrators and narratives and embedded stories (see Jucker and Locher 2017).

Sell (1985) illustrates these levels and the concepts of tellability and politeness with Geoffrey Chaucer's Miller's Tale, one of the tales in the *Canterbury Tales*. The (intradiegetic) I-narrator of the *Canterbury Tales* relates the story of pilgrim narrators who take part in a storytelling competition and tell a diverse range of stories. The miller tells a *fabliau* of a carpenter, his beautiful young wife Alison and their lodger Nicholas. In order to apply the notion of politeness, Sell (1985: 504) distinguishes between selectional politeness and presentational politeness. Selectional politeness concerns the avoidance of taboos and the observance of social and moral decorum. Presentational politeness concerns the strict observance of Grice's Cooperative Principle. But Sell is quick to point out that authors do not strive for absolute politeness, but rather for the right level of politeness: 'Too much selectional politeness makes for obsequiousness, too much presentational politeness is merely dull' (1985: 505).

In this respect, Chaucer's Miller's Tale takes huge risks on the extradiegetical level. There are severe infringements of social decorum on several levels. The story takes great relish in Alison and Nicholas's adulterous adventures, in Nicholas's blasphemous abuse of the story of Noah's flood and the scatological farce of the misplaced kiss. The miller does not hesitate to use sexually explicit vocabulary, such as *swyved* ('copulate with'), *ers* ('buttocks') and *queynte* ('pudendum'). 'The miller's story, then, is a deliberate challenge to socially accepted standards of decorum' (Sell 1985: 507), but literary conventions and in particular literary genres, such as *fabliaux*, allow or even encourage such challenges. And often such instances of selectional impoliteness may be hedged by the introduction of additional intradiegetical levels. The I-narrator of the *Canterbury Tales* protests that he must relate the stories exactly as they were told and thus shifts the blame to the level of the pilgrim narrator, the miller. Sell also points out several violations of presentational politeness in the form of seemingly incoherent or abrupt developments in the story line, which he analyses as violations of Grice's Cooperative Principle and as such as infringements of presentational politeness.

The majority of politeness work on literary sources does not investigate the politeness *of* the literary text itself, however, but focuses on the behaviour of the characters depicted *within* the literary sources. In Brown and Gilman's (1989) early adaptation of Brown and Levinson's (1978, 1987) politeness theory, the focus was very much on the politeness between different characters in Shakespeare's tragedies *Hamlet*, *King Lear*, *Macbeth* and *Othello*. They were particularly interested in Brown and Levinson's formula for assessing the weightiness of a face-threatening act, which consists of the three dimensions: power (P), distance (D) and the ranked extremity (R) of this particular face-threatening act in a given society. They search these plays for pairs of speeches that differ on only one of these three dimensions but are identical on the other two. Both speeches in each dyad are then evaluated as to the amount of politeness work that is carried out by the speaker to offset relevant face-threatening acts. Culpeper (1996), to give another example, adapts Brown and Levinson's (1987) approach to account for impoliteness strategies in literary texts. He develops impoliteness strategies and correlates them with plot development that often moves from a situation of equilibrium through a situation of disequilibrium back to a situation of equilibrium. Impoliteness may be an important aspect in moving the plot from one situation to the next, as he demonstrates on the basis of a central banquet scene of Shakespeare's *Macbeth* (act 3, scene 4). At the beginning of the scene, Culpeper (1996: 364) argues, Macbeth and Lady Macbeth go out of their way to be polite to the assembled Lords and thus re-establish and maintain a situation of equilibrium which is violently threatened by the appearance of the ghost. In this situation, Lady Macbeth uses impoliteness towards her husband to goad his manliness and push him into action. She asks him: 'Are you a man?' and thus flouts Grice's maxim of quality with the implicature that he lacks certain typical manly characteristics.

2.6   Conclusion

Historical politeness studies generate very specific challenges both in terms of methodology and data, and, in fact, the different methodologies outlined above require different sets of data to some extent. Lexical studies that give us an insight into the politeness vocabulary used at specific points in the history of English rely, on the one hand, on previous research in the form of historical dictionaries and historical thesauri, and, on the other, on large-scale electronic corpora that can be used to establish the frequency of particular lexical items and their collocational patterns. Most of these sources are now easily available online, for instance the *Oxford English Dictionary* and the *Historical Thesaurus of the Oxford English Dictionary*, which are indispensable for such investigations. And for the earlier periods of the history of English, the *Anglo-Saxon Dictionary Online*, the Dictionary of Old English Web Corpus and the *Thesaurus of Old English* have proven invaluable (for an overview of electronic dictionaries, see Kytö 2010: 45–6). Some twenty-five years ago, in the early days of historical pragmatics, only the Helsinki Corpus was available as an easily searchable electronic corpus covering the history of the English language. Today the situation has changed, and a multitude of corpora are available, such as the Corpus of Early Modern Dialogues 1560–1760, the Corpus of Late Modern English Texts, the *Eighteenth Century Collections Online* and so on. They are considerably larger than the Helsinki Corpus but usually also more restricted in the time period that they cover. Together these sources provide researchers with an abundant wealth of material for their investigations, but they also provide their own challenges because they are often not compatible with each other. They cannot easily be combined to provide a longer diachrony because they often contain very different types of material. Their interfaces differ and not all of them are freely available. Some require expensive licences and are, therefore, not available to all researchers.

Discursive studies, in contrast, generally do not require very large corpora. They rely on carefully selected short extracts of texts, for instance plays, novels or private correspondence. Such material is generally easily available, but it poses challenges of a very different kind. How are the extracts to be chosen from all the material that is potentially available? Are the chosen extracts in any way representative of the time period in which they were written? The answer is, of course, that the selection principles can only be very unsystematic and haphazard, and that the extracts cannot be taken to be truly representative of their period. It is well known that only a tiny fraction of literary production of any given time period is still known today. The vast number of literary works that did not pass the test of time and disappeared from the scene was in all probability more typical and therefore more representative of its time. The artistically more successful works, in contrast, are accordingly less typical and less representative. And very often it is out of this non-representative sample that the researcher picks and chooses.

As will become clear in the subsequent chapters of this book, the selection of extracts is very personal. It includes well-established classics by such luminaries as Chaucer and Shakespeare, but it also includes somewhat lesser-known works, such as the plays by Richardson and Steele in the eighteenth century. In any case, an individual piece of literature is never claimed to be representative of a specific period. The picture of how politeness was conceived at a particular point in the history of the English language only emerges through a triangulation of different perspectives including large-scale corpus-based approaches and microscopic analyses of short extracts of text.

3   Medieval Britain

3.1   Introduction[1]

The Anglo-Saxon period lasted for over six hundred years, from the fifth century well into the eleventh. It started with the arrival of several Germanic tribes on British soil and ended with the Norman invasion in 1066. This is such a long period that any generalisations about the language of the Anglo-Saxons must necessarily be simplifications and quite possibly oversimplifications. Our knowledge about the language of these tribes is based on a very limited set of texts. Literacy rates were low, and written texts were rare and restricted to very specific communicative needs in a religious or legal context, for instance, or for official communication. Our knowledge of Old English, which outlived the Anglo-Saxon period by some hundred years, in all its variety and diversity, is therefore very limited. This is particularly true for pragmatic aspects of the language and even more so for aspects related to politeness and impoliteness, except for some pioneering work by Thomas Kohnen (2008a, 2008b, 2011, 2017). Kohnen (2008b) provides a detailed study of politeness and face in Anglo-Saxon England. On the basis of Old English terms of address, he discusses the question of whether there is any evidence in the extant sources of what we would today call politeness. He understands politeness explicitly in terms of facework, and his answer is largely negative. In Anglo-Saxon England, facework does not seem to have played any major role. He also warns his readers against any reductionist simplifications in view of all the major developments in society, religion, politics and communicative practices that took place during this period: 'All we can expect to get is selected snap-shots of some hopefully typical patterns of communicative behaviour in restricted sections of Anglo-Saxon society' (Kohnen 2008b: 142).

However, it seems clear that Anglo-Saxon society was a warlike and violent society. Mitchell (1995: 107) lists some archaeological evidence in the form of a large number of weapon finds and graves whose skeletons bear evidence of violent deaths. This society had a strictly hierarchical organisation within tribal

---

[1] This chapter draws on material in Jucker (2010, 2011a, 2014).

networks. It was characterised by frequent feuds. Individuals had their fixed place in society, and this place could be given a precise numerical value in the form of the so-called *wergild* (Kohnen 2008b: 142; Mitchell 1995: 133). It was – in this sense – 'a brutally commercial society' (Campbell 1991: 59). Against this background, Kohnen argues that

the fabric of society depended very much on mutual obligation and kin loyalty, a tie which seems to have been especially pervasive with regard to the bond between man and lord. Apparently, it was only this bond which could guarantee a relatively normal life in society because it implied protection and safety. (Kohnen 2008b: 142)

In this context, considerations of face (i.e. the individualised wish to be free from imposition and to be appreciated by others) did not play an important role. Kin loyalty and a recognition of one's place in society were more important:

Kin loyalty was important in a violent society where the standard of medicine was poor; where expectation of life was short and parents did not always see their children grow to maturity; where justice was primitive; and where the blood-feud was a way of establishing such loyalty by permitting vengeance when *wergild* . . . was not paid. (Mitchell 1995: 203)

Every member of society was expected to honour the duties within the tribal network and kin loyalty at whatever level of the hierarchy, and at the same time they could expect the same loyalty from all the other members of the tribal network. In such a context, freedom from imposition and appreciation from others are values that are very much backgrounded. Instead '"belonging to the network of the society" and "having good relations in this network" were central values' (Kohnen 2008b: 143).

But Anglo-Saxon society was not only a warlike and violent society, it was also gradually Christianised. In AD 597 Augustine, later Archbishop of Canterbury, arrived in Britain together with his fellow missionaries and started the process of Christianisation. Christianisation had profound effects on Anglo-Saxon society. It brought the development of an Old English script based on the Roman alphabet, which replaced the runic alphabet (Irvine 2006: 41), and it also brought new value systems that were very different from the values of the earlier warlike and heroic tribal society, values that Kohnen (2008b: 143) captures with the terms *humilitas* and *caritas*.

The linguistic evidence for these values must be assessed very carefully. It is important to remember that virtually all extant Old English texts – whether translations of Latin texts or original compositions – were written by Christians. To some extent, therefore, Christian values may be superimposed on the texts of earlier periods. The Old English heroic poem *Beowulf* is a particularly clear example of this with its theme of heroic fights in a Germanic context interwoven with Christian elements. Texts that were based on Latin originals may reflect communicative practices that were different from the native Anglo-Saxon ones.

3.2   Discernment Politeness and Politeness of Humility and Gentleness

The surviving vocabulary of Old English does not include such politeness-related terms as *courtesy, civility* or *politeness*. These terms entered the English language later under the influence of French. But there was a rich vocabulary which allows us a glimpse of what was considered to be 'polite' in the broad sense of the word, and from this we can deduce types of behaviour that I subsume under the headings of 'discernment politeness' and 'politeness of humility and gentleness' (see also Ridealgh and Jucker 2019). Kohnen (2008b) was the first scholar to argue that politeness in Old English was very different from the type of strategic non-imposition polite-ness familiar from present-day English, and he suggests that it is better described as a type of discernment politeness or politic behaviour (in the sense of Watts 2003; see also Ide 1989). Linguistic choices in Kohnen's data reflected not so much a desire to save or enhance the speaker's or the addressee's face, but rather basic structures of society and were, therefore, more or less obligatory choices.

Kohnen analyses a range of Old English address terms, in particular *leof*, *broþor* and *hlaford*. He finds that the emerging picture is not homogeneous. The terms *leof* and *broþor* cover 80 per cent of all the relevant items, and they indicate friendship and affection. The term *leof* is often used in combination with other terms of address. On its own, it is often translated as 'Sir', 'My Lord' or 'dear Sir' (Kohnen 2008b: 147), but Kohnen suggests that this may often be too formal and that 'dear one, friend' would be more appropriate. It is not restricted to intimate relationships, but neither is it a formal or authoritative term. The term *broþor* can be used to address a real brother, but it can also be used – particularly in a religious context – to address a fellow Christian or a fellow member of a religious order. The term *hlaford*, on the other hand, does not occur frequently as a primary item, but indicates a fixed rank. In a religious context, it is often used for God or Jesus and for saints. Thus, if the data really reflect everyday usage in Anglo-Saxon England, the attested use of address terms represents the particular Anglo-Saxon blend of a Germanic world of mutual obligation and kin loyalty and a Christian world of *caritas* and *humilitas*. The use of these terms did not reflect politeness in the sense of facework. They were the reflection of the fixed positions of the interlocutors in the Anglo-Saxon world.

Kohnen (2008a) adds further evidence to this conclusion on the basis of an analysis of directives in Old English. In present-day English, directives are regularly formulated in conventionally indirect ways, paying tribute to the addres-see's wish to remain free from impositions, for example, 'Could you say that again?' (BNC KPG 912) or 'Would you please ensure that the plug is correctly fitted with the right fuse?' (BNC FUU 281).[2] Such forms do not seem to have been available in Old English. Kohnen (2008a) focuses on four different forms of Old English directives: directive performatives, such as 'I ask you to . . . '; constructions involving a second-person pronoun plus *scealt/sculon*; constructions with *uton* ('let's') plus infinitive; and impersonal constructions with *neodþearf* or *þearf* plus a first- or second-person pronoun ('it is necessary for x'). The available evidence indicates that what to us may appear to be face-threatening performatives were relatively common, while indirect strategies or suggestory performative formulae were not available (cf. in present-day English, 'may I suggest that you return to Piccadilly' (BNC HTY 109) or 'I advise you to give it up' (BNC KGN 61)). In Old English, the authoritarian *þu scealt* construction with its lack of concern for considerations of face is particularly common in secular or Germanic contexts (Kohnen 2008a: 40). For speakers in an authoritative position, face concerns do not seem to have been important. The *uton* and the *(neod)þearf* constructions, on the other hand, were more common in religious contexts. In this sphere, the speaker includes himself in the required action or formulates it in an impersonal way:

In the monastic world of humility and obedience there are (or there should be) only limited face wants since Christians are not allowed to assume a rank above their fellow Christians, and everybody is bound to follow the requirements of a Christian life. (Kohnen 2008a: 40)

In both papers, Kohnen is careful with his conclusions. The evidence available so far does not support far-reaching claims about a lack of face concerns in Anglo-Saxon society, but it does suggest that the notions of positive and negative face are in all probability considerably less helpful for a pragmatic analysis of Old English. Face-saving strategies do not seem to have been important enough to be conventionalised into the linguistic structures of address terms or directives.

A detailed look at the relevant vocabulary provides some additional nuances to this picture, and a concern not only for discernment politeness, but what might be called the politeness of humility and gentleness. The starting point for this investigation can be found in the entries of the *Thesaurus of Old English*, which compiles the known Old English vocabulary into semantic classes. Together with the *Anglo-Saxon Dictionary Online*, these entries can be used to uncover the relevant text passages in which these terms were used. Figure 3.1 gives an extract of a relevant entry of the *Thesaurus of Old English* together with meaning labels drawn from the *Anglo-Saxon Dictionary Online*.

---

[2] These examples are taken from the British National Corpus. The references indicate the relevant file name and line number.

11.05.02.02 Humanity, courtesy, civility

Manscipe 'humanity, kindness, civility'
Wærnes 'prudence, circumspection, caution'
Manþwærnes 'gentleness, meekness, courtesy'
Wynsumnes 'pleasantness, agreeableness, delight'
Swetnes 'pleasantness; kindliness, goodness'
þeáw-fæst 'of good manners, of well-ordered life, moral, virtuous'

Figure 3.1 Politeness vocabulary in Old English according to the *Thesaurus of Old English*

These terms refer to gentle, kind, meek and pleasant behaviour. There is only one instance for which the *Anglo-Saxon Dictionary Online* suggests 'courtesy' as an appropriate meaning label, despite the heading of the entry. The selection of terms and the meaning labels depend, of course, on the choices made by the thesaurus and dictionary compilers, but they strongly suggest that courtesy, and by implication politeness, were of a rather different type in Old English than in later periods, and I would like to suggest the term 'politeness of humility and gentleness' to capture this type of politeness. The following extracts illustrate how two of these terms, *manþwærnesse* and *þeawfæstnesse*, were used in actual contexts.

(1)   The Vercelli Homilies: Homily IV [0193 (323)] Ærest is an scyld wisdom & wærscipe & fæstrædnes on godum weorcum, & mildheortnesse & eaðmodnesse scyld, & ryhtes geleafan scyld & godra worca scild, & þæs halgan gastes sweord <þæt><syndon><Godes><word> þe men singaþ, & ælmessan & fæstenes scyld, & manþwærnesse & bilwitnesse scyld, & staðulfæstnesse scyld on godum weorcum. (HomU 9, ScraggVerc 4, B3.4.9)

[F]irst, one shield is wisdom, and caution, and constancy in good works, and mercy, and the shield of humility, and the shield of true faith, and the shield of good works, and the sword of the holy ghost that men sing of, and the shield of alms and fasting, and the shield of courtesy and innocence, and the shield of steadfastness in good works. (Nicholson 1991: 46)[3]

(2)   The Vercelli Homilies: Homily 14 [0055 (154)] Men ða leofestan, utan him sendan þa halgan & þa wynsuman lac, ærest þone rihtan geleafan & þa soðan lufan Godes & manna, & eaðmodnesse & geþyld & rihtwisnesse & soðfæstnesse & mildheortnesse & hyrsumnesse & æghwylce godnesse & manþwærnesse. (HomM 11, ScraggVerc 14, B3.5.11)

Dearly beloved, let us offer Him the holy and delightful gift; first, the right belief and the true love of God and of men and humility and patience and righteousness and faithfulness and mercy and obedience and every goodness and gentleness. (Nicholson 1991: 95)

---

[3]   The Vercelli examples are taken from Scragg (1992), the translations from Nicholson (1991).

Examples (1) and (2) are taken from the Vercelli Homilies. In both cases, the author admonishes his audience on how to lead a godly life. In (1), he lists all the shields that the audience should use to defend themselves against the arrows of the devil, such as those of pride, hatred, envy; theft, wantonness, drunkenness; adultery, witchcraft, avarice; greed and wrath. Against these arrows they should use the shields of humility, of true faith, of good works and also the shield of courtesy and innocence. In (2), the author lists the gifts that should be offered to God, including not only the true love of God and of men but also humility, patience, righteousness, faithfulness, mercy, obedience, goodness and gentleness. In (1), Nicholson (1991) translated the term *manþwærnesse* with 'courtesy' and in (2) with 'gentleness'. What is perhaps more significant is the fact that in both cases the term appears in a long list of related terms within the semantic field of humility and gentleness. Example (3), taken from the Psalms, is very similar to examples (1) and (2):

(3)   Psalms (PsGlI (Lindelöf) C7.11) [0664 (44.5)] Mid þinum hiwe wlite & fægernysse þinre begem gesundfullice gespediglice forðstæpe & rixa for soðfæstnesse & manþwærnesse & rihtwisnesse & gelæt þe wundorlice swiðre þin

Specie tua et pulchritudine tua intende prospere procede et regna propter ueritatem et mansuetudinem et iustitiam et deducet te mirabiliter dextera tua.

And in thy majesty ride prosperously because of truth and meekness and righteousness; and thy right hand shall teach thee terrible things. (King James Bible, Psalm 45:4)[4]

The term *manþwærnesse*, which the *King James Bible* here renders as 'meekness', again appears in a list of related terms: *truth* and *righteousness*. Examples (4) to (6) are taken from the *Rule of St Benet* and illustrate the use of the term *þeawfæstnesse*:

(4)   The Rule of St Benet (BenR B10.3.1.1) [0200 (7.23.9)] Seo arærede hlædder tacnað ure lif on ðisse weorulde, ðæt bið mid eaðmodre heortan þurh drihten aræred to heofonum; þære hlædre sidan tacniað lichoman and saule; on ðæm twam sidum, þæt is on saule and on lichoman, missenlice stæpas eaðmodnesse and þeawfæstnesse sio godcunde gelaðung to ðæm upstige gefæstnode.

And the ladder thus set up is our life in the world, which the Lord raises up to heaven if our heart is humbled. For we call our body and soul the sides of the ladder, and into these sides our divine vocation has inserted the different steps of humility and discipline we must climb. (Doyle 1948)[5]

(5)   The Rule of St Benet (BenR B10.3.1.1) [0653 (63.117.9)] Þa cild and seo geogoð mid steore and þeawfæstnesse hyra endebyrdnessum fylien, ge on

---

[4] The example from the Psalms is taken from Lindelöf (1909–14); the translation from the *King James Bible Online*.

[5] The examples from the Rule of St Benet are taken from Schröer and Gneuss (1964), the translations from Doyle (1948).

cyricean ge on beodernne; syn hy a behealdene mid steore and mid mycelre
heordrædenne, ægðer ge inne, ge ute, ge æghwær, oð þæt hy to andgyttolre
yldo cumen and to fulfremedre gestæþþignesse.

Boys, both small and adolescent, shall keep strictly to their rank in oratory and
at table. But outside of that, wherever they may be, let them be under super-
vision and discipline, until they come to the age of discretion. (Doyle 1948)

(6)   The Rule of St Benet (BenRGl C4) [0550 (62.103.15)] Nec occasione sacer-
dotii obliviscatur regule oboedientiam et disciplinam sed magis hac magis in
deum proficiat intingan preost

ne he na <forgimeleasie> regoles gehyrsumnesse & þeawfæstnesse ac swiðor
& swiðor on gode he geþeo.

Nor should he by reason of his priesthood forget the obedience and the
discipline required by the Rule, but make ever more and more progress
towards God. (Doyle 1948)

Doyle's translation renders *þeawfæstnesse* as 'discipline' and 'strictness', and it
occurs together with humility and obedience, and as in the case of examples (1)
to (3) illustrating *manþwærnesse*, the context is one of religious instruction.
Thus, the evidence that presents itself in Old English is a semantic field of terms
related to courtesy and politeness that appear exclusively in the context of
religious instruction. It describes God-fearing behaviour of innocence, humility,
kind-heartedness, obedience and goodness, qualities that I subsume under the
heading 'politeness of humility and gentleness' (cf. Ridealgh and Jucker 2019).

Thus, the limited available evidence for Old English suggests that politeness
in the modern sense did not play any significant role in this period in the history
of the English language. Instead there is evidence of discernment politeness. In
a strictly hierarchical society people knew how to address each other appropriately and with the appropriate terms of address. These forms were not
a matter of strategic choice to maintain or enhance the speaker's or the
addressee's face. And in the religious and didactic literature of the time there
is evidence of a politeness of humility and gentleness. These instructions did
not concern the outward manners of behaviour but the appropriate inner
feelings towards God and towards fellow human beings.

3.3   The French Court and the Concept of *Curteisie*

In 1066, William the Conqueror and his army defeated the British army and
within a few years, the English nobility and church leaders were completely
replaced by Normans. French became the language of the court while Latin
remained the language of the monasteries and English the language of the
peasant population. It took decades before French had a significant impact on
the English language, at least in the written texts that have survived from that
period, but in the long run the French impact on English was substantial. The

Old English declension system crumbled and in its place word order became more fixed. The Germanic vocabulary of Old English was enriched with a host of loanwords from French. On all these levels, Middle English links two systems that show marked differences. To modern readers, Old English looks and feels like a foreign language, while Early Modern English, the language of Shakespeare, sounds in many respects much more familiar and in any case recognisably English. All these changes have been studied in detail and are fairly well understood. On the level of pragmatics, however, we are still far from a comparable understanding of the changes that took place during the Middle English period. However, I would like to argue that in terms of politeness, Middle English also has a bridging function.

The *Historical Thesaurus of the Oxford English Dictionary* lists 1,704 expressions under the heading of 'good behaviour' and within that 781 under the heading of 'courtesy'. A considerable number of these expressions are first attested in the Middle English period. Jucker, Taavitsainen and Schneider (2012) investigated the development of the semantic field of courtesy and politeness in the history of the English language, and they found that the Middle English period was particularly rich in new courtesy and politeness related vocabulary. They retrieved sixty-seven terms from the *Historical Thesaurus* under the narrow headings 'courtesy, n', 'courteous, a' and 'courteously, adv'. Thirty of these sixty-seven expressions were first attested between 1150 and 1420 (Jucker, Taavitsainen and Schneider 2012: section 3.2). A search for these terms and their spelling variants in the Helsinki Corpus revealed that the semantic field of courtesy and politeness must have been particularly important in the Middle English period. In the Early Modern English period these terms are attested significantly less frequently (Jucker, Taavitsainen and Schneider 2012: section 3.4).

A particularly interesting term is 'courtesy', which is defined by the *Oxford English Dictionary* as 'courteous behaviour; courtly elegance and politeness of manners; graceful politeness or considerateness in intercourse with others' (*OED*, 'courtesy' *n*. 1a.). Its earliest occurrence is dated to 1215, and the word derives from Old French *cur-*, *cortesie*, later *courtesie*. In Chaucer's *Canterbury Tales*, it takes the form *curteisie* or *curtesye* (and some further spelling variants) and occurs twenty-seven times.[6] In addition, there are eleven occurrences of the adjective *curteis* and ten occurrences of the adverb *curteisly* (with spelling variants). The *Riverside Chaucer* glosses three senses of *curteisie/curtesye*: first, 'courtliness,

---

[6] All quotations as well as references and abbreviations are from Benson (1987: 779). Statistics are based on the search facilities available on the Harvard Geoffrey Chaucer website (http://sites .fas.harvard.edu/~chaucer/), which also uses the *Riverside Chaucer* as a textual basis. For a list of all spelling variants see www.courses.fas.harvard.edu/~chaucer/spelling.htm. Translations of the extracts in this section are my own.

good manners, courtesy as a moral ideal'; second, an 'act of good manners'; and third, in the locution *of (for) (your) curteisie* ('if you please'). The adjective *curteys* is glossed as 'courtly, refined, courteous', as 'generous, merciful' and as 'deferential'; and the adverb as 'politely' and as 'discreetly'.

Chaucer's *Canterbury Tales* are particularly suitable for such an investigation because they provide a panoply of characters from all walks of life. The frame narrative introduces a range of pilgrims from all three estates and from most ranks (for an overview of social life in Chaucer's England, see Singman and McLean 1995: 23). In the following I want to go beyond the semantics of the term *curteisie* (including the adjective and the adverb and spelling variants) and look at the sociolinguistic distribution of the term and at the pragmatics of how it is used in interactions between the fictional characters depicted on the various narrative levels of the *Canterbury Tales*.

A close analysis of all the occurrences of *curteisie* shows that Chaucer uses this term to refer to a virtue or moral ideal to be praised, as a personal quality ascribed to one of the characters and as a form of behaviour. In (7), for instance, the narrator of the General Prologue praises the knight, who strives for the ideals of chivalry, truth, honour, freedom and courtesy. In (8), he describes the prioress and her impeccable table manners. Her greatest pleasure was in *curteisie* ('courtly manners').

(7)   A KNYGHT ther was, and that a worthy man,
        That fro the tyme that he first bigan
        To riden out, he loved chivalrie,
        Trouthe and honour, fredom and curteisie. (GP I 43–6)[7]
        The KNIGHT was a very distinguished man, who, from the beginning of his career, loved chivalry, truth, honour, generosity and courtesy.

(8)   (The prioress)
        At mete wel ytaught was she with alle;
        She leet no morsel from hir lippes falle,
        Ne wette hir fyngres in hir sauce depe;
        Wel koude she carie a morsel and wel kepe
        That no drope ne fille upon hire brest.
        In curteisie was set ful muchel hir lest. (GP I 128–32)[8]
        At dinner she was well taught indeed; she allowed no morsel to fall from her lips, and did not dip her fingers too deeply into the sauce; she knew well how to carry a morsel and take good care that not the slightest drop would fall on her breast; her greatest pleasure was in good manners (courtesy).

The knight is a representative of the aristocracy and the highest-ranking pilgrim in the frame narrative. His introduction has been described as 'a portrait of ideal

---

[7] Benson (1987: 24) glosses *curteisie* here as 'refinement of manners'.

[8] Benson glosses line 132 as 'Her greatest pleasure (*lest*) was in good manners (*curteisie*)' (1987: 25).

Christian knighthood' (Cooper 1996: 35). It is, therefore, entirely appropriate for him to be aspiring to the virtues of chivalry, truth, honour, freedom and *curteisie*. The situation is different for the prioress, a member of the clergy. The narrator praises her mainly for her table manners, for her attractive appearance and for her compassion for her lap dogs. In this way the narrator draws a picture of innocent admiration but at the same time satirises her. She is praised, but for the wrong attributes. The positive features are those of a courtly lady and not of a devout nun (Cooper 1996: 37–9 and references cited there). In this context, the term *curteisie* contributes to the gentle satire. It is fitting for a lady of the court to strive for *curteisie*, but perhaps not for a nun.

The narrator of the frame narrative describes the squire, also a member of the aristocracy and the knight's son, as young, strong and in love, and with all the proper attributes of a young lover. One of these is that he is *curteis* 'courteous':

(9)   With hym ther was his sone, a yong SQUIER,
        A lovyere and a lusty bacheler,

        . . .

        He sleep namoore than dooth a nyghtyngale.
        Curteis he was, lowely, and servysable,
        And carf biforn his fader at the table. (GP I 79–80; 98–100)[9]
        With him there was his son, a young SQUIRE, a lover and a lively bachelor . . .
        He slept no more than does the nightingale. He was courteous, modest and
        attentive, and he carved for his father at the table.

Extract (10) is taken from the Shipman's Tale, a *fabliau* of a monk who borrows money from a merchant and sleeps with his wife. According to the tale he does business outside of his monastery and therefore presumably holds some office, perhaps that of a cellarer (Benson 1987: 911). The narrator of this tale introduces him as a good friend and frequent visitor in the merchant's house:

(10)   (The monk)
        And unto Seint-Denys he comth anon.
        Who was so welcome as my lord daun John,
        Oure deere cosyn, ful of curteisye? (CT ShipT VII 67–9)
        And anon he came to Saint Denis. Who was as welcome as my lord Sir John,
        our dear kinsman, full of courtesy?

The monk is *ful of curteisye*. Here, too, a member of the clergy is ascribed this quality. It can be argued that in this case there is also a touch of gentle satire in this description. The monk is described in very worldly rather than religious terms.

A similar case occurs in the Summoner's Tale, where the main protagonist, the hypocritical mendicant friar John, greets Master Thomas's wife. He gets up

---

[9] It was an honour for a squire to carve for his knight and in particular for his father (Benson 1987: 802).

curteisly when the wife approaches and embraces and kisses her. Benson comments: 'Although the kiss of peace was a normal greeting, the action here is rendered suspect by the comparison to the sparrow, a common symbol of lechery' (1987: 877). In this context, too, a member of the clergy is described as acting courteously, but the description appears in a context with satirical overtones:

(11)   *(Friar welcomes Thomas's wife)*
        'Ey, maister, welcome be ye, by Seint John!'
        Seyde this wyf, 'How fare ye, hertely?'
        The frere ariseth up ful curteisly,
        And hire embraceth in his armes narwe,
        And kiste hire sweete, and chirketh as a sparwe
        With his lyppes: 'Dame,' quod he, 'right weel'. (SumT III 1800–4)
        'Ey, master, welcome, by Saint John!' said the wife: 'How are you, cordially?' The friar rose full of courtesy, and tightly embraced her in his arms, and kissed her sweetly and chirped like a sparrow with his lips. 'Dame,' said he, 'right well'.

Thus, the evidence suggests that for members of the aristocracy, courtesy was something to strive for, while the descriptions of the members of the clergy who strive for courtesy or behave in a courteous manner appear to be somewhat ironical or satirical.

The *Canterbury Tales* frequently describe the behaviour of individual characters as courteous, and just as frequently characters are blamed for a lack of courtesy by other characters. These descriptions tend to concern lower ranks of society, as in the following example:

(12)   'But, sires, to yow it is no curteisye
        To speken to an old man vileynye,
        But he trespasse in word or elles in dede.
        In Hooly Writ ye may yourself wel rede:
        "Agayns an oold man, hoor upon his heed,
        Ye sholde arise"'. (PardT VI 739–44)
        'But sires, you show a lack of courtesy in speaking rudely to an old man, unless he has trespassed in word or deed. In the Bible you may well read yourself: "Before an old man, grey-haired with age, you shall rise up"'.

In this extract from the Pardoner's Tale, three rioters who are seeking a personified Death accost a poor old man whom they meet on the way and ask him in a very rude manner why he has lived so long. The old man explains that he must walk the earth because no young man wants to exchange his youth for his age and mother earth does not yet receive him. He then chides the rioters for their rude behaviour.

Extract (13) is taken from the very end of the Shipman's Tale, where the narration has already returned to the frame narrative and the host, Harry Bailey, turns to the prioress to invite her to tell a story. He puts on his best manners and speaks 'courteously as a maid', which invokes an image of innocence and lack of offence rather than courtly sophistication or refinement. It is also noteworthy that the host has just addressed the narrator of the previous tale, the shipman, with the pronoun *thou*, but he switches to the more polite *ye* when he talks to the prioress, and he manages to use the polite pronoun five times in five lines and adds two equally polite nominal forms of address, *my lady Prioresse*, and *my lady deere*. Thus there is a direct link between *curteis* speech and the use of *you* rather than *thou*, as I will show in more detail in the following chapter. Moreover, the host embellishes his request to the prioress with negative politeness strategies of the non-imposition type (see lines 448–51). He is concerned that his request might offend the prioress. He merely suggests that she might tell a tale on condition that she does not mind:

(13)   'But now passe over, and lat us seke aboute,
           Who shal now telle first of al this route
           Another tale;' and with that word he sayde,
           As curteisly as it had been a mayde,
           'My lady Prioresse, by youre leve,
           So that I wiste I sholde yow nat greve,
           I wolde demen that ye tellen sholde
           A tale next, if so were that ye wolde.
           Now wol ye vouche sauf, my lady deere?' (ShipT VII 443–51)
           'But now, pass on, and let us look who of all this company shall next tell another tale', and after that he said, as courteously as if he were a maid: 'My Lady Prioress, by your leave, if I knew it would not annoy you, I would suggest that you should tell the next tale, if you would not mind. Now will you agree, my lady dear?'

The term *curteisye* also regularly occurs in the phrase *of (for) (your) curteisye*, glossed in the *Riverside Chaucer* as 'if you please' (Benson 1987: 1234). In this form it might be suspected that it is no more than a polite speech-act formula, such as present-day English *please*, *thank you* or *you're welcome* (Biber et al. 1999: 1093). But the *Canterbury Tales*' narrators and characters tend to use this formula in contexts that are related to impoliteness, as the following extracts illustrate:

(14)   *(Implied author to implied reader (General Prologue))*
           And after wol I telle of our viage
           And al the remenaunt of oure pilgrimage.
           But first I pray yow, of youre curteisye,
           That ye n'arette it nat my vileynye,
           Thogh that I pleynly speke in this mateere,
           To telle yow hir wordes and hir cheere. (GP I 723–8)
           And afterwards I will tell of our journey and all the rest of our pilgrimage. But first I pray you of your courtesy, do not attribute it to my rudeness if I speak plainly in this matter in telling you their words and their behaviour.

In extract (14), the frame narrator asks the reader for forgiveness for crude tales and plain language, which in the interest of true narrations he is not at liberty to change. The request is accompanied by the phrase *of youre curteisye*. It is a polite request, but it asks the addressee in effect to endure impoliteness in what is to follow.

Extract (15) is taken from the Prologue to the Summoner's Tale. In the preceding tale the friar has deeply insulted the summoner of the frame narrative with a tale satirising summoners. As a result, the summoner stands up in his stirrups shaking from sheer outrage and requires the right to tell the next tale:

(15)   *(Pilgrim-narrator (Summoner) to fellow pilgrims)*
         This Somonour in his styropes hye stood;
         Upon this Frere his herte was so wood
         That lyk an aspen leef he quook for ire.
         'Lordynges,' quod he, 'but o thyng I desire;
         I yow biseke that, of youre curteisye,
         Syn ye han herd this false Frere lye,
         As suffreth me I may my tale telle. (SumP III 1665–71)
         The Summoner stood up high in his stirrups; his heart was so full of anger against this Friar that he shook like an aspen leaf from indignation. 'Gentlemen', he said, 'I desire only one thing: I beseech you, of your courtesy, since you have heard this false Friar lie, that I may be allowed to tell my tale'.

The phrase *of youre curteisye* is again used in a situation that at least the summoner has experienced as one of extreme impoliteness or improper behaviour. The same sense of improper behaviour can be seen in extract (16), taken from the Miller's Tale in which Nicholas, a student and lodger at the carpenter's house, indecently approaches his landlord's wife, Alison. She puts up some mock resistance, threatens to cry for help and appeals to his sense of *curteisye*. It is noteworthy that she switches to the pronoun *youre* in this case to maintain the pretence of decorum. It only takes Nicholas two more lines of begging for her to give in and grant him what he seeks:

(16)   *(Alison to Nicholas (Miller's Tale))*
         And she sproong as a colt dooth in the trave,
         And with hir heed she wryed faste awey,
         And seyde, 'I wol nat kisse thee, by my fey!
         Why, lat be!' quod she. 'Lat be, Nicholas,
         Or I wol crie "out, harrow" and "allas"!
         Do wey youre handes, for youre curteisye!' (MilT I 3282–7)
         And she sprang as a colt in the frame when being shod, and quickly turned her head away and said: 'I will not kiss you, by my faith! Why, let be', she said, 'let be, Nicholas, or I will cry "Help" and "Alas!" Take away your hands, by your courtesy!'

The phrase *for youre curteisye* is again used in a situation in which a sense of decorum and appropriate behaviour is set against the dangers of a breakdown of exactly this decorum.

In conclusion, we can say that the term *curteisie* and its related adjective and adverb refer to a virtue to be aspired to but also to a form of appropriate and expected behaviour that fits both the situation in which it occurs and the social status of the interactants. The phrase *for youre curteisie* is used in situations when the appropriate decorum has been violated or is in danger of being violated. The characters from a broad range of social ranks demonstrate an awareness or discernment of the behaviour that is appropriate in particular situations. For the aristocracy it is natural to strive for *curteisie* and for *curteis* behaviour. For members of the clergy it may be slightly less appropriate to pay too much attention to the outward appearance of decorum and appropriateness. When their behaviour is described as *curteis* or when they strive for *curteisie* there is often more than just a touch of irony involved. Craftsmen and other lower-ranking individuals, finally, tend to appeal to *curteisie* when the social decorum has already been lost or is in imminent danger of being compromised. *Curteisie* is thus a key term in the description of the discernment politeness as depicted by Geoffrey Chaucer in his *Canterbury Tales*.

3.4   The Discourse of Politeness

In the following I would like to shift the focus from the vocabulary of courtesy to the discourse of courtesy and politeness and analyse a series of interactions in which fictional characters discuss the courtly rules of behaviour. The interactions are taken from the late fourteenth-century Middle English alliterative romance, *Sir Gawain and the Green Knight*. It is the Arthurian story of a beheading game, but it is also a story of honour and chivalry and as such it depicts courtly behaviour and, in fact, in many scenes problematises the dilemmas of observing the multiple requirements of appropriate behaviour at court. I will focus my analysis on the three bedroom scenes of *Sir Gawain and the Green Knight*, in which Sir Gawain is tempted by the lady of the house and faces the dilemma of either being courteous towards the lady or loyal to his host, Bertilak de Hautdesert, and to his knightly ideals. Thus, it gives us a fictional and fairy-tale characterisation of courtly values at the end of the fourteenth century.

Sir Gawain, one of King Arthur's knights, accepts the Green Knight's challenge to an exchange of blows. Gawain can strike him with his axe if he is prepared to accept a blow in return in one year's time. Gawain strikes off the Green Knight's head, but in true fairy-tale fashion, the Green Knight picks up his head and, before he leaves, reminds Gawain to remember the appointment. After a long quest for the place of the encounter, Sir Gawain seeks refuge in Sir Bertilak de Hautdesert's castle. Sir Bertilak assures him that he can meet the Green Knight not far from the castle, so he can rest in the castle for the remaining three days before the appointment. Gawain does so. Meanwhile Sir Bertilak goes hunting after having proposed a playful bargain with Gawain. In the evening they will exchange their winnings of the day. While Sir Bertilak is away, Sir Gawain is visited by the lady of the house in his bedchamber, where she tries to seduce him. However, Sir Gawain resists her seductive efforts. On the first day they exchange only one single kiss. In the evening, Sir Bertilak brings home a deer, which he presents to Sir Gawain. In return he receives a kiss from Gawain, but Gawain does not reveal how he won the kiss because that was not part of the bargain. On the second day, the lady continues her seductive efforts, and this time she exchanges two kisses with Gawain, who trades them for a boar in the evening. On the third day, finally, the lady redoubles her efforts once again but ultimately accepts defeat, except that in addition to three kisses she also gives Sir Gawain a girdle of green and gold silk which, as she assures him, will protect his life if he keeps it secret. In the evening, Sir Gawain trades the three kisses for a fox, but he conceals the girdle.

The narrative in general is an account of a severe test of Sir Gawain's chivalry, loyalty and honour. First of all, having accepted the Green Knight's challenge, he is faced with a serious dilemma. If he backs out, he loses his honour, and if he does not, he is certain he will lose his life. And within this test he is faced with an almost equally serious dilemma, the lady's seductive advances. If he gives in to her seduction, he loses his honour, and if he does not, he is discourteous towards his hostess:

His knightly honor is forfeit if he backs out [of the encounter with the Green Knight]; his life, so far as he knows, is forfeit if he does not. But despite this dilemma, he must attend to the lady. He cannot, in all courtesy, refuse her request for dalliance; and yet, out of loyalty to his host he cannot really dally either. (Evans 1967: 42)

In the end he passes both tests, or at least almost. He resists the lady's temptation and dutifully relinquishes the kisses he has received from her, and he does not shy away from the renewed encounter with the Green Knight. He only fails to the extent that he has not revealed the girdle. As a result, he receives only a very mild punishment at the hands of the Green Knight. The first two blows do not strike him and the third, on account of the girdle, inflicts only a minor wound.

The three bedroom scenes are the focal points of his trial. The lady approaches Gawain when he is in a vulnerable position. He is still in bed, presumably undressed under his covers and, therefore, unable to get up and address the lady in an appropriate posture. Moreover, he is alone with the lady of the castle. Her husband has left for the day with his retinue and will not return before the evening. And the door to the bedroom is locked. This is certainly not a situation prescribed by courtly formality. In this situation, it seems paramount but at the same time exceedingly problematic to uphold the prescribed formality and courtesy of interaction.

On the first morning Sir Gawain wakes up and becomes aware that the lady of the house has entered his room. The narrator describes how Gawain pretends to still be asleep and how he deliberates his options in this precarious situation. Should he continue the pretence of being asleep or should he wake up and address the lady? He decides in his thoughts, 'More semly hit were / To aspye wyth my spelle in space quat ho wolde' (SGGK III, 48, lines 1198–9)[10] ('More seemly 'twould be / in due course with question to enquire what she wishes'), and thus the narrator immediately introduces the issue of 'seemly' behaviour.

The lady teases him for his carelessness in letting somebody approach him in his sleep, and she refuses his request to let him get up and get dressed. And within the first few lines she touches on the topic of courtesy. She praises Sir Gawain for his courtesy and for his reputation for being courteous (line 1229). Thus, she focuses on his dilemma right from the start. If he is courteous, he must serve her and fulfil her wishes, but at the same time such a course of action is unthinkable:

(17)   For I wene wel, iwysse, Sir Wowen ȝe are,
         Þat alle þe worlde worchipez quere-so ȝe ride;
         Your honour, your hendelayk is hendely praysed
         With lordez, with ladyes, with alle þat lyf bere.
         And now ȝe ar here, iwysse, and we bot oure one. (SGGK III, 49, lines 1226–30)
         For I wot well indeed that Sir Wawain you are,
         to whom all men pay homage wherever you ride;
         your honour, your courtesy, by the courteous is praised,
         by lords, by ladies, by all living people.
         And right here you now are, and we all by ourselves.

She praises him not for his deeds, but for his reputation, his honour and what she calls his 'hendelayk' ('courtliness, courtesy').[11] She immediately adds that they are now alone. In the continuation of the passage reproduced in (17), she points out that her husband and his men are away hunting, everybody else is still in bed and the door to his bedroom is securely locked. But Gawain does not give in to the temptation. He disclaims being worthy of such a reputation and praises the lady of the house for her own honour and reputation. The narrator

---

[10] The original text follows the edition by Tolkien and Gordon (1925), whose second edition was edited by Davis (1967); the translation is taken from Tolkien's translation (ed. by Christopher Tolkien 2006). The reference indicates the part of the manuscript, the stanza (numbers taken from the translation) and the line numbers (taken from the Davis edition).

[11] See Chapter 4, Section 5 for an analysis of the nominal and pronominal terms of address that Sir Gawain and the lady use for each other in these three bedroom scenes.

summarises a long interaction by saying that they continued to talk of many matters until late into the morning. Finally, the lady prepares to take her leave, and again she puts him in a dilemma. Once again, she reminds him of his reputation of courtesy but asserts that courtesy towards a lady should have induced him to crave a kiss from her during such a long interaction:

(18)   Þenne ho gef hym god day, and wyth a glent laȝed,
         And as ho stod, ho stonyed hym wyth ful stor wordez:
         'Now he þat spedez vche speech þis disport ȝelde yow!
         Bot þat ȝe be Gawan, hit gotz in mynde.'
         'Querfore?'quoþ þe freke, and freschly he askez,
         Ferde lest he hade fayled in fourme of his castes;
         Bot þe burde hym blessed, and 'Bi þis skyl' sayde:
         'So god as Gawayn gaynly is halden,
         And cortaysye is closed so clene in hymseluen,
         Couth not lyȝtly haf lenged so long wyth a lady,
         Bot he had craued a cosse, bi his courtaysye,
         Bi sum towch of summe tryfle at sum talez ende.'
         Þen quoþ Wowen: 'Iwysse, worþe as yow lykez;
         I schal kysse at your comaundement, as a knyȝt fallez,
         And fire, lest he displese yow, so plede hit no more.'
         Ho comes nerre with þat, and cachez hym in armez,
         Loutez luflych adoun and þe leude kyssez.
         Þay comly bykennen to Kryst ayþer oþer;
         Ho dos hir forth at þe dore without dyn more. (SGGK III, 52, 1290–1308)
         Then she gave him 'good day', and with a glance she laughed,
         and as she stood she astonished him with the strength of her words:
         'Now He that prospers all speech for this disport repay you!
         But that you should be Gawain, it gives me much thought.'
         'Why so?', then eagerly the knight asked her,
         afraid that he had failed in the form of his converse.
         But 'God bless you! For this reason', blithely she answered,
         'that one so good as Gawain the gracious is held,
         who all the compass of courtesy includes in his person
         so long with a lady could hardly have lingered
         without craving a kiss, as a courteous knight,
         by some tactful turn that their talk led to.'
         Then said Wawain, 'Very well, as you wish be it done.
         I will kiss at your command, as becometh a knight,
         and more, lest he displease you, so plead it no longer.'
         She came near thereupon and caught him in her arms,
         and down daintily bending dearly she kissed him.
         They courteously commended each other to Christ.
         Without more ado through the door she withdrew and departed.

Thus, the laws of courtesy impose contradictory demands on Gawain. The lady explicitly refers to courtesy that should have been a motivation for Sir Gawain to give in to her advances. Gawain's restraint is interpreted as discourteous, perhaps even an insult towards her, the lady of the house. At the same time, Gawain is aware that giving in to her temptations would be an extreme act of discourteousness and disloyalty towards his host, Sir Bertilak de Hautdesert. On this first morning he emerges unscathed. He has exchanged a kiss with the lady of the house, but in the evening he will pass on the kiss to Sir Bertilak as part of their bargain to exchange the winnings of the day.

On the second morning, the lady visits him again and redoubles her efforts to seduce him. Again, she sits down by his side on his bed. And this time she refers even more explicitly to the rules of courteous behaviour, the customs of the gentle (*of companye þe costez*). Tolkien here translates *companye* as 'the gentle' and glosses it as '(polite) society' (Davis 1967: 172):

(19) 'Sir, ʒif ʒe be Wawen, wonder me þynkkez,
      Wyʒe þat is so wel wrast alway to god,
      And connez not of compaynye þe costez vndertake,
      And if mon kennes yow hom to knowe, ʒe kest hom of your mynde;
      Þou hatz forʒeten ʒederly þat ʒisterday I taʒtte
      Bi alder-truest token of talk þat I cowþe.'
      'What is þat?' quoþ þe wyghe, 'Iwysse I wot neuer;
      If hit be soothe þat ʒe breue, þe blame is myn awen.'
      'ʒet I kende yow of kyssyng,' quoþ þe clere þenne,
      'Quere-so countenaunce is couþe quikly to clayme;
      Þat bicumes vche a knyʒt þat cortaysy vses.' (SGGK III, 59, 1481–91)
      'Sir, if you are Wawain, a wonder I think it
      that a man so well-meaning, ever mindful of good,
      yet cannot comprehend the customs of the gentle;
      and if one acquaints you therewith, you do not keep them in mind:
      thou hast forgot altogether what a day ago I taught
      by the plainest points I could put into words!'
      'What is that?' he said at once. 'I am not aware of it at all.
      But if you are telling the truth, I must take all the blame.'
      'And yet as to kisses', she quoth, 'this counsel I gave you:
      wherever favour is found, defer not to claim them:
      that becomes all who care for courteous manners.'

If he is well-meaning and concerned about being good, she argues, he should follow the customs of polite society and not refuse a favour that is offered to him. Everybody who cares about courteous manners (*þat cortaysy vses*) should accept such favours. This increases the pressure on Gawain, who now must even more explicitly break what the lady presents as the rules of courtesy. He argues that he did not dare accept the favour because he feared that he would be rejected. But the lady does not accept this argument. She points out that he would be strong enough to take a favour if anybody were so ill-bred to refuse him (*ʒif any were so vilanous þat yow devaye wolde*; SGGK III, 59, 1497), insinuating that he could

have kissed her even against her will, had he so wished, but that she would not
have been so discourteous as to refuse him. He protests that where he comes
from people do not take favours by force but only exchange them of their own
free will, but he is ready (*at your comaundement*) (SGGK III, 59, 1501) to kiss
her whenever she wishes. So, they kiss again.

But the lady is not yet satisfied. She again refers to his breeding, his chivalry
and the famous art of knightly love, and wonders why he has not talked to her
about the art of courtly love:

(20)   'And yow wrathed not þerwyth, what were þe skylle
          Þat so ȝong and so ȝepe as ȝe at þis tyme,
          So cortayse, so knyȝtyly, as ȝe ar knowen oute –
          And of alle cheualry to chose, þe chef þyng alosed
          Is þe lel layk of luf, þe lettrure of armes. (SGGK III, 60, 1509–13)
          '[I]f you would not mind my asking, what is the meaning of this:
          that one so young as are you in years, and so gay,
          by renown so well known for knighthood and breeding,
          while of all chivalry the choice, the chief thing of praise,
          is the loyal practice of love: very lore of knighthood.

So, once again, she challenges him to behave according to the code of chivalry
and courtly love, but he is well aware that if he were to do so, he would violate
exactly this code of chivalry and courtly love. On the surface, he is in a double
bind in which he can only lose. He breaks the code both if he gives in to her
wooing and if he withstands it. But on closer inspection, the choice is between
the code of chivalry and the code of courtesy. The code of chivalry requires him
to remain true to his principles, loyal to his host and faithful to the Arthurian
ideals of knightly behaviour. The code of courtesy that the lady insists upon, on
the other hand, requires him to accept her favours and to yield to her desires. He
is caught between two paradigmatic codes (Burlin 1995: 12–13). Before the
lady leaves, she kisses him a second time, and again Sir Gawain retains his
innocence by exchanging the two kisses of the second encounter with Sir
Bertilak's winnings of the day, a boar.

On the third day, the lady greets him with a kiss, and starts to press him even
harder:

(21)   For þat prynces of pris depressed hym so þikke,
          Nurned hym so neȝe þe þred, þat need hym bihoued
          Oþer lach þer hir luf, oþer lodly refuse.
          He cared for his cortaysye, lest craþayn he were,
          And more for his meschef ȝif he schulde make synne,
          And be traytor to þat tolke þat telde aȝt. (SGGK III, 71, 1770–5)
          For she, queenly and peerless, pressed him so closely,
          led him so near the line, that at last he must needs
          either refuse her with offence or her favours there take.

He cared for his courtesy, lest a caitiff he proved,
yet more for his sad case, if he should sin commit
and to the owner of the house, to his host, be a traitor.

The narrator describes Gawain's dilemma in very clear terms. On the one hand, there are the obligations of courtesy, according to which he cannot refuse the requests of the lady of the house, and on the other his own innocence, which makes it impossible to betray his host. He cannot observe both codes, he must decide whether to *lach per hir luf* ('take her favours') or whether to *lodly refuse* ('refuse with offence'). At this point she suspects that he must love another lady. When he denies this, she is finally defeated. If he refuses her without being tied to some other lady, there can be no hope for her. They kiss again, and she prepares to leave, but not before having asked him for a love token. He refuses on the grounds that he does not have anything that would be worthy of her. So she offers him a precious ring, but he refuses again. When she offers him a magic girdle that would protect him in the encounter with the Green Knight, he accepts the gift. She urges him to keep the gift a secret and leaves him with the third kiss of the day.

Thus, in the fourteenth-century romance *Sir Gawain and the Green Knight*, courtesy in its etymological sense of 'courtly behaviour' or 'courtly elegance and politeness of manners' (*OED*, 'courtesy', n.) is of essential importance. Sir Gawain is caught in the dilemma of having to choose between courteous behaviour towards the lady of the house and his loyalty to the code of chivalry, which forces him to be loyal and true to his host, Sir Bertilak, and it seems impossible – both to him and to the reader – to escape unscathed. He almost succeeds, and his lapse is only a minor one. In the words of Burlin, 'Gawain's lapse, then, results from being caught between two paradigmatic codes' (1995: 12–13) – the code of chivalry and the code of courtesy.

In the fairy-tale context of this romance, courtesy is a form of expected behaviour. But even in this highly regulated context, these expectations are not fixed in terms of the specific linguistic forms that have to be used. The terms of courteous interaction are negotiable. Sir Gawain and the lady thematise the rules of courteous behaviour. The lady refers to Gawain's reputation and courteousness to lead him into accepting her advances, and he refers to the ideals of courteousness and chivalry to justify why he does not give in to her temptations.

3.5   Conclusion

The picture that emerges from the data presented in this chapter is a multifaceted one. For Anglo-Saxon England, the studies by Kohnen (in particular 2008b) provide evidence for discernment politeness in the form of linguistic choices that were not based on strategic considerations of face wants but on the basic structures of a strictly hierarchically organised society where mutual obligation and kin loyalty were paramount. In a Christian context and in the teaching of the Church, the ideals of *humilitas* and *caritas* were important. I have called this the politeness of humility and gentleness. The evidence for this can be found in the rich vocabulary that the *Thesaurus of Old English* lists under the heading of 'Humanity, courtesy, civility'. This vocabulary, however, is almost entirely restricted to religious genres. Kohnen is certainly right to point out that the findings on politeness in Anglo-Saxon England are both preliminary and incomplete. The reasons he gives for the limitations of his own investigation also apply in this context:

First, there may have been face work (especially positive face work, similar to the strategies employed today) in Anglo-Saxon England after all, but it was expressed with different linguistic means which have not yet been discovered and examined. Secondly, face work and linguistic politeness in (secular) Anglo-Saxon England may have followed different underlying assumptions and customs. The prevalent picture of a warlike society, the many instances of proud, defiant behaviour found in the documents suggest that face-threatening acts were not felt as a menace but rather as an accomplishment and that face-enhancing acts, like boasting and self-praise, were not considered embarrassing and awkward. Here self-assertion and even provocation were probably major constituents of a person's face. (Kohnen 2008b: 155)

We must also remember that literacy was very much restricted and that the surviving textual evidence from Anglo-Saxon England is severely limited both in its total amount and in the range of genres. After the Norman Conquest and with the increasing cultural and linguistic influence from French, the politeness situation changed considerably, and we find a new type of courtly politeness. Chaucer's *Canterbury Tales* and the anonymous *Sir Gawain and the Green Knight* provide ample evidence of a concern with appropriate behaviour. In the *Canterbury Tales*, the term *curteisie* is not restricted to the aristocratic characters of the tales; it is also regularly appealed to by characters of lower ranks, especially if the normal forms of decent behaviour are violated or are in danger of being violated. In *Sir Gawain and the Green Knight*, the characters spend a great deal of time discussing matters of behaviour that is appropriate for a knight in a courtly context. Thus, it was the behaviour at the court that set the example. The influence from French also introduced the distinction with two pronouns of address, *ye* and *thou*. Single addressees – depending on the communicative circumstances – came to be addressed with a plural pronoun. This will be the topic of the following chapter.

4 Terms of Address in Middle English

4.1 Introduction[1]

Addressing people is one of the most prominent interactive features of language use and it is closely related to issues of politeness. With terms of address speakers appeal directly to their hearer(s), and two principal kinds can be distinguished: nominal and pronominal address. In some cases, the pronominal and nominal forms co-occur, as for instance in particularly deferential forms, such as *your lordship*, or in scolding forms, such as *you rascal*. Mostly, however, they perform slightly different functions and occur on their own. They are particularly relevant for considerations of politeness if there is a choice between different forms. Many modern European languages offer a choice between different pronouns to address one single addressee, as for instance in modern French *tu* and *vous* (see Jucker and Taavitsainen 2003). In English, this choice existed only for a time and then disappeared.

In Old English the pronoun *þu* and its associated forms *þe* (acc. and dat.) and *þin* (gen.) were used as the second person singular while *ge*, *eow* (acc. and dat.) and *eower* (gen.) were used as the second person plural. In Middle English, under the influence of French, the plural pronoun extended its use to singular contexts (cf. Blake 1992: 536; Mustanoja 1960: 126; Jucker 2000: 153). Middle English speakers thus had a choice of singular or plural pronouns when addressing a single individual. The use of the plural pronoun in a singular context is first attested in the second half of the thirteenth century (i.e. two hundred years after the Norman Conquest). And in the course of the seventeenth century the choice disappeared, except for some very restricted uses (e.g. in religious contexts or in some rural dialects). The pronoun *thou* was ousted, and *you* took over as the only pronominal term of address for single addressees. It is, therefore, particularly interesting to investigate the basis on which one or the other pronoun was used when a choice existed. Was it a question of discernment politeness (i.e. a more or less obligatory choice given any particular constellation of speaker and addressee)? Or was it

---

[1] This chapter reuses material originally published in Jucker (2006a, 2010, 2011b and 2014) and Taavitsainen and Jucker (2016).

a question of strategic politeness in which the speaker could freely express his or her attitude towards the addressee?

A fresh look at the evidence in Chaucer's *Canterbury Tales* and in the anonymous *Sir Gawain and the Green Knight* suggests that the use was more principled than previously assumed but that it is based on principles that deviate considerably from those that govern the use of pronoun choices in modern languages such as German or French. Traditionally the distinction has been argued to be based primarily on the social status of the interactants. A higher-status addressee and/or a courtly context – according to this inter-pretation – called for the use of the plural pronoun, whereas a lower-status addressee, negative emotions such as contempt or prayers to God were marked by the use of the singular pronoun. However, I want to argue that we should shift our focus from the social roles of the interactants to their interactional status, which is based partly on the social status of the interactants but also on the momentary status gained in a particular conversation (see also Jucker 2000). The choice among different nominal terms of address is considerably more diverse and complex, but this choice, too, has been connected to issues of politeness (see Section 4.4).

4.2   Pronominal Terms of Address

Research on Middle English address terms has focused on the choice between the pronouns *thou* and *ye* (and their case forms) (Burnley 2003; Knappe and Schümann 2006). As pointed out above, the usage pattern of the choice between the plural or the singular pronoun for specific addressees differs considerably from the patterns in modern languages which still make this distinction, and scholars have tried to establish the precise pattern involving status difference between the speakers (Burnley 2003), but also within more discursive approaches according to situational factors. Skeat has described the difference as follows: '*Thou* is the language of the lord to a servant, of an equal to an equal, and expresses also companionship, love, permission, defiance, scorn, threatening; whilst *ye* is the language of a servant to a lord, and of compliment, and further expresses honour, submission, or entreaty' (1894: V, 175). This description has generally been accepted by the few scholars who have investigated the use of personal pronouns in Chaucer's work.

Finkenstaedt (1963: 74–6) takes this as a starting point, and deduces two main types of use of the pronoun of address. The first is the plural of deference, which is used towards an addressee of higher social standing, and the plural of politeness. And the second is the pronoun of affect, that is to say the *thou* of 'companionship, love, defiance' in Skeat's formulation. The pronoun of defer-ence ('Plural referentiae') is used both for addressees of high social standing and for addressees that happen to be superior to the speaker. Chaucer's knight is always addressed as *ye*. The host uses *ye* for the knight, the prioress, the man of law and the monk, even though he occasionally switches to *thou* when he argues with the monk. But the miller and the pardoner always receive *thou* from him. The 'pronoun of affect' accounts for deviations from this system. Finkenstaedt, referring to work by Nathan (1956, 1959), points out that switches between *ye* and *thou* are common in Chaucer but that they are generally very systematic.

Nathan (1959) also takes Skeat's quotation reproduced above as the starting point for his paper. He summarises the above quotation as follows: '*Thou* would be informal, while *ye* would be formal' (Nathan 1959: 193), and then determines for the 2,281 uses of the pronouns of address in the singular in the *Canterbury Tales* whether they are used 'correctly' or 'incorrectly' according to this distinction. He finds that ninety-eight per cent of all uses are 'correct' and spends the rest of the paper analysing the two per cent which are 'not correct'. He considers, for instance, the evidence of scribal variation in the different manuscripts. In most cases he finds little variation in the use of these pronouns, and in those where there is variation he finds that Robinson's (1933) reading, which he used as the basis for his investigation, is corroborated. He also considers the possibility of an influence of a French source, but he can show that Chaucer treated pronouns of address with a free hand and did not stick to the choices indicated in the source texts (Nathan 1959: 198; see also Nathan 1956).

From a modern point of view, and from a pragmatic one, it is regrettable that Nathan focused exclusively on the 'incorrect' uses of the singular pronouns. It is of course possible that some 'correct' uses – according to Nathan – were only accidentally so. The scribes of the better manuscripts may have normalised Chaucer's usage according to a more recent system. Thus the textual evidence may be more systematic than Chaucer's actual usage. In addition, it may be rather surprising that it was possible to distinguish so precisely between what Nathan calls 'correct' and 'incorrect' uses. The definition by Skeat, quoted above, leaves considerable room for interpretation. It would have been interesting to see the details of the 'correct' uses.

Wilcockson (1980) analyses the use of *thou* and *ye* in Chaucer's Clerk's Tale. He argues that *ye* is commonly used as the plural of respect among people of high social rank, while *thou* is ambiguous and has the opposite potential of expressing intimacy and alienation. He, too, notes that Chaucer's use of pronouns deviates from the usage in the foreign source texts and thus indicates a conscious choice.

Burnley (1983), in his introduction to Chaucer's language, argues for the flexibility in Chaucer's system of using pronouns of address:

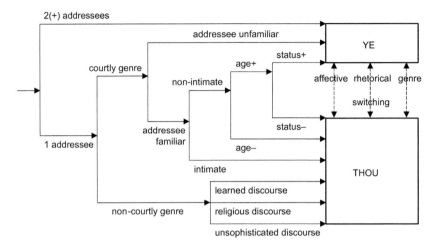

Figure 4.1 Flow chart of the choice between *ye* and *thou* (Burnley 2003: 29;
see also Burnley 1983: 20)

Although general hints on the factors governing the choice of *ye* or *thou* can be given, it
is important to realise that no unbreakable rules exist. The choice between *ye* and *thou*
when addressing a single individual is not a grammatical one, but a stylistic one
governed not only by institutionalised forms of social structure, but also by transient
emotions and attitudes arising from a relationship. (1983: 19)

Nevertheless, he presents a flow chart that depicts the choice between *ye* and
thou (see Figure 4.1).

   This chart likewise focuses on the social roles. For singular addressees, it
distinguishes between courtly style and non-courtly style. For the non-courtly
style, *thou* is the rule. For the courtly style, a further distinction decides
between intimates (friends), for whom *thou* is appropriate, while for non-
intimates the question of age is a further criterion. If the addressee is younger
than the speaker, *thou* is again appropriate. If the addressee is older, the final
question concerns status. Thus, *ye* is appropriate for singular addressees if
they are either unfamiliar or older and of higher status than the speaker. In all
other cases, *thou* is the default option. The flow chart allows for switches
between the two forms for reasons of affection, rhetoric and style. However,
the double-headed arrows between the two options leave it open in which
direction speakers may switch for which reasons. Thus, married couples in
the courtly sphere use *ye* to address each other. Does this choice indicate
a lack of intimacy and therefore a default choice of *ye* or does the flow chart
indicate that the default would have to be *thou* but for reasons of affection
they switch to *ye*?

Table 4.1 *Occurrences of pronouns of address in the* Canterbury Tales
(Mazzon 2000: 136; column and row totals added)

thou-forms		*ye*-forms singular		*ye*-forms plural		Impersonal *you*		Total
thou	743	ye	567	ye	290	singular	55	1,655
thee	308	you	377	you	251	plural	19	955
thy	683	your	492					1,175
	1,734		1,436		541		74	3,785

Blake (1992: 538) points out that polite *ye* as well as nominal forms of address, such as *madame*, are characteristic of the genre of courtly romances in the *Canterbury Tales*. But 'inevitably there is switching between *you* and *thou* forms, and in most cases it can be attributed to the author attempting to manipulate an effective response on the part of the reader' (Blake 1992: 539). He surmises that shifts are not frequent in romances because the polite pronoun is a marker of the genre and large shifts in attitude are not characteristic of courtly romance.

Mazzon (2000: 149) also points out that 'the pragmatic element of the situation seems as important as the social status of the addressee' both for nominal and pronominal forms of address. She provides detailed statistics to demonstrate the widespread use of *ye* forms for singular addressees. In total, she analyses 3,785 pronouns as summarised in Table 4.1.

It is interesting to note that Mazzon found a total of 3,170 pronouns of address in the singular in the *Canterbury Tales* where Nathan (1959), whom she does not mention in her paper, had only found 2,281. It may be advisable, therefore, to use these figures with care.

Mazzon (2000: 139) also points out that there is some random variation in the use of *ye* and *thou* forms to address deities, which in the case of the *Canterbury Tales* are generally pagan deities. Ancient heroes and other famous characters are regularly addressed with *thou* forms (Mazzon 2000: 166, fn 3). She also provides some interesting correlations between nominal and pronominal forms of address. Thus, the terms *sire*, *lord*, *lady*, *dame* and *madame* regularly co-occur with *ye* forms, while category names, such as *Cook*, *Squier*, *Somonour*, *Messager*, *Juge* and *Preest*, and terms of insult, such as *false traitour*, *olde dotard*, *false theef*, *unsely wrecche*, and *olde stot* co-occur with *thou* forms (Mazzon 2000: 149–50).

Honegger (2003) deals with forms of address in Chaucer's Knight's Tale. This tale has long been seen as problematic for such an analysis because of the seemingly arbitrary switches between *thou* and *ye* forms. However, Honegger also focuses on the situational status of the interactants in his analysis. The

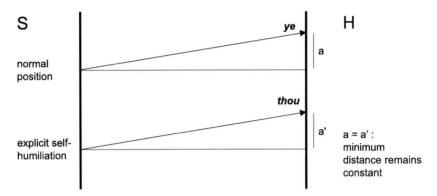

Figure 4.2 Minimum polite distance. S = speaker, H = hearer (Honegger 2003: 68)

characters may gain or lose status in an interaction with other characters and, on that basis, address terms may vary on a local level. In addition, he also includes nominal forms of address and even gestures. Thus, the Theban women who intercept Theseus on his triumphant return from his wars make manifest their low interactional position (their husbands were killed in action) by presenting themselves physically in prostrate position. They further reinforce the situation by starting their address with the polite plural form *ye* to address Theseus and the respectful nominal form *lord*. 'It is only within this firmly established framework of "respect" that the speaker varies the pronoun, and addresses Theseus with the *thou* of solidarity' (Honegger 2003: 68).

Honegger visualises this in Figure 4.2. The ladies' explicit self-humbling makes it possible for them to address Theseus with *thou*, because even with this term of address they still maintain the necessary polite distance and the basic tone of respect is guaranteed.

In the following I want to argue that the dichotomy between formal and informal suggested by Nathan (1959) and the approaches that focus primarily on the social roles of the interactants are inadequate. They seem to be influenced by the T/V distinction[2] in modern languages such as German and French (Brown and Gilman 1960; Jucker and Taavitsainen 2003). In these languages, choices of the appropriate pronouns remain relatively stable for any two people. Speakers must remember for every single person whom they know whether they are on T-terms or on V-terms. Mistakes in this respect are social blunders which can have considerable consequences for the social standing of the person perpetrating the blunder.

---

[2] T stands for the more familiar form as in French *tu* and V for the more formal form as in French *vous*.

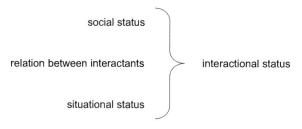

Figure 4.3 Interactional status of interactants

The Middle English system as evidenced in Chaucer's *Canterbury Tales* is flexible and, therefore, requires an approach that takes situational considerations seriously. The choices of the appropriate pronouns of address between two interactants are not fixed, but retractable (Mazzon 2000: 135). The speakers have to decide on the spot. Depending on the development of their interaction, they might have to reassess their decisions perhaps several times throughout one single conversation. The decisions depend not only on the relatively stable social statuses of the interactants and their relationship, but also on their temporary (and fluctuating) situational status.

The aspect of the social statuses of two speakers is only part of the more important aspect of the speakers' interactional status. The other two aspects that make up the interactional statuses of two interactants are their relationship to each other and the momentary situational status (see Figure 4.3).

The *social status* is relatively fixed for each person throughout their entire adult life. According to medieval social theory, medieval society was divided into three 'estates': the clergy, the aristocracy and the commons (see e.g. Singman and McLean 1995: 9). The clergy were responsible for spiritual well-being. The aristocracy fought for the country and defended it. And the commons produced the country's wealth through their labour. Every English man and woman had their fixed place in this social hierarchy, even though precise gradations were not always clear. Social mobility was possible but not easy. This social status was reflected, for instance, in their clothing and in the right to enter church first on Sunday.

The *relation between the interactants* is also relatively fixed for any given dyad of speakers. This dimension includes the central aspects of Burnley's flow chart reproduced in Figure 4.1. However, in contrast to Burnley's figure, I do not see these aspects as dichotomies that can be decided in a plus/minus fashion. They are rather scales whose combined weight tips the balance one way or the other. If an addressee is unfamiliar, of higher social standing and older than the speaker, the speaker is likely to use *ye*.

The *situational status*, finally, includes more temporary balances of power, which on occasion may disrupt the other two balances (see e.g. Watts 1991; Itakura 2001). A person may have temporary power over her interlocutor because he needs her help. Perhaps she has some information that he lacks but needs. The speaker may also have power over her addressee because she bettered him in a verbal dispute and he can no longer retaliate to her arguments.

Thus, Chaucer's characters make the choice between *ye* and *thou* not on a default basis for each possible interactant from which they may deviate on occasions, but instead take on-the-spot decisions depending on the interactional status reached at a specific point in an interaction.

Thus the function of *ye* can be described as a deference marker, where deference indicates respect and politeness. The choice of *ye* as a pronoun of address for a single addressee expresses the speaker's deference, the use of *thou* in the same situation indicates that deference in this situation is not necessary. Affection and intimacy, on the other hand, do not play the role that is often assigned to them by scholars such as Wilcockson (1980) or Burnley (1983, 2003). On the background of modern T/V systems, we may find it odd that married couples address each other with *ye* because in the modern systems intimacy calls for the T-form rather than the V-form, but Chaucer's characters use a different system. Deference and intimacy are not mutually exclusive. Husband and wife, if they are both of a higher social class, address each other with respect and politeness, that is to say with deference and therefore with the pronoun *ye*.

4.3   *Ye* and *Thou* in Chaucer's *Canterbury Tales*

In the following I want to support the above argument on the basis of relatively detailed sample analyses of a range of different tales of different literary genres in order to show that the switches of pronoun usage are not only well motivated but also serve dramatic purposes and often coincide with turning points in the narrative.

The Wife of Bath is introduced in the General Prologue of the *Canterbury Tales* as a particularly colourful character. She is from a small parish near Bath, where she works in the weaving and cloth-making business. She is well travelled and has visited all the main destinations for pilgrimages of the day. She has had five husbands. In all respects she is described as a little larger than life. Even her headgear weighs five pounds. In a lengthy prologue to her own tale she relates the stories of how she got and lost each of her five husbands. It is fitting for her somewhat pompous and presumptuous demeanour that she finally tells a romance, that is to say a story of a genre that normally would be reserved for more socially elevated characters, such as the squire or the knight.

The tale gives us several interactions between the characters in direct speech, and there are a total of eighty pronouns of address in this tale.[3] Six pronouns are addressed to several addressees (e.g. the implied readers of the tale). In these cases, the plural pronoun *ye* or the appropriate case forms *yow* or *youre* and spelling variants are used. In thirty cases, a single addressee is addressed by the singular pronoun *thou* or appropriate case forms (*thee, thy, thyne*). And in forty-four cases, a single addressee is addressed by the plural pronoun *ye* (*yow, youre, yourselven, yourself*). In two cases, there are verb forms that imply either a singular or a plural pronoun. In the verb form *hastow* (line 903), the singular pronoun *thou* is enclitically attached to the verb to form an interrogative construction ('have you?'), and the verb form *thenketh* (line 1165) is a plural imperative addressed to a single addressee implying a polite plural pronoun *ye*. I treat these verb forms as equivalent to the corresponding pronouns (see Fries 1985: sections 3.3.1 and 3.7.1).

The story is set in King Arthur's time and the main character is a lusty young knight who raped a young maiden. He is condemned to die by the king, but on Queen Guenevere's intervention he is pardoned and put into the queen's power. In order to save his life, he must find a satisfactory answer to the question of what it is that women desire most, and he is given one year to find the answer. When the year is almost up, he has still not found the answer, but he must return to the court. On the way back, he encounters an old lady who is described as being remarkably ugly. On this first encounter, the lady addresses the knight as *Sire knyght* ('Sir Knight') and uses the pronoun *ye* (WoBT III 1001–2).[4] The knight in return addresses the lady as *my leeve moooder* ('Good mother') and, despite the fact that she is obviously of a lower social status, also uses the pronoun *ye* (WoBT III 1006, 1008). Both show deference to the other; the lady because of the knight's higher social status, and the knight because of the lady's old age. At this point he tells her his problems and promises to reward her handsomely if she can help him. With this move he has made clear that she has power over him. Thus, she gains interactional status, and in this position she does not need to show deference, so she switches to the non-deferential address form *thou*. She promises to tell him if he in return promises to do whatever she asks if it is in his power. At this point he does not use a personal pronoun to address her:

(1)   Agayn the knyght this olde wyf gan ryse,
        And seyde, 'Sire knyght, heer forth ne lith no wey.
        Tel me what that ye seken, by youre fey!

---

[3] Based on a careful reading of the tale and a manual search.

[4] Quotations from Chaucer's *Canterbury Tales* are based on Benson (1987). The references and abbreviations follow the conventions of this edition (see Benson 1987: 779). Translations are my own.

Paraventure it may the bettre be;
Thise olde folk kan muchel thyng,' quod she.
   'My leeve mooder,' quod this knyght, 'certeyn
I nam but deed but if that I kan seyn
What thyng it is that wommen moost desire.
Koude ye me wisse, I wolde wel quite youre hire.' (WoBT III 1000–8)
This old woman got up to meet the knight and said, 'Sir Knight, there is no road from here on. Tell me truly what you are looking for; perhaps that may be best; we old folk know a great many things', she said. 'Good mother', the knight replied, 'the truth is I am as good as dead unless I can say what it is that women most desire. If you could tell me that, I would reward your efforts well'.

When they return to the court, the knight announces the right answer. What women desire most is to have sovereignty over both their husbands and their lovers. The ladies at court agree that this is the right answer and that he deserves to live. But the loathly old lady intervenes and reminds him of his promise:

(2)   Bifore the court thanne preye I thee, sir knyght,'
        quod she, 'that thou me take unto thy wyf,
        For wel thou woost that I have kept thy lyf.
        If I seye fals, sey nay, upon thy fey!' (WoBT III 1054–7)
        Before the court, I entreat you, sir knight', she said, 'to take me for your wife; because you know well that I have saved your life. If what I say is false, deny it upon your word of honour'.

At this point she has even more interactional superiority. He must do what she asks. Here in the formal context of the court, the use of *thou* by an old and apparently lower-class woman to a knight of much higher social status must have had a very strong impact. It communicates the woman's power over him in no uncertain terms. Again, he does not address her directly with a personal pronoun. He is very unhappy about her wish, but he has no choice and must marry her. There are no festivities and at night they are brought to bed. From this point onwards, the lady addresses her new husband invariably with the deferential pronoun *ye* and the address term *deere husbonde* ('dear husband'). The fact that she is his wife overrides other considerations. She shows respect and politeness towards her husband. The knight, on the other hand, uses the non-deferential form *thou* to explain to her why he is unhappy to be married to her:

(3)   Thou art so loothly, and so oold also
        And therto comen of so lough a kynde,
        That litel wonder is thogh I walwe and wynde.
        So wolde God myn herte wolde breste! (WoBT III 1100–3)
        You are so loathsome and so old, and in addition descended from such low-born lineage. It is little wonder if I twist and turn. I wish to God my heart would burst!

At this point she launches into a long and brilliant speech in which she chides him for his social arrogance. In the end, she lets him decide in true fairy-tale fashion whether he wants to have her old and faithful, or whether he would prefer her young and beautiful, but in the latter case he would have to take his chances as to her fidelity.

It is only now that the knight has learnt the true impact of the answer that he gave at court. He has learnt to leave the decision to his wife, and – perhaps even more importantly – he has learnt to address her in the appropriate deferential terms:

(4)   My lady and my love, and wyf so deere,
         I put me in youre wise governance;
         Cheseth youreself which may be moost plesance
         And most honour to yow and me also.
         I do no fors the wheither of the two,
         For as yow liketh, it suffiseth me. (WoBT III 1230–5)
         My lady and my love, and my dearest wife, I put myself into your wise governance; choose yourself whichever may be the most pleasing and most honourable for you and for me. I do not care which of the two you choose, for whatever pleases you is sufficient for me.

The discrepancy between his earlier *thou art so loothly* and his *My lady and my love, and wyf so deere* could not be bigger. It reflects the interactional status that has changed radically as a result of the lady's chiding speech. He is no longer in a position of (assumed) superiority but accepts her as his wife and therefore treats her with the respect and politeness that befits the situation.

Thus, the lady's and the knight's use of *ye* and *thou* closely reflects the interactional status of these two characters within this tale. *Ye* is used as a marker of deference to indicate politeness and respect, while *thou* does not indicate any deference. It is used in situations of real or assumed interactional superiority. Its use therefore does not depend primarily on the social roles of the lady and the knight. Their relationship changes when they are married, but this does not explain the behaviour. The intimacy between the characters also changes. They get to know each other better through their conversation, but in the end they both use *ye* rather than *thou*.

The next case study takes us away from the aristocratic fairy-tale characters of the Wife of Bath's romance to the rural characters of a *fabliau* told by the miller. The main characters of the Miller's Tale are the old and jealous carpenter John, his young and beautiful wife Alison, and Nicholas, their lodger, who is a poor student; there are also some supporting characters, such as Absolon, a village dandy who holds a small office in the church, John's servant Robyn and a blacksmith called Gerveys. Carpenter John and Nicholas always use *thou* when they address other characters. Robyn uses *ye* to address his master. But Alison, Absolon and Gerveys use both pronouns depending on their addressee and the current situation.

In the first conversation of the narration Nicholas seduces Alison:

(5)   Now, sire, and eft, sire, so bifel the cas
           That on a day this hende Nicholas
           Fil with this yonge wyf to rage and pleye,
           Whil that hir housbonde was at Oseneye,
           As clerkes ben ful subtile and ful queynte;
           And prively he caughte hire by the queynte,
           And seyde, 'Ywis, but if ich have my wille,
           For deerne love of thee, lemman, I spille.' (MilT I 3271–8)
           Now, gentlemen, and again, gentlemen, it so happened that one day this
           gracious Nicholas happened to sport and play with this young wife while
           her husband was away at Oseney – as these clerks are very cunning and
           clever – and secretly he groped her private parts, and said, 'Certainly, unless
           I have my way, I'll perish for secret love of you, sweetheart'.

He uses *thou* for her and also addresses her by the nominal term of address
lemman ('loved one, sweetheart, mistress'), which usually has the connotations
of 'adultery, lust, treacherous love, and rape' (Benson 1987: 954, note to MancT
IX 204). In her first reaction of shock and indignation, she addresses him also by
thou: 'I wol nat kisse thee, by my fey!' ('I won't kiss you, by my faith!'; MilT
I 3284) but immediately afterwards regains her composure and puts on a show of
decorum: 'Do wey youre handes, for youre curteisye!' ('Take away your hands,
by your courtesy'; MilT I 3287). When immediately afterwards they make their
plans to deceive her husband, Alison sticks to *ye*, but later on, when they are in
bed, she uses *thou* for him. Thus, she skilfully adapts to the situation and uses the
polite *ye* only as a pretence of decorum and formality, but when they consum-
mate their affair, such pretences are no longer needed.

Absolon the village dandy repeatedly serenades Alison outside the window
of her house. First he addresses her politely with the nominal term of address
deere lady, but he mixes *thou* and *ye*:

(6)   Now, deere lady, if thy wille be,
           I praye yow that ye wole rewe on me. (MilT I 3362–3)
           Now, dearest lady, if you care, I pray you to have mercy on me.

It is interesting that Absolon here actually uses negative politeness of the non-
imposition type ('if thy wille be') in his request that she have pity on him. The
request itself is formulated with the polite pronoun *ye*. But he is sent off by
Alison's husband John.

When Absolon mistakenly believes that Alison is on her own in her bedroom, he serenades her a second time. This time he sticks to *ye* and again uses
a range of nominal terms of address:

(7)   What do ye, hony-comb, sweete Alisoun,
           My faire bryd, my sweete cynamome?

Awaketh, lemman myn, and spekketh to me!
Wel litel thynken ye upon my wo,
That for youre love I swete ther I go. (MilT I 3698–702)
Where are you, honeycomb, sweet Alison, my pretty bird, my sweet cinnamon? Awake, my sweetheart, and speak to me! You give little thought to my unhappiness, though I'm sweating for your love wherever I go.

But Alison is not alone. This time, she is in bed with Nicholas the lodger. Her answer to Absolon is brief and to the point, and she uses *thou* to address him and send him away. Absolon is not dismissed so easily and asks for a kiss. As soon as he thinks he will get at least a kiss from her, Absolon addresses her with *thou*. His interactional status seems to have risen and therefore he thinks that he can now afford to address her with *thou*:

(8)   This Absolon doun sette hym on his knees
        And seyde, 'I am a lord at alle degrees;
        For after this I hope ther cometh moore.
        Lemman, thy grace, and sweete bryd, thyn oore!' (MilT I 3723–6)
        Absolon went down on his knees and said, 'In every way I'm well off because after this, I hope, there will be more to come. Sweetheart, your favour, and sweet bird, your grace!'

When he finds himself deceived because in the pitch-dark night she has offered him her bottom rather than her mouth to kiss, he sticks to *thou*: 'I shall thee quyte' ('I'll pay you back for this!'; MilT I 3746). He no longer cares for respect and decorum. When he returns again to serenade her a third time, he uses fewer nominal terms of address and only uses *thou*. He tries to deceive her by offering a present for another kiss:

(9)   'Why, nay,' quod he, 'God woot, my sweete leef,
        I am thyn Absolon, my deerelyng.
        Of gold,' quod he, 'I have thee broght a ryng.
        My mooder yaf it me, so God me save;
        Ful fyn it is, and therto wel ygrave.
        This wol I yeve thee, if thou me kisse.' (MilT I 3792–7)
        'Why, no', he said. 'God knows, my sweet beloved, it is your Absolon, my darling. I have brought you a ring of gold. My mother gave it to me, so God may help me. It is very precious and beautifully engraved. I'll give it to you if you kiss me'.

Perhaps Alison should have noted his change in attitude. He still addresses her as *my sweete leef* ('my sweet chick') and he praises the present that he wants to give her, but he no longer uses the polite *ye*. Thus, Absolon adapts his politeness level to his perceived interactional status. While he is wooing her, he uses *ye*, but as soon as he believes himself successful he uses *thou*, and he sticks to *thou* when he finds himself deceived.

In order to take revenge, Absolon seeks the blacksmith and borrows a hot plough blade. The smith, Gerveys, first shouts, 'What, who artow?' ('What! Who's there?'; MilT I 3766) using *thou* when Absolon calls at the gate, but when he realises that it is Absolon, he switches to *ye* and asks him in an elaborate way why he is up so early, and how he is doing. Absolon issues his request, and Gerveys answers as follows:

(10) Certes, were it gold,
   Or in a poke nobles alle untold,
   Thou sholdest have, as I am trewe smyth.
   Ey, Cristes foo! What wol ye do therwith? (MilT I 3779–82)
   Of course! You shall have it, even if it were gold or countless gold coins in a bag, as I'm an honest smith. Ah, by Christ's foe [i.e. the devil], what do you want it for?

Thus Gerveys grants the request with *thou* and asks what Absolon wants to do with the hot plough blade with *ye*. This may seem like an unmotivated switch between *thou* and *ye*, but it can also be seen as responsive to the different speech act values of granting a request and asking for information. In the former, the speaker is in a higher interactional position and can use *thou*, and in the latter he is in a somewhat lower position and therefore uses *ye*.

The third case study of this section, finally, is an exemplum told by the friar. According to Cooper, it is 'an exemplary tale about rapacity and intent' (Cooper 1996: 168). It is the story of a summoner who is on his way to extort money from a poor old widow when he chances on a fellow traveller who later turns out to be a fiend. The summoner pretends to be a bailiff because he is ashamed to admit to his true profession. The devil in the guise of a yeoman also claims to be a bailiff. It is interesting to note that the devil addresses the summoner with *thou*, while the summoner first uses the deferential pronoun *ye*. It appears that their respective guises do not extend to pronoun usage. The fiend does not need to show deference to somebody whom he knows to be a summoner and whom he hopes will be his next victim. The summoner, on the other hand, only pretends to be a bailiff and therefore uses the deferential pronoun that presumably would be appropriate from a summoner to a bailiff. He addresses his supposed fellow bailiff very politely as *brother* and with the deferential pronoun *yow*. He hopes to learn some new tricks of the trade, which gives the fellow traveller the situational advantage of having more information. The fiend is one-up, the summoner is one-down and the difference is reflected in the pronoun of address:

(11) 'Now, brother,' quod this somonour, 'I yow preye
   Teche me, whil that we ryden by the weye,
   Syn that ye been a baillif as am I,
   Som subtiltee, and tel me feithfully

In myn office how that I may moost wynne;
And spareth nat for conscience ne synne,
But as my brother tel me, how do ye.' (FrT III 1417–23)
'Now, brother', the summoner said, 'I pray you, teach me some of your tricks, while we ride along on our way, since you are a bailiff like myself, and tell me frankly how I can profit most in my business. And do not let conscience or sin hold you back but as a brother tell me how you do it'.

The fiend, who has earlier boasted about his wealth of gold and silver, now claims that his lord is so hard on him that he has to resort to extortion to make a living. To the summoner, who also makes a decent living from extortion, this line of argumentation sounds very familiar. He seems to have found a fellow after his own heart and consequently he switches to *thou*. Their shared way of living makes them more familiar with each other. The interactional status shifts accordingly:

(12)   Wel be we met, by God and by Seint Jame!
        But, leeve brother, tel me thanne thy name. (FrT III 1443–4)
        By God and St James, we are well met! But, dear brother, tell me your name.

At this point the fellow traveller reveals himself as a fiend, and immediately the summoner returns to *ye*:

(13)   'A!' quod this somonour, 'benedicite! What sey ye?
        I wende ye were a yeman trewely. (FrT III 1456–7)
        'Ah!' the summoner said. 'Good gracious! What are you saying? I really thought you were a yeoman'.

This is a first turning point in the tale. The devil's identity is revealed to the summoner. The interactional status shifts considerably. They are no longer on the same level, and the summoner can no longer address his fellow traveller with the familiar pronoun *thou*. He is surprised about the devil's human shape and asks him how it is that fiends can change their appearance. Throughout this discussion he sticks to the pronoun *ye*, until the fiend suggests that they should continue on their way, 'til it be so that thou forsake me' ('till it may be so that you forsake me'; FrT III 1522). This stirs the summoner's pride. He will not forsake his fellow traveller. They have sworn brotherhood, and he will stick to his pledge even if it was given to a fiend. They are still brothers, and therefore he switches back to the pronoun *thou*. They agree on a deal. They want to find out who is better at the trade of extorting money. The summoner tries to intimidate a poor old widow to pay twelve pence on some bogus charge. He uses *thou* to her and she addresses him with *ye*, which reflects their respective social status and their relationship to each other. He is in a position of dominance. But she cannot pay, and the summoner resorts to increasingly insulting accusations culminating in the charge that she has made her husband a cuckold. This provokes an outburst. The summoner has lost all credibility and the widow curses him, and from this point onwards she addresses him with *thou*:

(14)   'Thou lixt!' quod she, 'by my savacioun,
         Ne was I never er now, wydwe ne wyf,
         Somoned unto youre court in al my lyf;
         Ne nevere I nas but of my body trewe!
         Unto the devel blak and rough of hewe
         Yeve I thy body and my panne also!' (FrT III 1618–23)
         'You lie!' she said. 'By my salvation, up till now I have never been summoned to your court in all my life, whether as a wife or as a widow. Nor has my body ever been anything but faithful! To the black devil with his rough appearance I give your body and my frying pan!'

This is of course another turning point in the tale. With this curse, the devil has won both the summoner's life and the widow's frying pan. In the tale, both the summoner and the wife switch their pronouns in accordance with the momentary interactional status. The devil in his superior position uses *thou* throughout the tale when he addresses the summoner, but he addresses the widow very politely with *ye*. She is not his victim, but someone who yields him his profit with her curse of the summoner (cf. Nathan 1956; Finkenstaedt 1963: 75).

From these sample analyses several points emerge.[5] First, Chaucer's system of pronouns of address as manifest in the *Canterbury Tales* is characterised by retractable choices. Interlocutors may switch from *ye* to *thou* forms depending on the development of a spoken exchange. This contrasts with many of the systems in modern European languages, such as German, French, Polish or Czech, where the choice of pronoun is not usually retractable. In the *Canterbury Tales*, the choice of the appropriate pronoun is not fixed for each dyad of interlocutors. It is inconceivable for Chaucerian characters to go through the initiation ritual to switch from mutual *Sie* to mutual *du*, as it is known from modern German, for instance. Chaucerian characters are depicted as taking on-the-spot decisions. They may switch from *ye* to *thou*, or from *thou* to *ye*, in the course of a single conversation, depending on the interactional status reached at any given point.

Second, as Burnley (1983, 2003) suggests, the basic dimensions of the choice of the appropriate pronoun are the familiarity, social status and age of the interlocutors. But, contrary to the implications of his flow chart, none of these dimensions is a clear-cut dichotomy. On the contrary, they are scales, and it is the combined weight of all three dimensions that determines the basic choice of *ye* or *thou*. In addition, situational status may override these considerations. In the Wife of Bath's Tale, the old woman gains interactional status because she can impose her will on the knight after he is declared free. And he

---

[5] See Jucker (2006a) for similar analyses of two further tales, the Second Nun's Tale (a saint's life) and the Nun's Priest's Tale (a beast fable).

concedes her superiority after her long chiding speech. In the Friar's Tale, the summoner believes he has gained status when his fellow traveller admits to making a living by extortion. He loses this status when it becomes clear that this fellow traveller is a fiend, and regains it when he confirms the brotherhood that he has sworn.

Third, the sample analyses have shown that affection and intimacy are not appropriate criteria for the choice between *ye* and *thou*. The decision is rather governed by considerations of deference (i.e. respect and politeness). The Wife of Bath's Tale, for instance, shows clearly that pronoun usage does not coincide with the intimacy of the characters. In the bedroom scene, the knight first uses *thou* forms for his newly-wed wife because he despises her. After her chiding speech, when he has learnt his lesson of submission, he switches to the deferential *ye* forms.

And fourth, switches in pronoun usage often coincide with critical points in the narrative. Blake (1992) claims that major shifts in attitude are not common in courtly romances, but in the Wife of Bath's Tale the pronoun switches coincide clearly with major shifts in the characters' attitudes.

4.4   Nominal Terms of Address

Nominal terms of address have been placed on various scales of intimacy and politeness, ranging in their semantic types from intimate terms of endearment to more distant expressions with deference, and from polite communication to abuse with derogative name-calling. Raumolin-Brunberg (1996) suggests a scale from negative to positive politeness terms on the basis of Brown and Levinson's (1987) distinction between negative and positive politeness. On this scale, honorific titles are placed at the negative end of a sliding scale because they represent Brown and Levinson's (1987: 178–87) 'give deference' strategy, while terms of endearment and nicknames are placed at the positive end of the scale representing Brown and Levinson's 'use in-group identity markers', 'joke' and 'give gifts' strategies (Raumolin-Brunberg 1996: 171). Professional or occupational titles and kinship terms occupy less extreme positions on this scale (see Figure 4.4).

Negative		Positive	
Honorific titles (*lord*)	Other titles (*captain*)	Family (*brother*)	Terms of endearment (*sweetheart*) nicknames (*Will*)

Figure 4.4 The politeness continuum (Raumolin-Brunberg 1996: 171, slightly simplified)

This provides a useful way of thinking about the inherent qualities of different types of address terms, but, as pointed out in Chapter 1, in more recent years politeness theory has moved away from Brown and Levinson's essentialist ascription of fixed politeness values to specific expressions (see Locher and Watts 2005; Mills 2011, 2017). In specific contexts (e.g. in ironic, humorous or reprimanding contexts), address terms may adopt very different politeness, or indeed impoliteness, values.

The shades of meaning are often difficult to catch, particularly in historical texts, but the context helps and allows a discursive interpretation. In some cases, we have first-hand textual evidence of the use of *Madam* as a status symbol in late Middle English. According to the *Oxford English Dictionary* (s. v. madam), the noun was originally used by servants in speaking to their mistress, and more generally in speaking to a woman of high rank. English *madame* was also commonly used by children to their mother, a queen or a lady of very high rank in the extant examples. The desire to enhance one's social esteem by using a fine term of address was regarded as a sin of vanity:

(15)   Or ȝe wymmen also, comunly, wulde be kallede 'madame' or 'lady'; Al þys comþ of grete pryde. (Robert Mannyng, *Handlyng Synne*, lines 413–15)

   Or you women also commonly would like to be called 'madam' or 'lady'. All this comes of great pride.

Chaucer makes the same point, and in his time to be addressed as *madame* was one of the advantages of a citizen's wife if her husband was made alderman (*OED*):

(16)   It is ful fair to been ycleped 'madame,'
   And goon to vigilies al before,
   And have a mantel roialliche ybore. (GP I 376–8)
   It is very nice to be called 'my lady', and go to vigils[6] before everyone, and wear a cloak like a queen.

Madame is used almost exclusively in the address function, but such words are rare. The masculine counterpart *Sir* is not only an address term, but also a title. It is placed before the proper name or a common noun, forming with it a term of address, as *Sir Clerk, Sir King, Sir Knight*. The *OED* records it from the thirteenth century, and contemptuous and ironic uses emerged soon after (e.g. 'Sire olde lecchour, let thy japes be!' ('Old sir womaniser, stop your ploys'; WBT III 242)). The following passage contains *Sir* both as a title and an address term in polite conversation:

(17)   'Not so, syrs,' seyde sir Gaherys, 'hit was sir Launcelot that slew hym worshipfully with his owne hondys, and he gretys you all well and prayeth you to haste you to the courte. And as unto you, sir Lyonell and sir Ector de

---

[6] Vigils (i.e. public religious gatherings) on the evening before prescribed holy days (*MED, OED*).

Marys, he prayeth you to abyde hym at the courte of kynge Arthure.' (Malory, *Sir Launcelot du Lake*, pp. 268–9)

'Not so, sirs', Sir Gaherys said. 'It was Sir Launcelot who nobly slew him with his own hands, and he greets you all and entreats you to hurry to the court. And to you, Sir Lionel and Sir Ector de Maris, he entreats you to wait for him at King Arthur's court'.[7]

Address terms have been found to be sensitive interpersonal devices in the history of English. They have been studied as indicators of appropriate behaviour between people and social class distinctions have been discussed. The distribution of some central nominal address terms, like *leof, hlaford* and *ealdorman*, have been studied by Kohnen (2008b) on the basis of the Dictionary of Old English Corpus. Address terms are mainly found in sermons and poetry, and kinship terms and religious designations are particularly common in extant data. Kohnen's focus was on what attitudes these forms conveyed in various communicative situations. According to his study, friendship and affection-invoking family bonds prevail in the data, but authoritative language use based on hierarchical society is also prominent. Politeness in the way it is found in later periods was absent, and Kohnen did not find patterns of courteous behaviour. Instead, the use of address terms in Anglo-Saxon communication reflects mutual obligation and kinship loyalty, and the examples enhanced Christian values of *humilitas* and *caritas*. The following scene from the anonymous *Apollonius of Tyre* contains an address to the king, with native respectful nominal terms:

(18)   and eode into þam cynge and cwæð: Hlaford cyngc, glada nu and blissa, forðam þe Apollonius him ondræt þines rices mægna swa þæt he ne dear . . . (lines 179–81) (*Apollonius of Tyre* [0052 (7.17)])

and went to the king and said: 'Lord King, be glad and happy now because Apollonius is so much afraid of your kingdom's greatness that he dare not . . .'

Chapman's (2008) study on the same materials examines epithets used as insults in connection with second person pronouns. The following example comes from the debate between the body and the soul, and the insult is thrown by the soul as an accusation for getting them both damned:

(19)   La, ðu eorðan lamb & dust & wyrma gifel, & þu wambscyldiga fætels & gealstor & fulnes & hræw, hwig forgeate ðu me & þa toweardan tide? (HomU9 (ScraggVerc 4) 207)

Hey, you mud of the earth and dust and food for worms, and you bellyguilty bag and pestilence and foulness and corpse, why did you forget me and the future?[8]

Insults were also found in saints' lives and in addresses to devils and sinners. Most expressions proved conventional and were repeated in various contexts, yet some showed originality and creativity like that quoted above.

---

[7] The translations of extracts (17) and (18) are my own.   [8] Translation by Chapman (2008: 2).

Honegger (2004) focuses on one specific type of nominal forms of address in Middle English: pet names and terms of endearment between lovers. In dialogues between lovers, Honegger (2004) argues, forms of address are used that reflect the various stages of courtship. In the initial stages of an amorous relationship the typical terms for a woman would be *dame*, *madame* or *lady*, and for a man *sir* or *lord*, often with the qualifying adjective *swete* or *dere*, or the possessive pronoun *my*, and Honegger connects this usage to hierarchy and power and the concern for the negative face of the addressee (2004: 44). Beyond the initial stages of an amorous relationship the terms of address may change very significantly. They turn to the positive face needs of the addressee. Honegger quotes *hony*, *sweting*, *derling*, *herte* or *lif* from *William of Palerne* (2004: 48), but he also points out that the negatively polite *sire* persists as an address term used by Melior, the female protagonist, for her lover William well beyond the initial stages of their relationship.

In "'Wyȝe welcum iwys to this place" – and never mind the alliteration' (2005), Honegger investigated the influence of the alliterative metre in two Middle English romances, *Sir Gawain and the Green Knight* and *William of Palerne*, on the choice of specific nouns in direct address. He points out that nominal and pronominal forms of address regularly reinforce each other. The *thou* forms of solidarity and affection correlate with nominal terms such as *my leeve brother* and the *thou* forms of scorn correlate with address terms such as *false Arcite*, while the formal *ye* forms co-occur with more formal nominal terms of address, such as *lord* (in Chaucer's Knight's Tale; Honegger 2005: 171), but nominal and pronominal forms may also be used for variation rather than reinforcement. Against this background Honegger argues that the choice in *Sir Gawain and the Green Knight* and *William of Palerne* is often governed by the formal constraints of the alliterative poetry rather than pragmatic considerations.

4.5   Terms of Address in *Sir Gawain and the Green Knight*

In this section, I am going to provide a case study in which the two perspectives are combined to show how nominal and pronominal terms of address together provide a nuanced and complex picture of the interpersonal relationship between the characters in *Sir Gawain and the Green Knight*. De Roo (1997) has pointed out how names exert power, and how an unidentified character has power over an identified character. This is one of the driving forces in *Sir Gawain and the Green Knight*, in which the identities of the main characters (the Green Knight, Sir Bertilak de Hautdesert, Morgan Le Fay) are only revealed at the very end of the poem.[9] In this context it is also significant that the lady who visits Sir Gawain in his chamber is never named:

---

[9] See Chapter 3, Section 3 for an outline of the poem and a case study of the discourse of courtesy between Sir Gawain and the lady.

Table 4.2 *Nominal terms of address between Sir Gawain and Lady Bertilak*

	The lady to Sir Gawain	Sir Gawain to the lady
First encounter	Sir Gawayn	gay
	beau sir	lady louely
	my kny3t	Madame
	Sir Wowen	my souerayn
	Sir Gawayn	
	hende	
	kny3t	
	Gawan	
Second encounter	Sir	me dere
Third encounter	mon	lade
	dere	my gay
	mon	

Her anonymity does nothing to diminish the possibilities she represents from romance tradition on her initial entrance into the bedroom – a woman seduced by the knight's reputation; a lady in distress; a seductress; the wife of the 'Generous Host'; a Potiphar's wife; an agent of the devil. Isn't the power of her actions augmented by these multiple possibilities of the unidentified? (De Roo 1997: 242)

Table 4.2 gives an overview of the nominal terms of address that the lady and Sir Gawain use for each other in the three bedroom scenes. They also include some adjectives that are used nominally as terms of address.

In the very first line that the lady addresses to Sir Gawain, she addresses him with his name: '"God moroun, Sir Gawayn," sayde þat gay lady' ('"Good morning, Sir Gawain!" said that gracious lady'; SGGK III, 49, line 1208).[10] This may seem trivial as she obviously knows who he is, but it is also significant. In the sense of De Roo (1997), she exerts power over him. This conforms to the fairy-tale reality where figures, such as Rumpelstiltskin, lose their power as soon as they are named. She continues to address Gawain with his name in various spelling variations throughout the encounter. In an alliterative poem such as *Sir Gawain and the Green Knight*, the choice of terms of address is presumably not only based on considerations of the semantic and pragmatic impact of a particular name, but also on the formal constraints of

---

[10] As in Chapter 3, the original text is quoted from the edition by Tolkien and Gordon (1925), edited for its second edition by Davis (1967), and the Modern English version from Tolkien's translation (edited by Christopher Tolkien 1975). References are to the part of the manuscript, the stanza (numbers taken from the translation) and the line number (taken from the Davis edition).

alliterative form. A particular term must conform to the requirements of a particular poetic line (see Honegger 2005), and this may account for some of the variability, but the nominal terms that are not his name, *beau sir*, *hende* ('courteous, gracious (one))' and *knyʒt*, indicate how she frames him. Through these names she reminds him of his duties as a courteous knight and thus increases the pressure on him not to distress her by opposing her wishes.

Sir Gawain's terms in the first encounter are somewhat less varied. He addresses her as *gay* ('fair lady'), *lady louely*, *Madame* and *souerayn* ('liege lady') and thereby stresses her social position and the fact that he is obliged to serve her. In the second encounter only two nominal terms of address are used. The lady addresses Sir Gawain as *Sir*, and he addresses her as *me dere*. And in the third encounter, finally, the lady uses only *mon* and *dere*. In the opening line of their third interaction when she greets him, she calls him *mon* ('man'):

(20)   A! mon, how may þou slepe,
        Þis morning is so clere? (SGGK III, 69, 1746–7)
        Ah! man, how canst thou sleep,
        the morning is so clear!

She no longer addresses him with his name as in the first encounter. Her strategy has changed. In the first encounter, she used his name and nominal terms that stressed chivalry. At this point she uses very plain terms. She no longer appeals to his chivalry but merely to his gender as a man and to her feelings for him. It is also significant that at this point she does not use the expected pronoun *ye* but addresses him with *thou*.

De Roo argues that mutual *ye* between aristocrats conveys 'respect through the solidarity of mutual formality' (1997: 234) and he explicitly mentions the dyad of Sir Gawain and the lady. Mutual reciprocal *thou* between aristocrats conveys 'the solidarity of mutual intimacy', and for this usage De Roo also lists the dyad of Sir Gawain and the lady, although he notes that this occurs only rarely (1997: 233). However, I think it is more adequate to argue that they never exchange reciprocal *thou*, even though they both use *thou* for the other on a few occasions: the lady on several occasions in all three encounters and Sir Gawain only once in the third encounter.

Between Sir Gawain and the lady, the use of *ye* is the default in this courtly setting, and both speakers predominantly adhere to this choice. However, it is interesting that they do not always use the expected pronoun. The lady uses *thou* eight times against forty-two instances of *ye*; Gawain uses *thou* only once against thirty-five uses of the expected *ye* (see Table 4.3).

It might be hypothesised that these deviations indicate a greater intimacy. On the lady's side it might be an insistence on intimacy even where it is unseemly, and in the case of Sir Gawain one might speculate that in the third encounter he is on the brink of giving in to the lady's advances and,

Table 4.3 *Pronominal terms of address between Sir Gawain and Lady Bertilak (including different case forms, such as* thee, thine *or* your)

	Lady Bertilak to Sir Gawain		Sir Gawain to Lady Bertilak	
First encounter	*thou*	3	*thou*	-
	ye	17	*ye*	19
Second encounter	*thou*	1	*thou*	-
	ye	18	*ye*	13
Third encounter	*thou*	4	*thou*	1
	ye	7	*ye*	3

therefore, slips into the more intimate *thou*. But a closer reading indicates that respect and dominance are the guiding principles for the choice of *ye* and *thou*, respectively.

At the beginning of their first encounter, both the knight and the lady use the expected pronoun *ye*. Despite the unusual setting of the bedroom, they address each other with respect and courtesy. The lady first gives a few hints that her husband is away and then explicitly invites him to take advantage of the situation, and she uses *ye* throughout this first offer. When Gawain shows reluctance, she increases her enticement by pointing out that he is actually in her power, and at this point she switches to *thou*. Other ladies would be happy to have him in their power in the same way as she has him now:

(21)   Bot hit ar ladyes innoȝe þat leuer wer nowþe
         Haf þe, hende, in hor holde, as I þe habbe here. (SGGK III, 50, 1251–2)
         But there are ladies in number who liever would now
         have thee in their hold, sir, as I have thee here.

She continues with *thou* a little later when she tells him that if she had to choose a husband she would prefer him before all others. Immediately afterwards she reduces her insistence, becomes more playful again and switches back to *ye* to steal the first kiss from him.

In the second encounter the lady again greets Gawain with *ye*, but she only takes a few lines to switch to *thou* when she playfully reproaches him for having forgotten the lesson of the previous day:

(22)   Þou hatz forȝeten ȝederly þat ȝisterday I taȝtte
         Bi alder-truest token of talk þat I cowþe. (SGGK III, 59, 1485–6)
         [T]hou hast forgot altogether what a day ago I taught
         by the plainest points I could put into words!

Gawain is intimidated by the reproach and perhaps also by her choice of pronoun. He does not know why he is – playfully – chided by the lady of the house. She switches back to *ye* and reminds him that he should not refuse favours offered to him. She points out that he is so strong that he could even have taken the favour by force, and she certainly would not have refused it. She wants to learn from him the art of courtly love. Thus, she only uses *thou* for him when she reproaches him but not in her more submissive wooing strategy.

In the third encounter, finally, there are more switches. She immediately addresses him with *thou*, and this time reproaches him for sleeping:

(23)   A! mon, how may þou slepe,
            Þis morning is so clere? (SGGK III, 69, 1746–7)
            Ah! man, how canst thou sleep,
            the morning is so clear!

And before he is fully awake she kisses him for the first time during this third encounter. When she tells him how wounded she is in her heart and when she asks him whether he serves another lady, she adheres to *ye*. It is only at the point where she realises that he refuses her without serving another lady that she accepts defeat, but she requests a love token from him, and for this she switches back to *thou* and uses it three times in two lines (*þy gifte, þi gloue, on þe*) to increase the effect and the insistence of the request:

(24)   Now, dere, at þis departyng do me þis ese,
            Gif me sumqvat of þy gifte, þi gloue if hit were,
            Þat I may mynne on þe, mon, my mournyng to lassen. (SGGK III, 72,
            1798–800)
            Now, my dear, at this parting do me this pleasure,
            give me something as thy gift, thy glove it might be,
            that I may remember thee, dear man, my mourning to lessen.

For the remaining lines, in which the lady first offers a precious ring and then the protective girdle as love tokens, she returns to the use of *ye*.

Sir Gawain only once uses a *thou* pronoun for the lady, otherwise he always addresses her by *ye*. This one instance occurs in the third encounter, when Gawain refuses to give her a love token:

(25)   'Now iwysse,' quoþ þat wyʒe, 'I wolde I hade here
            Þe leuest þing for þy luf þat I in londe welde,
            For ʒe haf deserued, for soþe, sellyly ofte
            More rewarde bi resoun þen I reche myʒt;
            Bot to dele yow for drurye þat dawed bot neked,
            Hit is not your honour to haf at þis tyme
            A gloue for a garysoun of Gawaynez giftez. (SGGK III, 72, 1801–7)
            'Now on my word,' then said he, 'I wish I had here
            the loveliest thing for thy delight that in my land I possess;
            for worthily have you earned wondrously often
            more reward by rights than within my reach would now be,
            save to allot you as love-token thing of little value.
            Beneath your honour it is to have here and now
            a glove for a guerdon as the gift of Sir Gawain'.

At this point, the lady has relinquished her wooing, and he has survived the precarious situation she put him in unscathed – as far as he is aware at this point. He has remained both courteous towards her and true to his chivalric ideals. He has no love token to offer her, though he wishes that he had something 'for þy luf' ('for thy delight'), and with this choice of pronoun he both asserts his momentary interactional dominance and – by using þy instead of the more respectful *your* – depreciates her feelings for him. To do something 'for her delight' apparently does not deserve the pronoun of respect. But in the following utterances, he immediately switches back to the courtly courtesy of using the expected *ye* to the lady of the house.

4.6 Conclusion

Terms of address can be very sensitive to issues of politeness. This is true for both pronominal and nominal terms of address but to different degrees. Pronominal terms of address draw most of their interactive potential from situations in which there is a choice between two different terms. The sample analyses presented above show that the choice is not an obligatory one imposed by any given dyad of speaker and addressee, but one that carefully reflects the interactional status between the interactants. The characters in Chaucer's *Canterbury Tales* and those in *Sir Gawain and the Green Knight* choose the pronoun *ye* or *thou* to address their interlocutors on the basis of the interactional status of speaker and addressee and they adjust their judgement of the situation – or discernment – on the micro-level of their conversations. They switch back and forth, if necessary, in response to their developing interactional status throughout the conversation. Nominal terms of address are more varied. The lady in *Sir Gawain and the Green Knight*, as we have seen, carefully adjusts her choice from *Sir Gawayn, beau sir* or *my knyʒt* to a simple *mon* according to the developing relationship between her and Gawain, and combines them with appropriate choices of *ye* or *thou*. Thus, all these choices must be seen in their discursive contexts. They do not have fixed politeness values, but they are part of the discursive negotiations of the relationship between the interactants. I will come back to the use of terms of address in the context of Shakespeare's plays in Chapter 6, where the system of the choice between *ye* and *thou* has already changed considerably and shows the first signs of its impending disintegration.

5   Renaissance and Early Modern England

5.1   Introduction[1]

The year 1500 has traditionally been seen as the dividing line between the Middle English and the Early Modern English periods. It also marks the beginning of the Renaissance in England. It was, of course, not a hard and fast boundary, but there are several events in the late fifteenth century and the early sixteenth that had a lasting influence on the cultural and social development in England and on the development of the English language. In the 1470s Caxton introduced the printing press in England. He had learned the art of printing on the Continent, where he had also printed the first book in English, his own 700-page translation of *The Recuyell of the Historyes of Troy*. Printing soon replaced the production of handwritten books and made books more affordable, which led to an extension of literacy and ultimately also to increased standardisation of written English.

The Renaissance was characterised by a new interest in the classical languages and literatures. The number of publications in English increased considerably, including also scientific treatises. And there was a growing demand for translations, not only from Latin and Greek but also from Italian, French, Spanish and Portuguese. The English Reformation was the result of the pope's refusal to annul Henry VIII's marriage to Catherine of Aragon, which had not produced a male heir for the English throne. Unlike the Reformation in Germany and elsewhere, it was not so much motivated by the desire to change Catholic doctrine but by political considerations. It also led to an increase in the demand for new Bible translations.

The sixteenth century was also a time of great prosperity for England. In 1558, Elizabeth I succeeded to the throne. Under her rule, England saw the golden age of English music with the composers Thomas Tallis, William Byrd and Thomas Morley. Public theatres were built in London, and towards the end of the century and into the beginning of the seventeenth century William Shakespeare was active as a playwright and actor in London. In 1588,

---

[1] This chapter includes material from Jucker (2010, 2012b, 2015).

England had asserted its place on the seas by defeating the Spanish Armada, an event that opened up the world for English explorers and colonisers and ultimately led to the worldwide spread of the English language.

5.2   The Art of *Sprezzatura*

The Renaissance also brought new influences in terms of polite or refined behaviour. In the middle of the sixteenth century, English translations of three important Italian conduct manuals were published: Baldesar Castiglione's *Il Cortegiano* (originally published in 1528, translated by Thomas Hoby and published as *The Courtyer* in 1561); Giovanni della Casa's *Il Galateo* (originally published in 1558, translated by Robert Peterson and published as *Galateo ... A treatise of the maners and behauiours, it behoueth a man to vse and eschewe, in his familiar conversation* ... in 1576) and Stefano Guazzo's *La Civil Conversazione* (originally published in 1574, translated by George Petttie and published as *The Civil Conversation* in 1581) (see Culpeper 2017: 199). Thus, there must have been a strong interest for such books, particularly from Italy. The translations were published soon after the original publications. Burke (2002) gives an outline of how *Il Cortegiano* quickly disseminated across Europe both in its Italian original and in various translations, including Latin ones. Culpeper (2017: 200) relates the interest in Italian publications, rather than Spanish, French or German publications, to the fact that Italy as a conglomeration of many individual states was no threat to England and had considerable cultural prestige. The consolidation of the middle ranks led to an interest in courtly or courteous behaviour in order to display a particular social rank. It is interesting to note that all three books are still in print today with relatively recent translations.

Baldesar Castiglione's *Il Cortegiano*, for instance, consists of a series of conversations in which the reader gets the picture of a perfect courtier, his language, his posture and his gestures. This book had a considerable influence on the perception of a gentleman among the higher social classes in England:

> The *uomo universale* ('well-rounded person') should do all things with what Castiglione calls *sprezzatura. Sprezzatura*, which is almost impossible to translate into a single English word, means something like 'effortless mastery'. The courtier, unlike the pedant, wears learning lightly, while his mastery of sword and horse has none of the fierce clumsiness of the common soldier in the ranks. The courtier does everything equally well but with an air of unhurried and graceful effortlessness. (Cunningham and Reich 2006: 330)

Berger Jr unravels the complexities of the term *sprezzatura* into several different aspects. First, he describes it as 'an art that hides art, the cultivated ability to display artful artlessness, to perform any act or gesture with an insouciant or careless mastery' (Berger Jr 2002: 295–6). This he calls the aesthetic aspect of *sprezzatura*, to which he adds the aspect of modesty, which serves to suggest a greater reality behind the actual images conveyed through the behaviour. The term also involves 'an attitude of slightly superior disdain' (Berger Jr 2002: 296). The courtier who knows how to behave with *sprezzatura* demonstrates his superiority to those of his peers unable to decipher the code. And finally, Berger Jr suggests, *sprezzatura* also involves the aspect of disguise or deceit, or better perhaps, the suggestion of deceit, as 'it involves not deceit *tout court* but rather the menace of deceit, the display of the ability to deceive' (2002: 297). *Sprezzatura* may mask unpleasant truths. The courtier presents himself as someone who may have secrets and knows how to hide them.

Here, we may actually see some of the seeds of the ambivalence of politeness, which combines pleasant behaviour with an intention to hide unpleasant motives. The polished surface of politeness covers the underlying realities. In Brown and Levinson's (1987) conceptualisation of politeness, this is expressed in terms of politeness strategies that mitigate face-threatening acts. In fact, Culpeper (2017: 204ff) uncovers interesting similarities between Della Casa's *Galateo* and present-day politeness theories. He finds that Della Casa's advice to his readers often corresponds to Brown and Levinson's (1987) strategies of positive or negative politeness or to Leech's (1983) maxims of politeness. It has to be remembered that Della Casa gives advice to his readers on how they should behave while Brown and Levinson as well as Leech provide descriptions that rationalise actual behaviour, but the similarities are striking. As an example of positive politeness, Culpeper gives, in his own formulation, Della Casa's advice to 'avoid disparagement of the other, speak kindly' (2017: 206), which essentially corresponds to Brown and Levinson's (1987) positive politeness or Leech's (1983) 'approbation maxim'. Or, to take a more specific example, Della Casa's 'Don't question, contradict, rebuke, or correct' corresponds to Brown and Levinson's positive politeness strategy, 'Avoid disagreement', and to Leech's agreement maxim. There are also examples of negative politeness. Della Casa's advice, again in Culpeper's formulation, 'Show respect, don't use ridicule' (2017: 208), can be seen as a rough equivalent of Brown and Levinson's negative politeness strategy, 'Give deference' or Leech's 'modesty maxim'.

According to Cunningham and Reich (2006), Castiglione's influence can be clearly seen in the plays of William Shakespeare and Ben Jonson (see also Alexander 2007: 84). Shakespeare's *Hamlet* is set in Denmark in the context of a feudal court, but the young courtiers are perfect examples of the Renaissance gentleman:

Hamlet goes to considerable lengths to establish that Prince Hamlet is a student at Wittenberg; his friendship with Horatio is both a sign and an effect of that status. In this respect, the play and its title character are synecdoches for the gentrification of learning that transformed the European aristocracy from a martial class to a highly literate, governing one in the early modern period. (Hanson 2011: 207)

Rosencrantz and Guildenstern also fit this picture. They were fellow students at Wittenberg. Like Hamlet and Horatio, they are interested in music and plays, and they speak a smooth and courtly language. Hanson (2011: 222) points out that within the thirty-five lines of their initial interview with Claudius and Gertrude, they are given the epithet 'gentle' five times. They are smooth and proficient courtiers of the new type.

Osric, on the other hand, is presented as an inept courtier despite the fact that he has studied all the courtesy books, as Brown and Gilman (1989: 204) argue. What he lacks is exactly this essential quality, *sprezzatura*:

It was cruel of the courtesy books to lay down all manner of rules and strategies to be learned and then say (almost) that it was all in vain because the most perfectly prepared performance had no value without effortlessness. And there was some suggestion that effortlessness or sprezzatura might, just possibly, not be teachable. (Brown and Gilman 1989: 204)

Cunningham und Reich (2006: 330) refer to Ophelia's dismay at Hamlet's strange behaviour as an illustration of the influence of Castiglione's *Courtier* on *Hamlet*:

(1)   OPH. O, what a noble mind is here o'erthrown!
The courtier's, soldier's, scholar's eye, tongue, sword,
Th' expectation and rose of the fair state,
The glass of fashion and the mould of form,
Th' observ'd of all observers, quite, quite down! (*Hamlet* 3.1.150–4)[2]

Ophelia has just witnessed Hamlet's 'To be or not to be' soliloquy followed by a short interaction with him in which she wanted to return the gifts he had given her. However, his replies were enigmatic to her. He told her that he had never loved her and advised her to go to a nunnery. At this point, Ophelia is still dumbfounded and tries to make sense of what has just happened. Hamlet has lost his *sprezzatura*, he no longer behaves like the Renaissance gentleman who combines the roles of courtier, soldier and scholar. He no longer observes the courtly forms and fashions of the day. The hopes and ornaments of the state have vanished together with his courtly behaviour.

At several points, Hamlet's loss of *sprezzatura* is contrasted with the behaviour of his courtly friends, who try to maintain it:

(2)   HOR. Here, sweet lord, at your service.
HAM. Horatio, thou art e'en as just a man
As e'er my conversation cop'd withal.
HOR. O my dear lord–
HAM.   Nay, do not think I flatter,
For what advancement may I hope from thee
That no revenue hast but thy good spirits
To feed and clothe thee? Why should the poor be flatter'd? (*Hamlet* 3.2.53–9)

---

[2] The Shakespeare quotations in this section follow the Riverside edition edited by Evans (1974).

Hamlet has just instructed the players about how they should perform the play that they are going to stage in front of the king, when he is first intercepted by Polonius, Guildenstern and Rosencrantz, whom he sends off on errands connected to the performance of the play. Once they have left, Horatio enters and submissively offers his services in the faultless style of the courtier. In fact, the two lines he is given in this extract contain no more than polite terms of address and courteous formalities. These are met by Hamlet's ridicule and scorn. It is also noteworthy that Horatio uses the polite *you* to address Hamlet and receives *thou* in return (see Chapter 6).

Later in the same scene, Guildenstern is given a very similar treatment:

(3)   GUIL. Good my lord, voutsafe me a word with you.
       HAM. Sir, a whole history
       GUIL. The King, sir –
       HAM. Ay, sir, what of him?
       GUIL. Is in his retirement marvellous distemp'red.
       HAM. With drink, sir?
       GUIL. No, my lord, with choler.
       HAM. Your wisdom should show itself more richer to signify this to the
       doctor, for for me to put him to his purgation would perhaps plunge him into
       more choler.
       GUIL. Good my lord, put your discourse into some frame, and (start) not so
       wildly from my affair.
       HAM. I am tame, sir. Pronounce.
       GUIL. The Queen, your mother, in most great affliction of spirit, hath sent me
       to you.
       HAM. You are welcome.
       GUIL. Nay, good my lord, this courtesy is not of the right breed. If it shall
       please you to make me a wholesome answer, I will do your mother's
       commandment; if not, your pardon and my return shall be the end of (my)
       business. (*Hamlet* 3.2.296–318)

Guildenstern's mode of address is carefully deferential. He is the perfect courtier and addresses Hamlet with the appropriate titles (three times 'Good my lord', plus 'sir' and 'my lord' in just seven utterances). It seems possible that Guildenstern's language is not only rather formal but even a little pretentious here. Hamlet mocks Guildenstern's formality by imitating it but wilfully misinterpreting Guildenstern's entreaties. On the surface, Hamlet's replies appear to be courteous but on the basis of Guildenstern's response we may assume that they are not in fact, and may well be performed with noticeable irony by the actor. Finally, Guildenstern protests that Hamlet's courtesy 'is not of the right breed', it is a mocking pretence of courtesy.

5.3   Positive and Negative Politeness in Early Modern English

Much of the existing research on politeness in Early Modern English is based on the politeness framework proposed by Brown and Levinson (1987). In this section, I am going to review some of this work before then proposing a more discursive approach to two plays by Ben Jonson. Brown and Gilman (1989) were the first to propose a systematic, politeness-based analysis of Early Modern English data. They used Brown and Levinson's (1987) model for an analysis of four tragedies by William Shakespeare: *Hamlet, King Lear, Macbeth* and *Othello*. They were particularly interested in Brown and Levinson's claims that the weightiness of a face threat can be established on the basis of the power relationship between the speaker and the addressee, the distance between them and the ranked degree of the face threat in a given society. In order to test this claim, they analysed pairs of scenes which differ only on one of these dimensions. They scored these scenes for politeness and then assessed whether the result conformed with the prediction of the theory. On the basis of their data, they concluded that the results for the power dimension and the intrinsic degree of the face threat were those predicted by the theory, but those for the dimension of distance between the interlocutors were not. In fact, they found that it is the affect between the speaker and the addressee which most clearly influences the politeness level. If characters like each other, they are polite; if they don't, they aren't; or, in Brown and Gilman's rather more careful wording, 'increased liking increases politeness and decreased liking decreases politeness' (1989: 159).

In order to assess the politeness of the passages, Brown and Gilman relied on a categorisation of sub-strategies of positive and negative politeness. These were modelled on the basis of Brown and Levinson's strategies and their distinction between positive and negative politeness, where positive politeness is addressed to the positive face wants of the addressee (i.e. his or her wish to be appreciated and liked by others), and negative politeness to the negative face wants of the addressee (i.e. his or her wish to be free from imposition). The following examples illustrate their categorisation:

(4)   Notice admirable qualities, possession, etc.

> FIRST SENATOR: Adieu, brave Moor. (*Othello*, I, *iii*, 286)
> DESDEMONA: Alas, thrice-gentle Cassio. (*Othello*, III, *iv*, 122)

(5)   Use in-group identity markers in speech.

> HAMLET [to Horatio]: Sir, my good friend, I'll change that name with you. (I, *ii*, 163)

(6)   Avoid possible disagreement by hedging your statements.

> KNIGHT [to King Lear]: My lord, I know not what the matter is; but to my judgement. (I, *iv*, 57–8) (Brown and Gilman 1989: 167)

Examples (4) to (6) illustrate sub-strategies of positive politeness that are addressed to the addressee's wish to be appreciated and liked by others. Examples (7) to (9) illustrate sub-strategies of negative politeness:

(7)   Be conventionally indirect.

IAGO [to Othello]: You were best go in. (I, *ii*, 29)
BANQUO: Worthy Macbeth, we stay upon your leisure [convenience]. (I, *iii*, 148)

(8)   Give deference.

OTHELLO [to the Duke and Venetian Senators]: Most potent, grave, and reverend signiors, My very noble and approved good masters. (I, *iii*, 76–7)

(9)   Go on record as incurring a debt

QUEEN [to Rosencrantz and Guildenstern]: Your visitation shall receive such thanks as fits a king's remembrance. (*Hamlet* II, *ii*, 25–6) (Brown and Gilman 1989: 168)

In extract (7), the speakers of the two examples state their request in an indirect way, and thus make it clear that they are not imposing on the addressee. In (8), the speaker uses a deferential formulation to address the duke and the Venetian Senators. This, too, is seen as a sign of non-imposition. And in (9), the speaker explicitly refers to her indebtedness to Rosencrantz and Guildenstern.

Brown and Gilman's study has been replicated and extended to Shakespeare's comedies by Kopytko (1993, 1995) and Bouchara (2009). Kopytko (1993, 1995) used more or less the same classification of sub-strategies in order to investigate a larger set of plays by Shakespeare. To the four tragedies analysed by Brown and Gilman, he added four comedies: *The Taming of the Shrew*, *A Midsummer Night's Dream*, *The Merchant of Venice* and *Twelfth Night*. In contrast to Brown and Gilman, who used the model only to assess minimally contrasting scenes, Kopytko counted the frequency of the sub-strategies in his data in order to quantify the politeness level of the individual plays and to contrast tragedies and comedies. In both types of play he found a significantly higher number of positive politeness strategies. He concluded:

I tentatively assume that the high rate of occurrence of positive politeness strategies in Shakespeare's plays characterises the interactional style or 'ethos' of Elizabethan society … If both claims, i.e. about the Elizabethan society and modern British society, are at least to some degree true, it may be tentatively proposed that the interactional style or 'ethos' of British society has evolved from the dominating positive politeness culture in the 16th century towards the modern negative politeness culture. (Kopytko 1995: 531–2)

The claim regarding the evolution from positive politeness to negative politeness from the Elizabethan to modern British society is appropriately hedged, but it must also be stressed that Kopytko here compares his results based on some very specific fictional dialogues with a very general stereotype of modern British society. The situation is, of course, considerably more complex both in Elizabethan and modern British society (see in particular Chapter 9).

Nevalainen and her research associates also rely on Brown and Levinson (1987), but they focus on very different material, personal letters written in the fifteenth century (e.g. Nevalainen and Raumolin-Brunberg 1995; Raumolin-Brunberg 1996; Nevala 2003) and in particular politeness issues as manifested in address formulae are at the centre of interest in these investigations; they come to conclusions within the Brown and Levinson framework that appear to differ from Kopytko's. Raumolin-Brunberg, for instance, argues for a predominantly negative politeness culture in the fifteenth century in which letter writers used elaborate designations for their addressees, such as those exemplified in (10) to (17):

(10)   Worshipful sir

(11)   Right worshipful mother

(12)   Right honourable and worshipful sir

(13)   Right worshipful and my right singular good master

(14)   Right entirely and my most special beloved husband

(15)   Right trusty sir and brother

(16)   Reverent and worshipful sir and my special friend and gossip

(17)   (Right) trusty and (right) well-beloved. (Raumolin-Brunberg 1996: 168–9; for
         a similar list see also Nevalainen and Raumolin-Brunberg 1995: 559–61)

Raumolin-Brunberg (1996: 171) suggests that such forms should not be seen as part of a dichotomy of negative and positive politeness. Instead she suggests a continuum on a sliding scale between negative and positive poles. The negative end of the scale comprises honorific titles and other terms indicating a person's social status (deference type of negative politeness), while the positive end comprises nicknames and terms of endearment. Other terms of address are situated between the two endpoints. Professional titles, such as *captain*, appear not far from the negative end, while kinship terms, such as *brother*, appear closer to the positive end. Personal names have an ambiguous position because they can either be used for non-titled individuals with a low social status or as in-group identity markers.

Over the centuries the concern for negative politeness gave way to more and more positive politeness:

The negative strategy of giving deference is simplified not only structurally but also socially. The spread of *sir* neutralizes power distinctions among the ranks below the nobility, and *madam* throughout the rank hierarchy ... Positive substrategies simplify and diversify, ranging from terms of endearment to marking in-group identity by the use of first names and even nicknames. (Raumolin-Brunberg 1996: 180)

Nevala (2003: 160) modifies this picture in some of the details for her data focusing on letters written between family members. The trend towards positive politeness differs according to the dyads. It is, for instance, not very strong in letters written by fathers and mothers to their children, but it is more pronounced among children writing to their parents. A general trend towards an increase of positive politeness from the fifteenth century to the seventeenth is nevertheless confirmed.

On the surface, this development seems to run counter to the development identified by Kopytko (1995) from a positive politeness culture at Shakespeare's time to the present-day negative politeness culture. The reason for this development might be in the increased privacy of private mail. In the fifteenth and early sixteenth centuries letters were still carried by personal messengers and often written by amanuenses and possibly even read out to the addressee, and thus were not really private. With the increased privacy of the mail system in the later sixteenth and seventeenth centuries, positive politeness increased. However, the same facts can also be seen in a different light. What has been described as negative politeness by Nevalainen, Raumolin-Brunberg and Nevala in the publications cited above should perhaps better be seen as cases of discernment politeness. Nevalainen and Raumolin-Brunberg (1995: 588) point out that of the three factors, power (P), distance (D) and absolute ranking of the imposition (R), proposed by Brown and Levinson (1987) to work out the weightiness of an imposition, P is the most important while R appears to be insignificant: 'Even severe impositions (R) need not alter the form of address' (Nevalainen and Raumolin-Brunberg 1995: 588). If Brown and Levinson's face-saving strategies are basically reduced to a consideration of the power differential between the writer and the addressee, the term discernment politeness seems more appropriate. Linguistic forms are chosen in response to the social context, and not as a strategy to avert a face threat. Thus the deference type of negative politeness can be seen as having its origin in forms of Middle English discernment politeness.

Nevalainen, Raumolin-Brunberg and Nevala in the works cited above argue for a heavy reliance on negative politeness strategies in their data from correspondence in the fifteenth century. If, as I argue, these forms of linguistic politeness should be interpreted as discernment politeness rather than negative face strategies, they would develop rather naturally from the Middle English concern for *curteisie* (see Chapter 3). Brown and Levinson (1987: 178) include 'Give deference' among their negative politeness strategies, but in situations in which the linguistic forms are chosen on the basis of interactional status rather than on the ranking of the imposition, the reanalysis as discernment politeness may be more plausible. And the non-imposition type of negative politeness can be seen as having a distinct history. As I have pointed out above, some instances of non-imposition politeness can be observed in the *Canterbury Tales*, but they are not very frequent and still far from the conventionalised forms of indirectness so prevalent in present-day English.

Culpeper (1996) also used Brown and Levinson's (1987) politeness approach as a basis for his analysis of impoliteness in a 'fly on the wall' documentary of an American army recruit training camp and in Shakespeare's *Macbeth*. He argues that both types of data are ideal for a study of impolite behaviour. In the army training camp, the rigid hierarchical power structure is rigorously maintained, often by the strategic use of impoliteness to destroy the recruits' individuality and self-esteem. In drama dialogues, verbal aggression and impoliteness are used as a source of entertainment. They are used to move the plot forward, in particular when it shifts from a state of equilibrium to a state of disequilibrium, and *Macbeth* can be seen as chains of equilibrium and disequilibrium, starting with the disequilibrium in the social structure created by the murder of Duncan, the former king. Culpeper cites an extract from the banquet scene. At the beginning of the scene, Macbeth and Lady Macbeth try to re-establish an equilibrium by using excessive politeness strategies, but the arrival of the ghost creates a new disequilibrium, causing Macbeth to lose his nerve and blame the lords on its appearance. This is when Lady Macbeth draws him aside and 'uses impoliteness to knock him back into line' (Culpeper 1996: 365):

(18)　LADY MACBETH:　　Are you a man?
　　　MACBETH:　Ay, and a bold one that dare look on that
　　　　Which might appal the Devil.
　　　LADY MACBETH:　　O proper stuff!
　　　　This is the very painting of your fear;
　　　　This is the air-drawn dagger which you said,
　　　　Led you to Duncan. O, these flaws and starts –
　　　　Impostors to true fear – would well become
　　　　A woman's story at a winter's fire,
　　　　Authoris'd by her grandam. Shame itself!
　　　　Why do you make such faces? When all's done,
　　　　You look but on a stool.
　　　MACBETH:　　　Prithee, see there.
　　　　Behold! look! lo! how say you?
　　　　Why, what care I? If thou canst nod, speak too.
　　　　If charnel-houses and our graves must send
　　　　Those that we bury back, our monuments
　　　　Shall be the maws of kites. *(Ghost disappears.)*
　　　LADY MACBETH:　　What! quite unmann'd in folly?
　　　MACBETH:　If I stand here, I saw him.
　　　LADY MACBETH:　　Fie! for shame! *(Macbeth* III.iv.57–73)

Culpeper argues that in this extract, Lady Macbeth consistently uses impoliteness to attack Macbeth's face in order to get him to pull himself together and

take action. She repeatedly attacks his masculinity ('Are you a man? ...
A woman's story at a winter's fire / Authoris'd by her grandam ... quite
unmann'd in folly?'), suggesting that he should be more masculine, which
for her means cold and ruthless and ready to perform murder. She also uses
sarcasm ('O proper stuff!'), scorn ('Shame itself' and 'Fie! For shame!') and
ridicule ('Impostors to true fear') in order to get him to regain his stability and
return to the banquet table.

Despite the criticism that has been levelled at Brown and Levinson's (1987)
politeness approach (see Chapter 2), it turns out to be a useful analytical tool
that focuses on some very specific politeness-related aspects of the plays under
investigation. It helps to highlight different types of politeness and it generates
useful hypotheses about the differences of politeness between Shakespeare's
time and our own. But the approach is also problematic, as suggested by its
critics, because it relies too much on a relatively simple match of specific
linguistic structures to specific politeness values and because it suggests that
such differences can even be quantified. In the following two sections, therefore, I propose a discursive approach that focuses more on the characters'
negotiations of specific politeness values and on their evaluations of each
other's behaviour. As case studies I use two plays by Ben Jonson.

5.4   Ben Jonson's *Volpone, or The Fox*

Ben Jonson (1572–1637) was, like his contemporary William Shakespeare,
a playwright, poet and actor. His play *Volpone, or The Fox* was first performed
in London in 1605. It is a play about greed and deceit. Volpone ('the Fox'),
a wealthy Venetian gentleman, feigns to be on his deathbed in order to attract
greedy fortune hunters. Voltore ('the Vulture'), Corbaccio ('the Raven') and
Corvino ('the Carrion Crow') try to ingratiate themselves in order to inherit
Volpone's fortunes. Mosca ('the Fly'), Volpone's servant, tells each of them
that Volpone has made him the sole heir in order to keep up their hopes and to
get them to bring even more presents. In the third scene of the first act, Volpone
receives one suitor after the other in what he would like his visitors to believe
are his last moments. In extract (19), Mosca announces Voltore, who presents
Volpone with an expensive plate:

(19)   VOLPONE   Bring him near, where is he?
            I long to feel his hand.
            MOSCA   The plate is here, sir.
            VOLTORE How fare you, sir?
            VOLPONE   I thank you, Signor Voltore;
            Where is the plate? Mine eyes are bad.
            VOLTORE (*gives the plate to Volpone*)   I'm sorry,
            To see you still thus weak.

MOSCA (*Aside.*)   That he is not weaker.
VOLPONE You are too munificent.
VOLTORE   No sir, would to heaven,
   I could as well give health to you, as that plate!
VOLPONE You give, sir, what you can. I thank you. Your love
   Hath taste in this, and shall not be unanswered.
   I pray you see me often.
VOLTORE   Yes, I shall sir. (*Volpone* 1.3.14–23)[3]

In this scene both Volpone and Voltore act with cunning and highly strategically. Volpone tries to project his terminal illness and his (conditional)
benevolence towards Voltore; Voltore tries to project his concern and good
will in order to be adopted as an heir. An analysis on the basis of Brown and
Gilman's (1989) and Kopytko's (1993, 1995) strategies of positive and
negative politeness would reveal very little here. All three characters use
the deferential term of address *sir*. Volpone and Voltore address each other
with this term (lines 16, 19, 21, 24) and Mosca uses it to address his master
(line 15). Volpone also uses the term of address 'Signor Voltore' (line 16). In
a Brown and Levinsonian framework this would be a negative politeness
strategy. In addition, Volpone uses a positive politeness strategy when he
gives reasons for his request to Mosca to show Voltore in ('I long to feel his
hand', line 15), and he uses a negative politeness strategy (to go on record as
incurring a debt) when he vaguely alludes that 'Your love … shall not be
unanswered' (lines 21, 22). If we add the concept of politic language use (e.g.
Watts 2003), we can observe that the terms of address are the forms that are
socially expected. They are not used strategically to avert some impending
face threat. Volpone's request to Mosca to show in Voltore is issued without
any adornment. It comes in the form of an unmitigated imperative ('bring him
near', line 15). In fact, the entire passage seems to take the form of politic
language use.

   However, discursively, a lot is going on in this passage and the spectators can
derive pleasure from seeing through the double layers. Voltore's question about
Volpone's health (line 16) is acknowledged ('I thank you') but not answered.
Presumably the actor will give some of the answer in his tone of voice,
suggesting that he is very weak and unlikely to rise again from his bed. The
humour also derives from the fact that the question, 'How fare you my sir' is
prototypically uttered in the hope to hear a positive answer, but the audience
knows that Voltore has high hopes to hear a negative answer. Volpone complies
with this wish but only in his gestures and his voice, not in the words he uses.
Volpone wants to touch the plate on the pretence of his bad eyesight.
Apparently, he also pretends to be too weak to hold the plate. So Voltore

---

[3] Quotations of *Volpone* follow Campbell's (1995) edition.

expresses his concern for Volpone's weakness, and the audience knows again that this weakness is exactly what Voltore had been hoping for, an interpretation that is reinforced by Mosca's aside to the audience in line 18 ('That he is not weaker'). Finally, Voltore expresses his wish to give his own health to Volpone, even though it is completely transparent that he wishes exactly the opposite. Finally, Volpone urges Voltore to visit him regularly ('I pray you see me often', line 24), which Voltore is likely to see as a positive sign in his quest to become Volpone's favourite and ultimately his heir, while for Volpone it is just a way of receiving more presents. Thus the veneer of civility and politic language thinly veils the motives of the characters, and the audience can enjoy the great contrast of the politic and polite interaction with the darker motives of the interactants.

Soon afterwards, the stratagems of intrigue and deceit reach a different level. Mosca persuades Corbaccio to disinherit his own son in favour of Volpone (1.4.87–123). This would convince Volpone of Corbaccio's love and it would seal Corbaccio's position as Volpone's heir. This would only be temporary, Mosca argues, since Volpone's death is imminent.

At the beginning of Act 3, Corbaccio's son Bonario arrives on the scene because he suspects some wrongdoing, and he strongly dislikes both Volpone and his servant Mosca. As yet, he does not know what has happened. He has not yet learned of the plot that would disinherit him. But he does not want to interact with Mosca because of his strong antipathy:

(20)   *Enter Bonario*
        MOSCA Who's this? Bonario? Old Corbaccio's son?
             The person I was bound to seek. Fair sir,
             You are happ'ly met.
        BONARIO   That cannot be by thee.
        MOSCA Why, sir?
        BONARIO   Nay, 'pray thee know thy way, and leave me;
             I would be loath to interchange discourse
             With such a mate as thou art.
        MOSCA   Courteous sir,
             Scorn not my poverty.
        BONARIO   Not I, by heaven—
             But thou shalt give me leave to hate thy baseness.
        MOSCA Baseness?
        BONARIO   Aye, answer me, is not thy sloth
             Sufficient argument? Thy flattery?
             Thy means of feeding?
        MOSCA   Heaven, be good to me.
             These imputations are too common, sir,
             And easily stuck on virtue when she's poor;
             You are unequal to me, and howe'er,
             Your sentence may be righteous, yet you are not,

> That ere you know me, thus proceed in censure;
> St Mark bear witness 'gainst you, 'tis inhuman.
> *(He weeps)*
> BONARIO *(aside)* What? Does he weep? The sign is soft and good!
> I do repent me that I was so harsh. (*Volpone* 3.2.1–19)

A Brown and Levinsonian analysis would again focus on positive and negative politeness strategies employed by both characters. Mosca, in his obsequious attempt to interact with Bonario, uses the positive politeness strategy of exaggerating sympathy and approval ('you are happ'ly met', line 3) and the negative politeness strategy of deferential terms of address (e.g. 'fair sir', line 2; 'courteous sir', line 6). Bonario also uses politeness strategies when he asks Mosca to move on. He uses the negatively polite phrase 'pray thee' (line 4), and provides a reason for his request (another negative politeness strategy), even if the justification for his request is a face-threatening act in itself. He uses a further negative politeness strategy when he veils the face threat of his unfavourable opinion of Mosca: 'Thou shalt give me leave to hate thy baseness' (line 8). But such an account would not do justice to the very different attitudes of the two characters. Mosca's obsequiousness contrasts with Bonario's more or less open hostility.

In contrast to the scene between Volpone and Voltore analysed above, Bonario does not hide his dislike of Mosca. He states openly that he does not want to talk to him, and that he hates his baseness, sloth, flattery and his position as a 'parasite' ('thy means of feeding', lines 8–11). But these sentiments are couched in polite, or perhaps rather politic, phrases. The terms of address that are used by Mosca and Bonario conform to expectations. Mosca, the servant, uses *you* to Bonario, the gentleman, while the gentleman uses *thou* to the servant. In a discursive approach, it is not sufficient to say that the phrases 'I pray thee' and 'thou shalt give me leave' are impolite in this scene. The effect of the scene derives from the fact that the default politeness of these phrases is diametrically opposed to the hostility towards his interlocutor of the character who uses them.

From the audience's point of view, Mosca's servile surface politeness comes across as insincere, while Bonario's polite hostility comes across as sincere and honourable. This is only possible because of the contrast of the inherent politeness value of the phrases, such as 'courteous sir' or 'thou shalt give me leave', with the context of their actual use. Mosca's use of such phrases is in conflict with his devious intentions, while in Bonario's case they reinforce the sincerity of the face-threatening and impolite attitudes that he expresses towards Mosca.

At the end of this passage, we get a rare comment by one of the characters on his politeness level. After Mosca's skilful strategy of redirecting Bonario's hostility to his own poverty and his weeping, Bonario regrets having been 'so harsh'. Thus, Bonario comments on the politeness level of his own utterances and evaluates them as 'harsh'. Clearly, he is concerned with the sentiments that he expressed about Mosca's baseness, sloth and flattery, and not about the veneer of polite phrases that he used for the purpose. This adds to our interpretation of the polite phrases ('I pray thee', 'thou shalt give me leave') as polite despite the hostility of the context.

Back in the second act, Volpone was enraptured by the beauty of Corvino's wife, Celia, and immediately decided that he wanted to have her for his own. Mosca, the parasite, is sent out to find a way of extricating Celia from her jealous husband. So Mosca tells Corvino that, for medical reasons, his master requires sex with a young woman, and he insinuates that Corvino's chances of becoming Volpone's heir would be greatly increased if he could provide a suitable woman for the purpose. Predictably Corvino can only think of his own wife and immediately proceeds to offer her to Volpone. However, Celia is horrified by her husband's indecent suggestion and subsequently by Volpone's advances. Volpone fails to seduce her and when he wants to take her by force, Bonario intervenes and rescues her. In the ensuing courtroom scene, Mosca, Volpone and the three dupes collude to utterly confuse the issues. Instead of Volpone, it is Celia and Bonario who seem to be accused. Corbaccio accuses his son and Corvino accuses his wife (extract 21):

(21)   NOTARO Your testimony's craved.
      CORBACCIO   Speak to the knave?
         I'll ha' my mouth first stopped with earth; my heart
         Abhors his knowledge; I disclaim in him.
      1ST AVVOCATO But for what cause?
      CORBACCIO   The mere portent of nature.
         He is an utter stranger to my loins.
      BONARIO Have they made you to this?
      CORBACCIO   I will not hear thee,
         Monster of men, swine, goat, wolf, parricide!
         Speak not, thou viper.
      BONARIO   Sir, I will sit down,
         And rather wish my innocence should suffer,
         Than I resist the authority of a father.
      VOLTORE Signor Corvino!
      2ND AVVOCATO   This is strange!
      1ST AVVOCATO   Who's this?
      NOTARO The husband.
      4TH AVVOCATO   Is he sworn?
      NOTARO   He is.
      3RD AVVOCATO   Speak then.

CORVINO This woman, please your fatherhoods, is a whore
   Of most hot exercise, more than a partridge,
   Upon recòrd—
1ST AVVOCATO No more.
CORVINO   Neighs like a jennet.
NOTARO Preserve the honour of the court.
CORVINO   I shall,
   And modesty of your most reverend ears.
   And yet I hope that I may say, these eyes
   Have seen her glued unto that piece of cedar,
      (Indicating Bonario)
   That fine well-timbered gallant: and that, here,
   The letters may be read, through the horn,
   That make the story perfect. (*Volpone* 4.5.105–26)

This is a violently impolite passage in which first Corbaccio seriously insults his own son, Bonario, and then Corvino follows suit by seriously insulting his own wife, Celia. They do this by calling them names. Corbaccio calls his son 'Monster of men, swine, goat, wolf, parricide' (line 111) and 'viper' (line 112). Corvino goes even further and calls his wife a 'whore' (line 117), a 'partridge' (line 118) and a 'jennet' (line 119). Campbell in his notes to the play points out that these animals are 'associated with filth (swine), lechery (goat and partridge), cruelty (wolf), filial ingratitude (viper), and resistance to discipline (jennet, a Spanish breed of horse)' (1995: 457). Corvino further claims to have seen his wife glued to Bonario, whom he calls a 'piece of cedar' (line 123), a tree which is characterised as 'tall, strong, and gluey' (Campbell 1995: 457). This seriously impolite and insulting use of language serves the dual purpose of confusing the judges by shifting the blame from Volpone to Celia and Bonario and of further ingratiating the speakers to Volpone. The dupes have not yet given up hope of becoming Volpone's heir and, therefore, they do everything to please Volpone; they even attack the dignity of their own families. In this case it is not polite language which covers up the hidden motives of the speakers but, on the contrary, violently offensive language which serves this purpose.

   In this extract we see again several reactions to politeness value. The 1st Avvocato first protests 'no more' (line 119), and the Notaro doubles up with 'preserve the honour of the court' (line 120). Corvino promises to oblige and also to preserve the 'modesty of your most reverend ears' (line 121). The statements by Corbaccio and Corvino are clearly meant to be outrageous in the context of a court. Thus, the analyst has discursive confirmation of the impoliteness value of what Corbaccio and Corvino say in the context of the court.

5.5   Ben Jonson's *Bartholomew Fair*

Ben Jonson's comedy *Bartholomew Fair* was first performed in London on 31 October 1614. It was the last of his four great comedies. It is set in the context of the annual fair held in London on Bartholomew's day, 24 August, and presents a detailed and turbulent picture of Londoners from very different social classes. The first act starts with the proctor John Littlewit and his friends, Winwife and Quarlous, who scheme to extract Littlewit's mother Dame Purcraft from the influence of the puritan Zeal-of-the-Land Busy. In Scene 4, they are joined by Humphry Wasp, a lively and irascible manservant. Wasp wants to collect a marriage licence for his master, the Esquire Bartholomew Cokes. Once he has received the licence, they are joined by Cokes, his fiancée Grace Wellborn and his sister Dame Overdo. Cokes is delighted to meet Wasp, but the sentiment does not appear to be mutual:

(22)   COKES O Numps! Are you here, Numps? Look where I am, Numps!
              And Mistress Grace, too! Nay, do not look angerly, Numps. My
              sister is here, and all; I do not come without her.
        WASP What the mischief, do you come with her? Or she with you?
        COKES We came all to seek you, Numps.
        WASP To seek me? Why, did you all think I was lost? Or run away
              with your fourteen shillings' worth of small ware, here? Or that I
              had changed it i' the Fair for hobby-horses? 'Sprecious—to seek me!
        MISTRESS OVERDO Nay, good Master Numps, do you show discretion,
              though he be exorbitant (as Master Overdo says) an't be but for
              conservation of the peace.
        WASP Mary gip, Goody She-Justice, Mistress French-hood! Turd
              i' your teeth; and turd i' your French-hood's teeth, too, to do you
              service, do you see? Must you quote your Adam to me? You think
              you are Madam Regent still, Mistress Overdo, when I am in
              place? No such matter, I assure you; your reign is out when I am
              in, dame.
        MISTRESS OVERDO I am content to be in abeyance, sir, and be
              governed by you; so should he too, if he did well; but 'twill be
              expected you should also govern your passions.
        WASP Wil't so forsooth? Good Lord! How sharp you are, with being
              at Bedlam yesterday! Whetstone has set an edge upon you, has he?
        MISTRESS OVERDO Nay, if you know not what belongs to your
              dignity, I do, yet, to mine.
        WASP Very well, then. (*Bartholomew Fair*, 1.5.1–29)[4]

Wasp uses a rather unfriendly tone to talk to his master and expresses his irritation that the party of three had come to seek him out at the fair. He asks his

---

[4] Quotations of *Bartholomew Fair* follow Campbell's (1995) edition.

master whether he had been worried that he, Wasp, would exchange his master's money for hobby horses, which is an ambiguous word that can refer both to a prostitute or to a toy horse (*OED*, 2nd ed., hobby-horse, *n.* meanings 3. b and 4.a). At this point Coke's sister, Dame Overdo, intervenes and asks Wasp to moderate his tone, thereby opening up a discourse on appropriate conversation. She urges him to show 'discretion' despite Coke's somewhat 'exorbitant' nature. 'Discretion' is here used in the meaning 'the quality of being discreet; the possession or demonstration of sound judgement in speech or action; prudence; tactfulness, trustworthiness' (*OED*, 3rd ed., discretion, *n.* II.4.a). Wasp, however, does not cooperate. He reacts by swearing at her and insulting her with such terms as *mary-gip* (a corruption of 'St Mary of Egypt') and *turd i' your teeth*, but she is not drawn in and wants to keep out of the exchange (to be in abeyance), but she also wants herself and her brother to be governed by Wasp's guidance, provided that Wasp manages to govern his passions. But he does not even think of doing so. He continues to insult her and associates her with the Hospital of St Mary of Bethlehem (Bedlam), an asylum for the mentally ill in London. Dame Overdo once again is not to be provoked. She prefers to keep her dignity even if he does not.

Here, too, the qualities of a gentleman – or Castiglione's *sprezzatura* – are discussed in a situation in which they are obviously missing. Discretion, dignity and control of emotions appear to be particularly important to Dame Overdo, and these qualities should appertain not only to a nobleman but also to the manservant Wasp, whom she seems to be treating as one of her own rather than as a servant, as she thinks it appropriate for her and her brother to be governed by him.

The second act opens in the commotion and hurly-burly of the fair. Judge Adam Overdo has appeared in disguise in order to observe the tricks and dealings of the people at the market. More visitors arrive on the scene, including Tom Quarlous and Ned Winwife, who chance upon Jordan Knockem, a horse-courser (with the double meaning of 'dealer in horses' and 'pimp'). And again, a brief discourse about proper behaviour ensues. Winwife and Quarlous debate the appropriateness of even talking to Knockem, but they are immediately accosted by him. He addresses them rather formally with their names and immediately offers them beer and tobacco:

(23)   WINWIFE Do not see him! He is the roaring horse-courser. Pray thee
       let's avoid him; turn down this way.
    QUARLOUS 'Slud, I'll see him, and roar with him too, an he roared
       as loud as Neptune; pray thee go with me.
    WINWIFE You may draw me to as likely an inconvenience, when you
       please, as this.
    QUARLOUS Go to the, come along we ha' nothing to do, man, but
       to see sights now.

> KNOCKEM Welcome Master Quarlous and Master Winwife! Will you
> take any froth and smoke with us?
> QUARLOUS Yes, sir, but you'll pardon us if we knew not of so much
> familiarity between us afore.
> KNOCKEM As what, sir?
> QUARLOUS To be so lightly invited to smoke and froth.
> KNOCKEM A good vapour! Will you sit down, sir? This is old
> Ursula's mansion. How like you her bower? Here you may ha'
> your punk and your pig in state, sir, both piping hot. (*Bartholomew Fair*,
> 2.5.22–38)

Quarlous takes offence at what he sees as too much familiarity in Knockem's
address to them despite the fact that he is happy to consider the offer of 'froth
and smoke', but Knockem does not know – or at least pretends not to know –
how to interpret the reproach of excessive familiarity. It could be his use of the
names of his guests in a context where they might have preferred to remain
anonymous (Gossett 2000: 9). But Quarlous clarifies that he has taken offence
at the immediacy of the offer of beer and tobacco. Knockem persists and asks
them to sit down; he introduces Ursula's market stall and describes it both as
a mansion and as a bower where both prostitutes and illegal pork meat can be
purchased 'piping hot' in the double meaning of 'sizzling, active' and 'infected
with the pox' (Gossett 2000: 85).

The third, slightly longer extract, is also taken from the fifth scene of
the second act. Quarlous and Winwife encounter Ursula, the large and heavy
pig woman, which leads to a sequence of reciprocal insults with absurd
metaphors and similes:

(24)   QUARLOUS Body o' the Fair! What's this? Mother o' the bawds?
         KNOCKEM No, she's mother o' the pigs, sir, mother o' the pigs.
         WINWIFE Mother o' the Furies, I think, by her firebrand.
         QUARLOUS Nay, she is too fat to be a Fury; sure some walking sow
           of tallow.
         WINWIFE An inspired vessel of kitchen stuff!
             She drinks this while.
         QUARLOUS She'll make excellent gear for the coach-makers here in
           Smithfield to anoint wheels and axletrees with.
         URSULA Ay, ay, gamesters, mock a plain plump soft wench o' the
           suburbs, do, because she's juicy and wholesome. You must ha'
           your thin pinched ware, pent up i' the compass of a dog collar – or
           'twill not do – that looks like a long laced conger, set upright; and
           a green feather, like fennel, i' the jowl on't.
         KNOCKEM Well said, Urs, my good Urs; to 'em, Urs.
         QUARLOUS Is she your quagmire, Dan Knockem? Is this your
           bog?
         NIGHTINGALE We shall have a quarrel presently.
         KNOCKEM How? Bog? Quagmire? Foul vapours! Hum'h!

QUARLOUS Yes, he that would venture for't, I assure him, might sink
into her and be drowned a week ere any friend he had could find
where he were.

WINWIFE And then he would be a fortnight weighing up again.

QUARLOUS 'Twere like falling into a whole shire of butter; they had
need be a team of Dutchmen should draw him out.

KNOCKEM Answer 'em, Urs, where's thy Bartholomew wit now?
Urs, they Bartholomew wit?

URSULA Hang 'em, rotten, roguy cheaters! I hope to see 'em plagued
one day (poxed they are already, I am sure) with lean playhouse
poultry, that has the bony rump sticking out like the ace of spades
or the point of a partisan, that every rib of 'em is like the tooth of
a saw and will so grate 'em with their hips and shoulders, as (take
'em altogether) they were as good lie with a hurdle. (*Bartholomew Fair*,
2.5.67–98)

The first insult relates to Ursula's business as the owner of a brothel ('Mother o'
the bawds') and as a dealer and consumer of alcohol, but the conversation
immediately turns to her oversized build. Quarlous and Winwife compete to
find the most ridiculous metaphors for her. She is described as a fat sow or an
inflated vessel for storing fat in the kitchen, which would also be useful for
coachmakers to grease their wheels and axles. Ursula reciprocates and
reproaches them for their preference of 'pinched ware' (i.e. women or prostitutes thin as a compass needle), a close-fitting collar, a streaked sea eel or some
fennel (Gossett 2000: 87). As a result, Quarlous becomes even more abusive
and asks Knockem whether Ursula is his quagmire, which, according to
Gossett, means 'anything soft, flabby, and yielding, here suggesting the vagina'
(2000: 87). Knockem is horrified, while Quarlous and Winwife gleefully
continue and extend the insulting metaphors: one might sink into her and be
drowned; it would feel like getting lost in a sea of butter and it would take
weeks to get out again. Ursula retorts with equally insulting metaphors and
associates them with venereal diseases and emaciated prostitutes whose ribs
stand out like the teeth of a saw.

This passage exemplifies the clash of different worlds but all of them rather
dubious and shady. The characters do not strive for politeness but for impoliteness. Quarlous and Winwife relish insulting Ursula, who defends herself with
her own creative impoliteness (Jucker and Taavitsainen 2000). Knockem contributes to the dispute on a meta level. He encourages Ursula to defend herself
('well said . . . to em Urs . . . Answer 'em, Urs, where's thy Bartholomew wit
now?'), while Ursula herself does not defend herself on a meta level but pays
back in the same currency as she has received.

Bartholomew Fair is not a realistic representation of the behaviour of
Londoners at the beginning of the seventeenth century, it is a fictional and
exaggerated caricature. As such it provides a rich spectrum of interpersonal

behaviours between people of different social classes that can be investigated on a scale of politeness and impoliteness. It differs clearly from Jonson's better-known *Volpone, or The Fox*. *Volpone*'s main character is a rich Venetian merchant who stages his own impending death in order to play off his legacy hunters against each other, which leads to a plot full of exceptionally polite interactions masking the scheming and intrigue. *Bartholomew Fair*, on the other hand, does not play in a distant Venice but in London. The characters do not hide behind deceiving politeness. They attack each other with open and often crude impoliteness.

But in both plays, there are passages in which the characters negotiate and discuss the appropriateness or politeness of individual utterances, and even if there is no explicit talk about politeness, the reactions of the characters provide some insights into the politeness value of specific utterances in the given contexts. In *Volpone* members of the higher levels of society are among their own and use politeness to disguise their impolite motives. In *Bartholomew Fair* different levels of London's society clash in direct and open hostility and impoliteness.

5.6   Conclusion

The beginning of this chapter identified the sixteenth century as a particularly important period in the development of politeness in the history of English. It was in this century that for the first time a large number of conduct manuals were published in England. Many of them were translations from Italian originals and they introduced a new understanding of how people should behave. The term *sprezzatura* describes a new ideal of a courtier who is well trained in the arts and sciences and who behaves with effortless ease and grace. At the same time, we can see some clear indications that such behaviour can also be a pleasing surface to somewhat less pleasing underlying motives. The chapter has also reviewed some of the early work that investigated politeness in historical sources. These scholars generally relied on Brown and Levinson's seminal work to identify instances of positive and negative politeness in Shakespeare's plays (Brown and Gilman 1989; Kopytko 1995) or in a corpus of sixteenth-century correspondence (Nevalainen and Raumolin-Brunberg 1995; Raumolin-Brunberg 1996; Raumolin-Brunberg 1995; Nevala 2003).

The analysis of Ben Jonson's plays in the second part of this chapter has shown several things. As a play full of deception and intrigue it has turned out to provide rich material for analyses of polite and impolite behaviour. Surface politeness is often in conflict with the characters' real intentions. The nature of a play as fictional language has the advantage of giving the analyst a better insight into the hidden motives of the characters and, therefore, it is easier to tease apart speaker intentions and actual behaviour. In real life, the analyst can only take communicative behaviour at its face value. He or she has no, or only limited, access to the real motives of the speakers. In a play, the author often provides clues for the audience. Characters often spell out their real intentions in other scenes, either in soliloquies or in interaction with other characters. In the context of the fictional world, Volpone projects a truer image of his own character when he interacts with Mosca, while he provides a deceptive image to all the other characters of the play. Part of the audience's pleasure derives from the conflict of the different levels. The audience knows more than the characters on the stage.

Obviously, the politeness and impoliteness patterns encountered in these plays cannot be taken in any straightforward way to be representative of everyday face-to-face communication in London at the time of Ben Jonson. The reality depicted in these plays is a stage reality. It is very likely that it is not entirely disconnected from Ben Jonson's real world, but an analysis of a play should be seen as saying something about this play and not necessarily about Early Modern English in general.

On a theoretical level, I have tried to show the potential of a discursive approach to historical data. In some cases we have explicit comments by the characters on the politeness level of the ongoing interactions. Such comments provide first-hand information on the politeness or impoliteness value of specific linguistic expressions and their actual use in specific situations. And in addition, a careful study of the 'discursive structuring and reproductions of forms of behaviour' (Locher and Watts 2005: 16) reveals much about the interaction of the semantic politeness values of linguistic expressions and the pragmatic politeness values of the utterances in the specific contexts in which they are used. This kind of approach does not lend itself to a quantitative analysis of politeness levels. It seems very unlikely that it could be used in the same way in which Kopytko (1993, 1995) used the approach by Brown and Levinson (1987) and Brown and Gilman (1989) to quantify politeness strategies in Shakespearean plays. But it can be used for microanalyses of specific scenes in order to dissect the linguistic behaviour of individual characters in contrast to their real motives. A discursive approach thus provides a particularly rich perspective on the structure of politeness and impoliteness in play texts.

6   Terms of Address in Early Modern English

6.1   Introduction[1]

By the time of Shakespeare, the choice between two pronominal terms of address for a single addressee had been in existence for over 300 years (see Chapter 4) and, in fact, it appears that at this time the use of *thou* was already a clearly marked form (see Walker 2003, 2007). In certain contexts, at least, *thou* had already acquired a sense of insult. In Shakespeare's comedy *Twelfth Night*, Sir Toby urges Sir Andrew, who is in love with Olivia, to compose a challenge to Cesario, whom Sir Andrew believes to be a suitor of Olivia.

(1)   SIR TO. Go, write it in a martial hand, be curst and brief. It is no matter how witty, so it be eloquent and full of invention. Taunt him with the license of ink. If thou thou'st him some thrice, it shall not be amiss; and as many lies as will lie in thy sheet of paper, although the sheet were big enough for the bed of Ware in England, set 'em down. Go, about it. Let there be gall enough in thy ink, though thou write with a goose-pen, no matter. About it. (*TN*, III.ii.42–50)[2]

From this passage it becomes clear what kind of politeness, or rather impoliteness, value Sir Toby assigns to the use of a *thou*-form. As a form of address from Sir Andrew to Cesario it would add to the insult of the challenge and it would amount to 'taunting' Cesario.

The next passage is drawn from the trial of Sir Walter Raleigh (1552–1618), the English courtier, explorer, writer, and favourite of Elizabeth I. He was imprisoned and tried for treason under James I, and beheaded in 1618:

(2)   RALEIGH: I do not hear yet, that you have spoken one word against me; here is no Treason of mine done: If my Lord Cabham be a Traitor, what is that to me? ATTORNEY: All that he did was by thy Instigation, thou Viper; for I thou thee, thou Traitor. (Helsinki Corpus: E2 XX TRI RALEIGH I, 208)

---

[1] This chapter is a revised and extended version of Jucker (2012c). It also includes short passages from Jucker (2012b).

[2] In this chapter, quotations of *Romeo and Juliet* are taken from Evans (2003). Other quotations of Shakespeare are taken from Evans (1974) unless otherwise indicated. Abbreviations for the plays' titles are taken from Evans (2003: viii).

The attorney here uses the *thou*-form for Sir Walter Raleigh and comments on his own usage. Normally the social status of the defendant and the formality of the court setting would require a *you*-form, but the attorney is convinced of Raleigh's guilt and, therefore, uses *thou* to address him, and, in fact, the insulting pronoun is accompanied by equally insulting nominal terms of address, 'viper' and 'traitor' (see also Taavitsainen and Jucker 2007: 125; Jucker and Taavitsainen 2013: 83).

These examples show that the system of terms of address has changed considerably between Chaucer's time and that of Shakespeare. By the time of Shakespeare, the system has become the topic of explicit comments by characters in plays or by interactants recorded in transcriptions of courtroom interaction. In the sources investigated in Chapter 4, *The Canterbury Tales* and *Sir Gawain and the Green Knight*, the choice between *ye* and *thou* reflected the social and situational power structure of the interactants and their level of respect for each other. By the time of Shakespeare, the system seems to have adopted an additional layer of emotionality. The choice is no longer just a matter of politeness and respect, but it is also a matter of emotional closeness or distance, of intimacy or insult. This is the topic of the current chapter. In addition, I will show how the pronominal terms of address correlate systematically with nominal terms of address. On this basis, I hypothesise that it is the increased emotionality which ultimately led to the demise of the pronoun *thou*. Its frequent use in highly emotional contexts gradually prevented its further use in neutral situations.

6.2   Pronominal Terms of Address

The case markings of the pronouns show that Shakespeare used a somewhat archaic system which reveals clear signs of erosion. He no longer consistently distinguishes between the subject and the non-subject forms of the pronouns of address (see U. Busse 1998). In the following speech, which the Nurse addresses to Romeo, she uses the pronouns *ye* and *you* indiscriminately in both subject and non-subject position. The first three occurrences are all instances of the expected *you* in non-subject position. This is followed by two cases of *ye*, the first in non-subject and the second in subject position. The last instance is again *you*, but this time in subject position:

(3)   NURSE Now afore God, I am so vexed that every part about me quivers. Scurvy knave! Pray **you**, sir, a word: and as I told **you**, my young lady bid me enquire **you** out; what she bid me say, I will keep to myself. But first let me tell **ye**, if **ye** should lead her into a fool's paradise, as they say, it were a very gross kind of behaviour, as they say; for the gentlewoman is young; and therefore, if **you** should deal double with her, truly it were an ill thing to be offered to any gentlewoman, and very weak dealing. (*Rom.* 2.4.133–40)

As a result of such morphological inconsistency, it is plausible to assume that Shakespeare also used the pragmatics of the pronoun choice less consistently than Chaucer. Micro-pragmatic, turn-by-turn explanations are more difficult. The system clearly had changed in the 200 years since Chaucer, but any attempt to ascertain the consistency of either Chaucer's or Shakespeare's system pre-supposes, of course, that we know the details of the underlying system from which the two authors might have deviated.

Hope describes the basic choice between the *thou*-forms and the *ye*-forms, or T and Y for short, as follows:

> The basic factor determining choice of *th-* or *y-* pronoun in Early Modern English is social relationship: *th*-forms are used *down* the social hierarchy; *y*-forms *up* it. This means that those in authority – kings, lords, husbands, fathers, masters – can use *th*-forms to those in subordinate roles: subjects, vassals, wives, children, servants. Subordinates use *y*-forms in return. Social equals usually exchange mutual *y*-forms in the Early Modern period. (2003: 73; italics original)

However, things are often more complex, as a brief analysis of the opening scenes of *Romeo and Juliet* clearly demonstrates. In the first scene Sampson and Gregory, two members of the house of Capulet, address each other with T, but when they encounter Abram and Balthasar, two servants of the house of Montague, Gregory switches to Y to address Abram and receives Y in return. When Benvolio, a Montague, and Tybalt, a Capulet, enter the scene, however, they immediately use T to each other. The tone is hostile, and they do not waste any efforts on unnecessary decorum. It is no surprise that later in the same scene, Montague, the head of the Veronese family, uses T to Benvolio, one of the members of his household, and receives Y in return (1.1.147–50). The interactions between Romeo, Montague's son, and Benvolio are again more complex. They start out with mutual T (1.1.174–80), but when Romeo threa-tens to leave, Benvolio switches to Y (1.1.187). In the next scene, however, Benvolio uses T to Romeo and receives Y in return (1.2.44–51, 82–7), but soon afterwards – without discernible reason – Benvolio switches back to Y, too. The interaction between Lady Capulet, the Nurse and Juliet in Scene 3 of the first act further follows the basic system as described by Hope. Lady Capulet uses T both to the Nurse and to Juliet, and she receives Y from both of them. The Nurse and Juliet, however, mostly use T to each other despite their status difference, but on certain occasions the Nurse switches to Y to address Juliet, such as when she announces her to her mother (1.3.6) or in a later scene when she calls Juliet away from her interaction with Romeo at the ball (1.5.110). In this case, the switch can easily be explained by the increased formality of the situation. Romeo and Juliet almost exclusively use T for each other except for Juliet, who uses Y to Romeo during their first encounter before they even know each other's identities (1.5.92–109).

Even this brief and cursory analysis shows that in many cases it is difficult to account for pronoun choices on a turn-by-turn basis. Many scholars have, therefore, tried to supplement or even replace the micro-pragmatic account with a more sociolinguistically informed approach focusing on relative frequencies of pronouns in different plays and in particular on the frequencies of the pronouns in specific dyads of characters. Thus, the choice of pronoun is accounted for on the basis of the constellation of a particular pair of interlocutors but not for each individual occurrence of a pronoun of address. The occurrences are accounted for on a sociolinguistic basis on their relative frequencies over longer stretches and often over entire plays (see Busse and Busse 2010 on historical pragmatic analyses of Shakespeare's plays, and Mazzon 2010 on address terms in general).

Stein (2003), for instance, uses a markedness approach to study the pronominal terms of address in Shakespeare's *As You Like It* and *King Lear*, that is to say he combines an approach that establishes general usage patterns with micro-pragmatic analyses that account for deviations from these patterns. He identifies socially defined dyads, such as fathers and daughters, servants and aristocrats, or lovers, and establishes the unmarked use of pronouns for each of them. Against the backdrop of this usage, he then focuses on specific cases of pronoun switches and studies them in detail within their dramatic context and the emotional involvement of the communicating characters. Positive or negative emotions may lead to a switch from an expected T to a Y or vice versa. He concludes that the pronoun usage in these two plays is in accordance with the general development that turned the Y pronouns into the default at the beginning of the seventeenth century.

Mazzon (2003), in a similar fashion, investigates the terms of address in *King Lear*, *Othello* and *Hamlet*. She also establishes usage patterns for specific types of relationships between characters, such as husband and wife, father and daughter or between equals. However, she looks not only at pronominal terms of address, but also considers their interaction with nominal terms of address, to which I shall turn in the next section.

6.3   Nominal Terms of Address and Vocatives

Juliet asks: 'What's in a name?', and adds: 'That which we call a rose / By any other word would smell as sweet' (*Rom.* 2.2.43–4). According to the traditional linguistic approach, signs are arbitrary. The word 'rose' does not smell like a rose, neither does it look or sound like one. But words have conventional meanings. They have denotative meanings, which specify the range of concepts that the word can refer to, and they have associative meanings, which concern language users' attitudes towards the concepts referred to by the word. As opposed to common nouns, proper nouns or names are generally said to have no sense but only reference. In *Romeo and Juliet*, names are particularly important and, therefore, worthy of investigation. In Act 3, Scene 3, Romeo very explicitly comments on the significance of names:

(4)   ROMEO   As if that name,
                Shot from the deadly level of a gun,
                Did murder her, as that name's cursèd hand
                Murdered her kinsman. O tell me, Friar, tell me,
                In what vile part of this anatomy
                Doth my name lodge? Tell me, that I may sack
                The hateful mansion. (*Rom.* 3.3.102–8)

In this extract, Romeo speaks to Friar Laurence just after killing Juliet's cousin Tybalt. Both Romeo and Juliet are concerned with the potent meaning of their family names. They are deeply in love but their love is impossible because of their family names and the hostility between the families which these two names represent.

Names of people are used both to refer to them when talking about them and as vocatives, or nominal terms of address, when talking to a person. Linguistically, a distinction is made between common nouns, proper nouns and names. Proper nouns generally refer to people, places, months, days, festivals and so on (Quirk et al. 1985: 288), and their formal characteristics differ from common nouns. Common nouns take articles (*rose, the rose, a rose*), while proper nouns generally do not (*Stratford, *the Stratford, *a Stratford*). In a given universe of discourse, proper nouns have unique denotation, that is to say they unambiguously refer to one specific entity only and from a synchronic point of view they do not have sense. Quirk et al. (1985: 288) define proper nouns as single words, while a name may consist of more than one word. Thus *Shakespeare* and *William Shakespeare* are both names consisting of one or two proper nouns.

Proper nouns, and by implication also names, generally refer to one specific entity and are semantically meaningless. In the words of Biber et al., 'The most typical proper nouns (e.g. *Tom, Hobart*) are arbitrary designations which have no lexical meaning. There are no defining characteristics for those who carry the name *Tom*, except that they are male' (1999: 245). In the context of a play, names have an important function for the audience, who need to keep track of who is who. For Romeo and Juliet clearly this is different. Their family names should be arbitrary labels ('What's in name?'), but they are full of significance standing in the way of their love. A name can even murder ('As if that name . . . did murder her').

Vocatives are used by speakers to refer directly to the person or thing to whom or to which they are speaking. Quirk et al. define the term 'vocative' as follows: 'A vocative is an optional element, usually a noun phrase, denoting the one or more persons to whom the sentence is addressed' (1985: 773; see also

Biber et al. 1999: 1108–13). The most detailed study of vocatives in the plays of William Shakespeare has been carried out by Beatrix Busse, who defines vocatives as follows:

[V]ocatives are direct attitudinal adjunct-like forms of address. Realised as a nominal group or head alone, vocatives are optional in form, they may be introduced in Shakespeare by the morphological marker *O*, and their position may be either initial, middle or final in the clause. (2006: 29)

Shakespeare often presents his characters as being very much aware of the significance and power of how they address each other. When used as vocatives, names are often embedded in standard phrases and used as more or less empty formulas, but on occasion they can regain their literal force (B. Busse 2006: 210), as in the following extract from *King Henry VI, Part 3* (see also Chapter 1, Extract (4)):

(5)   GLOU. Good day, my lord. What, at your book so hard?
         K. HEN. Ay, my good lord – my lord, I should say rather.
         'Tis sin to flatter; 'good' was little better:
         'Good Gloucester' and 'good devil' were alike,
         And both preposterous; therefore not 'good lord.' (*3H6* 5.6.1–5)

The exchange takes place in the tower where King Henry has been captured by Richard and his followers. It is one of the final interchanges between the two rivals before Henry's abdication and his death. Henry reflects on a variety of forms of address – including the use of the name *Gloucester* modified by the epithet *good*, and the reasons why the epithet does not seem to fit the formulaic address in this case. The extract shows how sensitive terms of address were or could be in Shakespeare's plays.

Beatrix Busse argues that besides their interpersonal and textual potential, 'Shakespearean vocatives, as so-called "experiential markers," semiotically re-construe and construe experience into meaning and are part of the experiential metafunction of language' (2006: 129). She distinguishes between a large range of different vocatives to account for all occurrences in Shakespeare's work. She distinguishes between name-based vocatives that are based on modified or unmodified proper nouns and non-name-based vocatives (see also Busse and Busse 2010: 259). The non-name-based vocatives can be further subdivided into the three categories of those that are related to human qualities, those that are not related to human qualities and a third category which Busse labels 'EPITHETS' in capital letters to distinguish it from epithets that are used as premodifiers of nouns or names. Figure 6.1, based on B. Busse (2006: 132), gives an overview of her categorisation.

The category of personal names comprises unmodified and modified personal names, such as *Benvolio, Balthasar, good Juliet* (5.3.159) or *gentle Romeo*

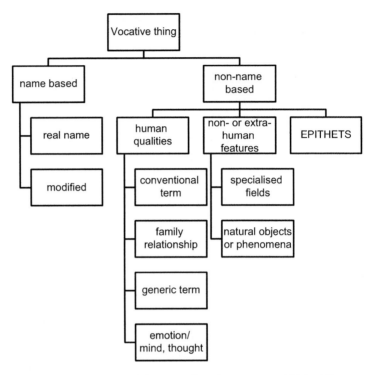

Figure 6.1 Vocatives in Shakespeare (based on B. Busse 2006: 132)

(1.4.13). Among the non-name-based names, the category of conventional terms describes those terms that are related to early modern England's hierarchical society and its social structures. Relevant examples would be *sir* (1.1.37, 38, 39), *my lord* (1.2.6) or *your ladyship* (3.5.106). Terms of family relationship are illustrated by examples such as *gentle coz* (1.5.64) or *daughter* (3.5.64). Generic terms are those that overtly refer to the male or female gender of the addressee and often to his or her age. Relevant examples are *boy*, *girl*, *good fellow* or *man* (5.3.1, 1.3.106, 5.3.42, 1.2.44). The category of 'emotion/ mind, thought' refers to expressions that designate an emotion or thought, such as *dear love* (2.2.136). There are two more categories under the non-name-based vocatives. There are those that refer to specialised fields (e.g. legal, medical, metaphysical), and there are those that refer to natural phenomena, such as sense and perception, parts of the body or food. Some of these terms are used to address humans, such as when Capulet addresses his daughter with *you green-sickness carrion* and *you baggage* (3.5.156). And some are used to address non-human entities as in the following example:

(6)   ROMEO ...

> Here's much to do with hate, but more with love:
> Why, then, O brawling love, O loving hate,
> O any thing of nothing first create!
> O heavy lightness, serious vanity,
> Misshapen chaos of well-seeming forms,
> Feather of lead, bright smoke, cold fire, sick health,
> Still-waking sleep, that is not what it is!
> This love feel I, that feel no love in this.
> Dost thou not laugh? (*Rom.* 1.1.166–74)

In his first substantial speech, Romeo addresses the feelings love and hate, and feelings evoked by them. At this point, he has not yet met Juliet and he is characterised as 'the lover in love with love (hence largely with himself)' (Evans 2003: 12).

EPITHETS, finally, refer to 'vocatives that describe a kind of quality already inherent in the semantics of the thing' (B. Busse 2006: 133, 137). As such they denote a quality that is more important than a generic quality. Beatrix Busse gives the example of the vocative *whore*, which denotes the female sex of the addressee and as such has generic qualities, but the quality of being a prostitute is the more important aspect of the term. *Sirrah* (4.2.2) or *good my friend* (5.3.124) are relevant examples in *Romeo and Juliet*.

Table 6.1 gives Beatrix Busse's statistics of the frequency of these categories in *Romeo and Juliet*. It appears that the conventional terms are the most frequent category. EPITHETS, personal names and specialised fields are next. The category 'Emotion/mind, thought' is the least frequent.

In the context of all the other plays by Shakespeare, *Romeo and Juliet* does not stand out in any way in its use of vocatives. The relative frequency of vocatives in the entire corpus investigated by Beatrix Busse (2006: 146) is

Table 6.1 *Vocative constructions in Shakespeare's* Romeo and Juliet *(extracted from B. Busse 2006: 148, Table 3)*

	Occurrences	Frequency per 100 words
Conventional terms	152	0.64
Emotion/mind, thought	24	0.10
EPITHET	91	0.38
Generic terms	27	0.11
Natural phenomena	74	0.31
Personal names	91	0.38
Specialised fields	81	0.34
Terms of family relationships	54	0.23
Total	594	2.48

2.31 per 100 words. In *Romeo and Juliet* it is slightly higher at 2.48 but considerably lower than the 3.38 vocatives per 100 words in *Titus Andronicus*, the play with the highest frequency.

6.4   Co-occurrence of Nominal and Pronominal Terms of Address

Ulrich Busse (2003) has developed a particularly clear way of visualising the correlation of pronominal and nominal terms of address. For each individual nominal term of address, he establishes how often it co-occurs with a T or a Y pronoun (i.e. its so-called *thou*- or *you*-fulness). In order to visualise the result, he uses the logarithm of the division of the frequencies of Y and T. If the frequencies are identical, the division equals 1 and the logarithm is 0. If the frequency of Y is higher than that of T, the division is larger than 1 and the logarithm positive, if Y is smaller, the division is smaller than 1 and the logarithm is negative. A logarithm of +1 indicates that Y is ten times as frequent as T, and a logarithm of −1 that T is ten times as frequent as Y. In order to enhance the visibility of the result, the logarithm is multiplied by one thousand (see U. Busse 2003: 217, fn 11). The results are bar charts with negative and positive bars representing what Ulrich Busse calls *you*-ful and *thou*-ful terms of address (i.e. terms of address that tend to co-occur more often with *you* or more often with *thou*).

Figure 6.2 represents the six categories of terms of address that Ulrich Busse distinguishes and the extent of their *thou*- or *you*-fulness. The three bars on the left of the diagram indicate negative values. These terms of address co-occur more often with the pronoun *thou* (U. Busse 2003: 196). Terms of endearment, such as *chuck*, *heart*, *joy*, *love* or *wag* show the highest predominance of *thou* over *you*. Terms of abuse, such as *devil*, *dog*, *fool*, *knave*, *rascal*, *rogue*, and generic terms of address, such as *boy*, *friend*, *gentleman*, *gentlewoman* or *lad*, also co-occur more often with *thou* than with *you* but not to the same extent as terms of endearment. The remaining three categories of terms of address co-occur more often with *you* than with *thou* in Shakespeare's work. These are terms indicating family relationships, such as *brother*, *cousin*, *coz*, *daughter*, *father* or *husband*; terms of address indicating occupation, such as *captain*, *doctor*, *esquire*, *justice*, *knight* or *nurse*; and titles of courtesy, such as *Your Grace*, *Your (Royal) Highness*, *Your Honour*, *Your Ladyship*, *Goodman*, *goodwife*, *lady*, *lord* or *sir*.

Ulrich Busse observes that the order of these categories echoes Brown and Levinson's (1987) politeness scale. The titles of honour and courtesy represent the extreme end of negative politeness or deference while the terms of endearment represent the extreme end of positive politeness.

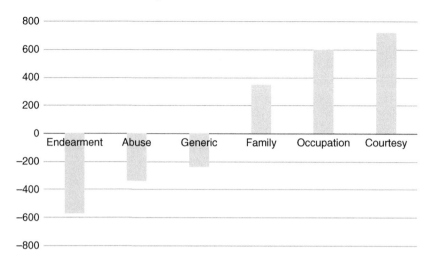

Figure 6.2 Co-occurrence of pronominal and nominal forms of address in Shakespeare's plays. Values: 1,000 * log(Y/T) (source: U. Busse 2003: 214)

The scale in Figure 6.2 suggests that the T pronouns are used together with terms of endearment to express intimacy, and with terms of abuse they express contempt and lack of respect. The predominant co-occurrence with terms of courtesy and occupation, on the other hand, indicates that Y pronouns are used to indicate deference and respect. The fact that terms of family relationship also occur more often with Y pronouns than with T pronouns indicates that solidarity in the sense of Brown and Gilman (1960, 1989) does not automatically call for T pronouns.

6.5 William Shakespeare's *Romeo and Juliet*

In Figure 6.3 I have applied Ulrich Busse's methodology to throw a more focused light on the six most frequent terms of address in *Romeo and Juliet*. The Nurse, Romeo and Juliet are more often addressed with T than with Y, and the term *villain*, which is used to address different characters also co-occurs more often with T than with Y. The terms *Madam* and *Sir*, on the other hand, co-occur more often with Y. They are *you*-ful terms in Ulrich Busse's terminology.

It is noteworthy that the extreme values in Figure 6.3, both positive and negative, are considerably higher (or lower) than in Figure 6.2. It is plausible to assume that this is the result of the much smaller basis on which these figures have been calculated. In contrast to Figure 6.2, the different bars in Figure 6.3

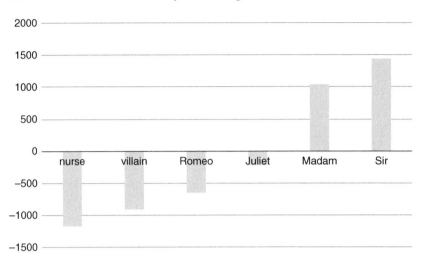

Figure 6.3 Co-occurrence of pronominal forms of address with selected nominal forms of address in *Romeo and Juliet*. Values: 1,000 * log(Y/T)

do not comprise the data of large categories of terms of address, but only the data of single characters (the Nurse, Romeo, Juliet) or one single term of address used for a range of different characters (*villain*, *Madam*, *Sir*). It is also significant that Romeo and Juliet receive most address terms from each other (almost exclusively T) and from the Friar, who also almost exclusively uses T to both of them. The Nurse, on the other hand, mostly addresses Juliet with Y (8 T/38 Y) but Romeo's and Juliet's *thou*-fulness depends mostly on their own address terms and those of the Friar.

For Romeo it is clearly T which is the unmarked pronoun of address. He uses 118 T pronouns and only seven Y. The Y pronouns are addressed to Juliet (twice), the Nurse (twice), Benvolio (twice) and Mercutio (once). But all four of them receive more T pronouns from Romeo: Juliet (thirty-two), the Nurse (thirteen), Benvolio (six) and Mercutio (three). This pattern shows Romeo to be a character who enjoys a fairly high social position and who only rarely cares for the social decorum of the Y pronoun.

Table 6.2 gives an overview of the pronoun choices between Romeo, Benvolio, Mercutio and Tybalt. This table once again reveals the multifunctionality of the T pronouns. Benvolio, Montague's nephew, and Mercutio, a kinsman of the Prince, are both friends of Romeo. Tybalt, Capulet's nephew, is one of Romeo's foes. Romeo addresses all of them mostly with T and only rarely with Y. He never uses the pronoun of respect for Tybalt. His friends also address him mostly with T but they use Y pronouns more often than Romeo. Tybalt only uses

Table 6.2 *Pronominal terms of address (T/Y) between friends and foes in* Romeo and Juliet

	Addressee			
Speaker	Romeo	Benvolio	Mercutio	Tybalt
Romeo		6 / 2	3 / 1	12 / 0
Benvolio	14 / 8		2 / 0	1 / 0
Mercutio	25 / 6	13 / 0		3 / 4
Tybalt	3 / 0	5 / 0	2 / 5	

Table 6.3 *Nominal terms of address between friends and foes in* Romeo and Juliet *(ordered in each cell according to their first occurrence)*

Speaker/ addressee	Romeo	Benvolio	Mercutio	Tybalt
Romeo		*my coz, cousin, good fellow*	*Mercutio, gentle Mercutio, man good Mercutio*	*Tybalt, good Capulet*
Benvolio	*cousin, coz, fair coz, man, Romeo*			
Mercutio	*gentle Romeo, Sir, madman, lover, Signor Romeo*	*Good Benvolio, Benvolio*		*Tybalt, you rat-catcher, good king of cats, sir*
Tybalt	*Romeo, boy, wretched boy*	*Benvolio*	*Sir*	

T to Benvolio. Benvolio and Mercutio only use T to each other. Among the foes, it is only Mercutio and Tybalt who switch between T and Y to address each other.

Table 6.3 tabulates the nominal terms of address used by the same four friends and foes as Table 6.2. The results are perhaps somewhat less clear-cut. They indicate that the friends tend to use each other's names or family relationships (*coz, cousin*), and they tend to premodify these terms with *good, fair* or *gentle*, while the foes either use mostly unadorned names or insults.

It is interesting to compare these usages with the more neutral stance of the Prince. The Prince rarely uses address terms that are modified by adjectives. He addresses his interlocutors mostly with their plain names: *Benvolio* (3.1.142), *Capulet* (1.1.90), *Montague* (1.1.81, 91). In one case, he uses the term 'old Capulet' (1.1.81). For the Prince, names are neutral designations. For the other characters, however, names are not neutral, and appropriate adjectives are used to connote the emotional value of the names themselves.

Table 6.4 *Nominal terms of address and referring expressions used by Romeo and Juliet for each other (ordered in each cell according to their first occurrence)*

Speaker	Terms of address	Referring expressions
Romeo	*Dear saint*	*The fair daughter of rich*
	Juliet	*Capulet*
	bright angel	*thy lady and mistress*
	fair saint	*thy lady*
	love	*sweet Juliet*
	my love, my wife	
Juliet	*Good pilgrim*	*My love*
	Romeo	*Romeo*
	gentle Romeo	*My dearer lord*
	fair Montague, gentleman	*Beautiful tyrant, Fiend*
	dear love	*angelical*
	sweet Montague	*Dove-feathered raven,*
	my Romeo	*wolvish-ravening lamb*
	Poor my lord	*Despised substance of*
	Love, lord, ay, husband,	*divinest show*
	friend	*A damned saint, an*
	Churl	*honourable villain*
		My husband
		That husband
		My sweet love

For Romeo and Juliet, names, terms of address and referring expressions are perhaps even more important. They use a variety of vocatives and nominal designations to address each other, and referring expressions when talking about each other to other characters. Table 6.4 lists all the vocatives and all the referring expressions that the two lovers use for each other.

The distinction between terms of address and referring expressions is not always as straightforward as it might seem. Romeo and Juliet address each other not only when they actually talk to each other but also in their soliloquies, for instance in Act 5, when Romeo encounters what he believes to be Juliet's dead body (5.3.74–120) and when Juliet wakes up to find her husband dead (5.3.160–70). But Juliet also seems to talk to her husband when she learns from the Nurse that he has killed Tybalt (see below). In such passages it is not entirely clear whether the nominal designations are used as address terms or as referring expressions.

In the light of the above considerations, I shall discuss two extracts from *Romeo and Juliet* in some more detail. In the first scene of Act 3, Benvolio and Mercutio encounter Tybalt. After a verbal fight, Romeo enters and tries to defuse the situation. Because of his secret love for Juliet he no longer pursues the struggle between the houses of Montague and Capulet. He very clearly hints at his changed feelings towards the house of Capulet but his allusions are not understood in the intended sense:

(7)   *Enter ROMEO*
> TYBALT   Well, peace be with **you**, **sir**, here comes my man.
> MERCUTIO   But I'll be hanged, **sir**, if he wear **your** livery.
>   Marry, go before to field, he'll be **your** follower;
>   **Your** worship in that sense may call him man.
> TYBALT   **Romeo**, the love I bear **thee** can afford
>   No better term than this: **thou** art a villain.
> ROMEO   **Tybalt**, the reason that I have to love **thee**
>   Doth much excuse the appertaining rage
>   To such a greeting. Villain am I none;
>   Therefore farewell, I see **thou** knowest me not.
> TYBALT   **Boy**, this shall not excuse the injuries
>   That **thou** hast done me, therefore turn and draw.
> ROMEO   I do protest I never injured **thee**,
>   But love **thee** better than **thou** canst devise,
>   Till **thou** shalt know the reason of my love;
>   And so, **good Capulet**, which name I tender
>   As dearly as my own, be satisfied.
> MERCUTIO   O calm, dishonourable, vile submission!
>   'Alla stoccata' carries it away. *(Draws.)*
>   Tybalt, **you rat-catcher**, will **you** walk?
> TYBALT   What wouldst **thou** have with me?
> MERCUTIO   **Good King of Cats**, nothing but one of **your** nine lives that
>   I mean to make bold withal, and as **you** shall use me hereafter,
>   dry-beat the rest of the eight. Will **you** pluck **your** sword out of
>   his pilcher by the ears? Make haste, lest mine be about **your** ears
>   ere it be out.
> TYBALT   I am for **you**. *(Drawing.)* (*Rom.* 3.1.49–75)

At the beginning of this extract, Mercutio and Tybalt address each other with Y pronouns and with the honorific *sir*, which is Shakespeare's most frequent vocative and used here as a neutral and socially safe term of address. The social decorum is still intact, but it immediately breaks down when Tybalt addresses Romeo. He switches to T and calls him a villain, which is a very serious insult 'carrying not only the sense of "depraved scoundrel" but undertones of "low-born fellow" (=villein)' (Evans 2003: 137, fn to line 3.1.54). The word 'love' in line 53 is highly ironic, and some editors prefer the reading *hate* from the first Quarto because such irony seems untypical of Tybalt (Evans 2003: 137, fn to line 3.1.53). Romeo, in his attempt to defuse the situation, ignores the insult and tries to end the risky interaction, but he also uses T to address Tybalt, possibly because he feels closer to Tybalt than Tybalt can understand at this point, but Tybalt is either not placated by Romeo's address or he takes the T pronoun as picking up the challenge he presented with his own T and the term 'villain'. Tybalt sticks to T and addresses Romeo as *boy*, a further insult (see Crystal and Crystal 2002: 52). In his response, Romeo uses five T pronouns and addresses Tybalt as 'good Capulet'. These signs are now clear enough for Mercutio, who is incensed by what he perceives as Romeo's submission to Tybalt's insults. So he verbally attacks Tybalt, calling him 'alla stoccata', which literally means 'at the thrust' and refers to an Italian type of fencing despised by Mercutio (Evans 2003: 138, fn to line 3.1.67). He addresses him as a cat with the terms 'rat-catcher' and 'good King of Cats' (according to Evans 2003: 119, 138 fn to lines 2.4.18 and 3.1.68, an allusion to a fictional cat called Tybert or Tibault) but, perhaps surprisingly, he sticks to the formal Y pronoun. In return Tybalt, who accepts the challenge for a fight, also addresses him with Y.

From this interaction it becomes clear why it is problematic to account for pronoun choices on a strict turn-by-turn basis. We might have expected Romeo to use a Y pronoun to show his new-found respect and 'love' for the house of Capulet and, therefore, for Tybalt. But as I have shown above, T is the unmarked choice for Romeo from which he does not deviate at this point. At the same time, we might have expected Mercutio and Tybalt to use T as an expression of their contempt for each other. The full significance of T and Y pronouns in this play can, therefore, not be gleaned easily from such examples. The broader perspectives provided above in which pronominal terms of address are correlated with nominal terms of address and tabulated for significant pairs of interlocutors or for specific categories of nominal terms of address provide a more comprehensive picture.

The second scene of Act 2, following the scene from which the previous extract is taken, is a turning point in the play. Juliet has been married to Romeo for only a few hours, and now she is to learn that her husband has killed Tybalt, one of her cousins. At the beginning of the scene, still unaware of the events, she awaits the Nurse's report on Romeo. However, on her return the Nurse is so overwhelmed by the calamity of the news she must convey that she presents a confusing and ambiguous account and it takes Juliet several turns to find out what has happened. When Juliet finally grasps the impact of the news, she is torn in her feelings:

(8)   NURSE Tybalt is gone and Romeo banishèd.
               Romeo that killed him, he is banishèd.
        JULIET O God, did Romeo's hand shed Tybalt's blood?
        NURSE It did, it did, alas the day, it did!

JULIET O serpent heart, hid with a flow'ring face!
        Did ever dragon keep so fair a cave?
        Beautiful tyrant, fiend angelical!
        Dove-feathered raven, wolvish-ravening lamb!
        Despisèd substance of divinest show!
        Just opposite to what thou justly seem'st,
        A damnèd saint, an honourable villain!
        O nature, what hadst thou to do in hell
        When thou didst bower the spirit of a fiend
        In mortal paradise of such sweet flesh?
        Was ever book containing such vile matter
        So fairly bound? O that deceit should dwell
        In such a gorgeous palace! (*Rom.* 3.2.71–84)

Juliet uses a string of pairs of referring expressions that are incompatible in themselves. Romeo is both a beautiful tyrant and an angelical fiend; he is both a raven and a lamb, but a dove-feathered raven and wolfish-raving lamb, and even a damned saint and honourable villain. Thus, Juliet's conflicting feelings find a very direct expression in the incongruity and incompatibility of the terms that she uses to refer to the man she married only a few hours ago. Romeo is not present in this scene, but Juliet's words seem to be addressed to him. Later in the scene she already regrets her words ('O what a beast was I to chide at him!', 3.2.94) but the phrasing suggests that they were addressed to her husband. It is, therefore, not quite clear whether these designations are terms of address or referring expressions. But they indicate once again the power of names (in the wider sense of the word).

6.6   Conclusion

This chapter has reviewed the use of pronominal and nominal terms of address at the time of Shakespeare. In Chapter 4, I presented the situation some 200 years earlier, at the time of Chaucer. In Chaucer's *Canterbury Tales* and the anonymous *Sir Gawain and the Green Knight*, terms of address turn out to be very sensitive linguistic devices that reflect issues of politeness. The characters carefully choose *ye* or *thou* and appropriate nominal terms of address to manifest their interactional status and, crucially, the level of respect warranted by this status. The forms themselves do not have fixed politeness values, but they have default values that are discursively negotiated in the interactions between the characters.

In Shakespeare's plays it proves more difficult to establish an underlying system of pronoun usage. Choices of pronouns or nominal terms of address cannot always be accounted for on a turn-by-turn basis but more plausibly only on a more global level for different dyads of speakers, which corresponds to

Ulrich Busse's claim about Shakespeare's use of nominal and pronominal terms of address:

Shakespeare uses both nominal and pronominal address in his plays and . . . a correlation between these categories in terms of variable rules can be established. However, [this paper] has also proved that pronoun use is not fully predictable, because on the micro level of analysis apart from intersocial relationships other factors have to be taken into account. Obviously, Shakespeare must have been well aware of the social conventions of the day, and he surely exploited them skilfully for dramatic purposes. Nonetheless, on the basis of this investigation we can only construct a 'social grammar' of Shakespeare, but we should not conclude that the language of drama with its carefully constructed speeches bore any close resemblance to real people talking, because it is not always possible to take such renditions at their face value. (2003: 216)

It seems that the impact of these devices has shifted from Chaucer to Shakespeare. In Chaucer's work, they are more clearly related to politeness; in Shakespeare's work, the emotional aspect is more important. Or, put more simply: Chaucer's characters often use Y in addressing another character in order to express politeness and respect, while Shakespeare's characters often use T to express their emotions, which may be emotions of closeness and intimacy or emotions of dislike, resentment or hatred. Such values are discursively created in specific situations which contrast against a backdrop of more or less unmarked usage, in which a specific choice does not have any specific politeness value or emotional value but corresponds to what Watts (1989) has called 'politic behaviour'.

Ultimately, it seems plausible to assume that the shift to an increased emotionality of the T pronouns was an important contributing factor in their demise in the seventeenth century (see also Walker 2007; Leitner 2013). Their emotional colouring increasingly became stronger and made it more and more difficult to use them in a neutral context. They survived in some specialised genres and varieties of English, for instance, in some dialectal usages and in the language of Quakers. They also survived well into the eighteenth century in fictional writing, where they continued to be useful as a device to indicate characters' emotions in their interpersonal relationships.

It is certainly important to repeat the point made above that Shakespeare's use of terms of address does not necessarily reflect the usage in everyday conversations at the turn from the sixteenth to the seventeenth century. The basis of our analysis is a fictional world, albeit a highly complex and intricate one. Even if we agree that Shakespeare exploited these resources 'skilfully for dramatic purposes', it is not always straightforward to interpret these purposes. The linguist's striving for generalisations of usage patterns may be seen to clash with the reader's or the literary scholar's wish to interpret each passage individually taking into account the unique constellation of the characters' emotional involvement at any particular point in a play.

7 The Eighteenth Century: The Age of Politeness

7.1 Introduction[1]

In eighteenth-century England, politeness played a particularly pertinent role as the country was undergoing major social and cultural change. The beginning of the Industrial Revolution, improvements in agricultural methods, new roads and canals and, in particular, rapidly increasing international commerce led to a new prosperity and, with it, a rise of the middle classes who now earned their income as lawyers, merchants or employees of the new trading companies. Against this backdrop of upward social mobility, it was important for the individual to know exactly how to behave in a way that was appropriate to his or her social position. Politeness was seen as an ideal that was aspired to in all aspects of daily life and included not only language but also gestures, postures, choice of conversational topics and all kinds of other general behaviours (Langford 1989; Klein 1994a, 1994b). The Earl of Chesterfield (1694–1773), one of the leading eighteenth-century authors of the relevant politeness literature wrote:

An aukward country fellow, when he comes into company better than himself, is exceedingly disconcerted. He knows not what to do with his hands, or his hat, … If spoken to, he is in a much worse situation, he answers with the utmost difficulty, and nearly stammers; whereas a gentleman, who is acquainted with life, enters a room with gracefulness, and a modest assurance; addresses even persons he does not know, in an easy and natural manner, and without the least embarrassment. This is the characteristic of good-breeding, a very necessary knowledge in our intercourse with men; for one of inferior parts, with the behaviour of a gentleman, is frequently better received than a man of sense, with the address and manners of a clown. (1778: 11)

In this chapter, based on Taavitsainen and Jucker (2010), I shall approach the study of politeness in eighteenth-century English through an analysis of some relevant expressive speech acts, in particular compliments and thanks. One important source for my analysis will be educational handbooks, such as books of etiquette and politeness, which were an important genre throughout

---

[1] This chapter is largely based on Taavitsainen and Jucker (2010). My thanks go to my co-author, who graciously allowed me to use our joint paper in this context.

the century. They were in great demand with frequent reprints and editions. In addition, I discuss material that comes from new genres of writing in the eighteenth century (i.e. newspapers and novels). As a result of the lapse of the licensing act and the end of formal censorship in 1695, the eighteenth century saw a great increase in the number of newspapers. In 1702, the first daily newspaper appeared in England, and soon many new newspapers were being published. They contained accounts of ceremonial speech acts in public settings. This century, sometimes described as the Age of Sentiment, also saw the rise of the novel, at first in the form of epistolary novels (e.g. Samuel Richardson's *Pamela*). The patronage system of earlier centuries was replaced by the commercialisation of book production; for the first time, authors could make a living by selling their works to a reading public and were no longer forced to depend on rich patrons. As a result, new topics and new genres developed and novels provided fictional accounts of verbal interactions and of politeness. All these genres provide access to a broad range of expressive speech acts of the eighteenth century, each with certain limitations, yet we may gain new insights into politeness as a social practice of the period.

Most of my examples come from the last quarter of the century, but my aim is to outline some special features of eighteenth-century politeness and how expressive, polite speech acts reveal the ideology of politeness and how they change over the course of time.

7.2   Politeness as an Ideology

The eighteenth century in England has been described as the age of politeness and commerce, but Langford (1989) stresses the dangers of misunderstanding these notions on the basis of present-day connotations of both these terms. It was a century that saw the rise and dramatic enrichment of the middle classes. Commerce, in this context, means more than just trade, it signifies also the new processes of production and exchange which drastically increased the wealth of the middle classes and improved living standards (Langford 1989: 2). Politeness was a direct result of commerce. In a feudal society, the lower classes could easily be controlled and the relations among the higher social classes regulated by an elaborate code of honour:

Politeness conveyed upper-class gentility, enlightenment, and sociability to a much wider elite whose only qualification was money, but who were glad to spend it on acquiring the status of gentleman ... Politeness was primarily about the control of the individual at a time of intense enthusiasm for individual rights and responsibilities. (Langford 1989: 4, 5)

Watts (1999) draws attention to the ideological dimension of politeness in the eighteenth century. Politeness, according to him, was closely associated with polished and refined language use. The higher social classes used it to distinguish themselves from the lower social classes. Admittance to higher social status was impossible without the appropriate variety of language (see also Watts 2002). Klein adds the normative aspect:

In later seventeenth- and early eighteenth-century England, the term 'politeness' came into particular prominence as a key word, used in a variety of settings, with a wide range of meanings. From the first, politeness was associated with and often identified with gentlemanliness since it applied to the social world of gentlemen and ladies ... Not all gentlemen were polite since 'politeness' was a criterion of *proper* behavior. The kernel of 'politeness' could be conveyed in the simple expression, 'the art of pleasing in company,' or, in a contemporary definition, 'a dextrous management of our Words and Actions, whereby we make other People have better Opinions of us and themselves.' (1994a: 3, 4; emphasis original)

Eighteenth-century handbooks of etiquette and politeness provide an ethnographic view of polite manners and elegant refinement in speech. The existence of such books in itself does not tell us how people actually behaved and how they spoke, but their popularity provides evidence for a widespread interest in matters of politeness and appropriate behaviour. Chesterfield reveals that it is 'a certain manner, phraseology, and general conversation, that distinguishes the man of fashion' and this manner of speaking and behaving 'can only be acquired by frequenting good company, and being particularly attentive to all that passes there' (1778: 38). Chesterfield continues with a passage about inherently polite speech acts and their appropriate wordings to meet the norms of polite society:

When invited to dine or sup at the house of any well-bred man, observe how he does the honours of his table, and mark his manner of treating his company. Attend to the compliments of congratulation or condolence that he pays; and take notice of his address to his superiors, his equals, and his inferiors; nay, his very looks and tone of voice are worth your attention, for we cannot please without a union of them all ... Saying to a man just married 'I wish you joy,' or to one who has lost his wife, 'I am sorry for your loss,' and both perhaps with an unmeaning countenance, may be civil, but it is nevertheless vulgar. A man of fashion will express the same thing more elegantly and with a look of sincerity, that shall attract the esteem of the person he speaks to. He will advance to the one, with warmth and cheerfulness, and perhaps, squeezing him by the hand, will say, 'Believe me, my dear sir, I have scarce words to express the joy I feel, upon your happy alliance with such and such a family,' &c. to the other affliction he will advance flower, and with a peculiar composure of voice and countenance, begin his compliment of condolence with, 'I hope, sir, you will do me the justice to be persuaded, that I am not insensible of your unhappiness, that I take part in your distress, and shall ever be affected where YOU are so.' (Chesterfield 1778: 38–9; emphasis original)

This particular book, *The Beauties of Chesterfield: or, Remarks on Politeness, and of Knowing the World: Containing Necessary Instructions To complete the Gentleman and Man of Fashion*, is a posthumous collection published in the last quarter of the eighteenth century, but the development towards the ideology of politeness described above had started well before Chesterfield's time. A century earlier, *Youths Behaviour, or Decency in Conversation Amongst Men* declared that 'EVery Action [*sic*] done in the view of the world, ought to be accompanied with some sign of reverence, which one beareth to all who are present' (1663: 1). This is the first of thirty-four short rules of behaviour, specifying appropriate and inappropriate body movements and facial expressions, how coughing was to be avoided, spitting and other rude manners restricted or abandoned, etc. Table manners, too, received a great deal of attention. The advice takes the form of maxims and requests, such as, 'It is an uncivil thing to stretch out thine arms at length, and writhe them hither and thither' (1663: 2), 'Turn not thy back to others, especially in speaking; Jog not the Table, or Desk, on which another doth read or write; Lean not upon any one; pull not him by his Cloak to speak to him; push him not with thine elbow' (1663: 5).

Similar maxims and general advice for better behaviour can be found more than two centuries earlier in late medieval courtesy literature. Instruction in the *Babee's Book, Stans puer ad mensam* and other courtesy books taught good manners and appropriate behaviour to aristocratic children and acquired a somewhat broader readership among the aspiring upper middle classes who were eager to improve their status in the world (Nicholls 1985). The same kind of enthusiasm to rise in the world can be found in the eighteenth-century handbooks of polite behaviour. What distinguished eighteenth-century politeness from the courtesy of the late medieval and Renaissance models was perhaps that its main emphasis was on a much bigger layer of society as the middle classes had become more prominent and accounted for a larger part of the population.

Politeness in eighteenth-century England, therefore, should be seen as a much wider notion in which face concerns in the modern sense played a different and less important role. Politeness was very directly linked to the ideology of the higher social classes, to the art of pleasing in conversation, the art of behaving properly in the right social circles and therefore to an ideology of dominance and of standard English. The picture that emerges of politeness in the eighteenth century can be summed up with the words of Lord Chesterfield: 'True politeness consists in making every body happy about you' (1778: 75). The distinction he makes is minute: he writes about genuine politeness, with emphasis on modesty and respect towards others. These qualities make the difference between politeness as a form of sociability and as mere ceremoniousness. The latter kind could cause tension, as pointed out by Klein

(1994a: 4), and provide a source of ridicule in comedy drama, or sparkle ironical remarks more widely in the literature.

7.3   Polite Speech Acts

Searle (1979: 12–18) divides speech acts into five different types: Assertives, Directives, Commissives, Expressives and Declarations. Of these, expressive speech acts reveal personal attitudes and feelings: 'The illocutionary point of this class is to express the psychological state specified in the sincerity condition about a state of affairs specified in the propositional content' (Searle 1979: 15). They deal with social and interpersonal relations. The list of expressives includes speech acts like greetings, thanks, congratulations, condolences and apologies. Politeness considerations are among the main factors that determine the realisations of these speech acts. In the eighteenth century, expressive speech acts received a great deal of attention and their linguistic manifestations received normative educational attention to the extent that they, with accompanying non-verbal signs of polished behaviour, became distinguishing features of status in society.

The speech acts in focus in this chapter express appreciation or gratitude about something related to the addressee (i.e. compliments and thanks), and they can thus be described as inherently polite speech acts. By default, they are supposed to work for the benefit of the addressee, but such default values do not always apply. Compliments and thanks can be used ironically or even sarcastically. In specific situations, they can appear to be inappropriate to the recipient even if they are well-intended by the speaker. Despite such situational re-evaluations, the unmarked default usage is one that generally is perceived as polite. Inherently polite speech acts can be seen as enhancing the positive face of the addressee, because they show the speaker's appreciation of the addressee. In Holmes's (1984) terms they are positively affective speech acts.

Compliments and thanks are neighbouring and partly overlapping speech acts; others in the same group include congratulations, invitations, greetings and farewells. The other end of the scale is occupied by inherently impolite speech acts, including insults and various other forms of verbal aggression, with the same qualification that in actual contexts, they often adopt different values (Jucker and Taavitsainen 2000; Taavitsainen and Jucker 2007).

However, for both compliments and thanks, we must ask whether the speech act in its modern form is identical in the scope of its function to that of its eighteenth-century precursors. I will argue that we must distinguish between the eighteenth-century ceremonious compliment with a much wider range of functions and the personal compliment which survives into present-day English. Perhaps this development illustrates changes in the notion of politeness: from eloquent formulations based on the observance of rules of elegant diction and decorative ceremonies, to more personal comments on looks and possessions, but it is also a fact that the two types already existed side by side at the dawn of the eighteenth century.[2] For thanks, the functional differences may be smaller in some respects as the core function is similar, but thanking has become routinised (*thank you*, *thanks*) and the short forms have gained a range of additional functions that seem to be later developments (see below). The examples gathered by Taavitsainen and Jucker (2010) show that compliments included thanks, and the field of inherently polite speech acts was not divided in the way it is now.

7.4   Compliments

In present-day English, compliments usually come in the form of what I call the 'personal compliment'. Holmes provides the standard definition of this speech act:

A compliment is a speech act which explicitly or implicitly attributes credit to someone other than the speaker, usually the person addressed, for some 'good' (possession, characteristic, skill etc.) which is positively valued by the speaker and the hearer. (1988: 446; see also Holmes 1995: 117)

This type of compliment is addressed to a single person, and it expresses a positive evaluation of some assessable good that is directly related to the addressee of the compliment. I want to distinguish this type of compliment from the earlier form, defined by the *Oxford English Dictionary* as

a ceremonial act or expression as a tribute of courtesy, 'usually understood to mean less than it declares' (J.); now, esp. a neatly-turned remark addressed to any one, implying or involving praise; but, also applied to a polite expression of praise or commendation in speaking *of* a person, or to any act taken as equivalent thereto. ('compliment', n., 1.a)

I call this the 'ceremonious compliment' (see also Taavitsainen and Jucker 2008). In present-day English, it is the personal compliment that seems to be what people expect when they talk about compliments. The ceremonious compliment still exists in phrases like 'with compliments', which has acquired the meaning of 'formal respects, remembrances, greetings'. In the eighteenth century, the ceremonious compliment was far more important. It extended to all aspects of polite interaction and courteous interaction (see Taavitsainen and Jucker 2008: section 4; Beetz 1990, 1999).

---

[2] In an earlier study on the topic (Taavitsainen and Jucker 2008), the best example of the personal compliment in our extensive historical material came from the year 1696 and the CED, in a dialogue between two newly married ladies. They pay compliments on looks and garments as social strokes to create intimacy and rapport, before a more serious discussion of moral issues begins.

Handbooks of etiquette and politeness provide a rich source of ceremonious compliments in private settings, including compliments of introductions and greetings, as well as compliments of invitation and of accepting invitations. The 1784 handbook *A New Academy of Compliments*, for instance, contains a section called 'Wit's Improvement' with instructions for various social situations, for instance how to become acquainted upon accidentally meeting a person, containing two alternative model conversations. The turns begin with polite addresses and expressive speech acts, descriptions of the state of mind, joy and pleasure at the event of the encounter. All model conversations contain ceremonious and elaborate diction, in accordance with the norms of the period. The idea was for the reader to study the conversations carefully in order to memorise them: the polite phrases could have had a wider currency as useful acknowledgements or uptakes after introductions and greetings more generally, and many of them fit the descriptions of compliments of both types as given above. The first model discussion, example (1), consists of three turns in negotiation of interpersonal relations to reciprocal satisfaction, paying compliments and returning them, with thanks to follow:

(1)   A: Sir, I esteem it a singular Happiness, to have met with such good Company, seeing I have by this Means obtained the Favour of being acquainted with you.

B: Sir, if the same Chance which brought us together in this place, did likewise render me capable of making my Friendship as useful to you as your Goodness is pleased to esteem it acceptable, I should think myself doubly happy; but till Opportunity presents itself, I shall pray you to accept of the good Will.

(2)   A: Sir, Your Merits oblige me highly to esteem your Acquaintance, and desire your Love. And my Intent was to make tender of my Service to you. But now I am doubly indebted to you, for preventing my Purpose, by proffering your affection. I humbly thank you for it, and desire you reciprocally to accept mine. (*A New Academy of Compliments* 1784: 9)

Similar short conversations are given for a whole range of communicative situations, like paying a visit, an invitation to dinner, acceptance of the invitation, end-of-dinner speeches, etc. Comments on personal appearance or characteristics are found as well: 'Others seem glimmering Stars when compared with you, who outshine them like bright *Luna*', 'You are the Glory of your Sex, and bear the Palm of Beauty from them all', 'The Music of the Spheres is not so ravishing as your Voice' or 'Not the Mountain Ice congealed to Chrystal, is more bright than you'. Acknowledgement of success in creating good relations could be phrased as, 'Sir, I must enrol you in the Catalogue of my dearest Friends'. Some of the sentences represent the other side of the witty duel with words, providing second turns to compliments, such as, 'Your Tongue is as smooth as Oil with courtly Flatteries', or even somewhat pejoratively as, 'Your

Language is more dubious than an Oracle' or, with disapproval, 'Sure Winter dwells upon your coy Lips, the Snow is not more cold' (these examples come from *A New Academy of Compliments* 1784: 18–19). An edition from three years earlier (1781) contains further astrological references like, 'Sir, you are the Star I reach at'. The currency of such compliments was wide, as witnessed by some comedies of the time, for instance.[3] Comments on women's looks include, 'Madam, Mortal eyes are never to be satisfied with the wonders of your beauty' (*The New Academy of Complements* 1781: 2–3, 14).

The ceremonious nature of eighteenth-century compliments is reflected in the way in which early newspapers use this term. Direct speech is, at least for the early decades, extremely rare (Jucker 2006b). Nevertheless the term 'compliment' (sometimes spelt 'complement') is often used, revealing a great deal about its development and its associated speech act in the history of English. An investigation of the data in the Zurich English Newspaper Corpus (ZEN, cf. Fries and Schneider 2000; Lehmann et al. 2006), which spans the period from 1671 to 1791, reveals that the term 'compliment' initially referred exclusively to acts of diplomacy. Compliments were an important part of international politics. Representatives of a state paid appropriate compliments to the dignitaries of another state. Royals, the pope or other members of the nobility were often the recipients of compliments. From the examples, it can be deduced that these compliments were always used as an expression of good wishes and good intentions. Particularly frequent were compliments on the coronation of a new king or the accession of a dignitary to a high office. Welcome compliments were also frequent, as were compliments of condolence and thanks (see below). Some relevant early examples are:

(3)   By these and our Artillery-Company (all in one Habit) he was Conducted hither, and Received, and Complimented by the Mayor and Aldermen in their Scarlet Gowns and Robes at the Guild-Hall. (1681, lgz0165)

(4)   The 3d Instant the Queen of Spain began to receive the Compliments of Condoleance for the Death of the late King. (1701, lgz0366)

(5)   Cardinal Gabrieli, is by the intercession of the Popes Sister, dispenced with from his journey to his Residency, for which favour he has paid his Compliments, and is now Treating for the Purchase of the Lands of Fiano, belonging to Prince Ludovisio. (1671, lgz0052)

---

[3] Such compliments belonged to the stock of complimentary phrases. An example from the seventeenth century contains the following sequence: '*Sir Timothy Compliment.* You are Lady, the Starre of your Sex. *Lady Amorous.* No truely, I am but a Meteor that soon goeth out' (LION; Newcastle, Margaret Cavendish, Duchess of, *Love's adventures* (1662): 5). An eighteenth-century example plays the compliment down: '*Dam.* Fair Nymph, that dost outshine the brightest Stars– *Phil.* Your Compliments are all thrown away upon me. You sail against the Wind, I assure you' (LION; Bellamy, Daniel, *The rival nymphs* (1739 [1740]): 60).

These examples deal with compliments that were paid in contexts of diplomacy. They report a welcome compliment, a compliment of condolence and a compliment of thanks. Compliments in the modern sense are not mentioned in any of the articles contained in the sections of the ZEN corpus covering the seventeenth and the early part of the eighteenth century. However, during these decades and in particular before the lapse of the licensing act in 1695, newspaper reporting was largely restricted to foreign news (see Studer 2008), and therefore the absence in the corpus of other meanings of the term 'compliment' is not very strong evidence for the absence of such meanings altogether. The year 1701, just after the turn of the century, contains an unusually large number of such compliments of diplomacy. In particular, the compliments of good wishes on the accession to a high office and those of the type given in the examples above are attested with numerous examples in this part of the ZEN corpus. In later years, the term 'compliment' is used for other types of polite speech encounter as well. In the early years of the eighteenth century, compliments, according to these newspaper reports, are frequently conferred on the birthdays of royals, on the weddings of dignitaries and on the occasion of the births of their offspring. The news reports are written as third-person narratives and they pay detailed attention to the correct form of titles (cf. address terms above):

(6)   On the 14th Instant his Royal Highness enter'd into the 45th Year of his Age, and receiv'd the Compliments of the Chief Officers of the Court, and all the Foreign Ministers on that Occasion. (1711, lgz0485)

(7)   Just now we hear, that the Courier from Spain, who arrived here on the 29th, brought the Consent of his Catholick Majesty and Council, to the Marriage of the Prince of Asturias, with Mademoiselle de Montpensier, Daughter of the Duke of Orleans, and the Marquis de Biron will set out the first Opportunity to Compliment their Catholick Majesties and Prince thereupon, in the Name of his Royal Highness. (1721, fpt0448)

(8)   All the Cardinals at Rome have been one after another to compliment the Pretender on the Birth of his Son. (1721, wjb0183)

It is interesting, however, that even in the early years there are occasionally either hints or very explicit indications that compliments are not always to be trusted:

(9)   Yesterday arrived some Deputies from two Provinces, and to day others from three more, whose business was to assure his Majesty that they would not appear in the Field in Arms till they knew against whom they were intended, and that here were none among them who had any thoughts of opposing his Majesty; but this is lookt on but as a complement, in regard the major part of Great and Little Poland are already in Arms, and wait only an advantage to give battel. (1671, cui0000)

(10)   That far from making a Mystery of his Intentions as the Queen's Rescript says, he explain'd them in a clear manner to the Marquess de Botta, who answer'd

them only by uncertain Assurances of that Princess's Friendship; so that we
were oblig'd, more than once, to give that Minister to understand, that mere
Compliments were not the Business in hand, but a very serious Affair. (1741,
dpt0668)

In (9), the protestations of the deputies from the provinces are obviously not
trusted: they are reported as being looked upon merely as compliments. In (10),
the same point is made. Uncertain assurances given by the Marquess de Botta
are seen as insufficient: 'mere compliments' are not enough to do business.

In novels, we can see both the ceremonious compliments of diplomacy and
those of refined and polite interactions in private settings. The following examples are taken from the Gothic novel *The Monk* by Matthew Lewis. It was first
published in 1796, and thus represents the very end of the period in focus:

(11)   Here She intended to throw a tender and significant look upon Don Christoval;
         But, as She unluckily happened to squint most abominably, the glance fell
         directly upon his Companion: Lorenzo took the compliment to himself, and
         answered it by a profound bow. (*The Monk*: 17)[4]

(12)   He saluted me with politeness; and having replied to the usual compliments of
         introduction, He motioned to Theodore to quit the chamber. The Page
         instantly with-drew. (*The Monk*: 77)

(13)   He saluted me without speaking; I returned the compliment, observing an
         equal silence. (*The Monk*: 82)

(14)   The marriage was therefore celebrated as soon as the needful preparations had
         been made, for the Marquis wished to have the ceremony performed with all
         possible splendour and publicity. This being over, and the Bride having
         received the compliments of Madrid, She departed with Don Raymond for
         his Castle in Andalusia. (*The Monk*: 267)

The compliments of the extracts (11), (12) and (13) are compliments of
greeting and introduction. It is noteworthy that gestures are just as important
as speech. In fact, in (11) and in (13) the compliments consist of gestures only.
Extract (11) relates the encounter of Don Lorenzo and Don Christoval with
Leonella and her niece Antonia in the Cathedral of Madrid. The two cavaliers
do not know the ladies, but they are attracted by the beauty of the younger of the
two. The compliments that are exchanged here are not more than an inclination
of the head or a glance. In extract (12), the narrator, Don Raymond, Marquis de
las Cisternas, relates an encounter with a stranger. The opening of the conversation is described as 'the usual compliments of introduction'. This testifies
both to the ceremoniousness of the speech act and to its ritual form. It is not
a creative and original speech act but one that is entirely appropriate and

---

[4] Page references for the extracts from Matthew Lewis's *The Monk* are to the electronic version
available at http://lion.chadwyck.co.uk/.

expected in this particular situation. In extract (13), which takes place only a few days after the first introduction described in extract (12), the narrator and the stranger meet again. The compliment of greeting and the reply are both acted out in silence and with gestures only. In extract (14), the compliments referred to are more like the diplomatic compliments reported in the newspapers. The marquis is a public figure, and his bride receives the compliments of the city on their happy marriage.

7.5   Thanks

In present-day English, as in our historical material, the speech act verb 'compliment' is rarely used performatively (i.e. to perform the speech act that it names), but it is used to report occasions on which compliments had been paid or to negotiate the illocutionary force of a speech act in interaction. In contrast, the speech act verb 'thank' is often used performatively, as an illocutionary force indicating device, to the extent that it has become a routinised speech act with formulaic expressions (Aijmer 1996). Thanking is an inherently polite speech act, and its force can be maximised by boosting, using intensifying adverbs or by prosodic devices (Aijmer 1996; Leech 1983: 84). We can add address terms to this list of maximisers used in the eighteenth century, as they often accompany this speech act as a focusing device to bring the speech act the adequate level of politeness. In speech act terms, thanking expresses gratitude and appreciation, as specified by a set of rules, defined by Searle (1969: 63) as:

> **Propositional content rule**: past act A done by H (hearer).
> **Preparatory rule**: A benefits S (speaker) and S believes A benefits S.
> **Sincerity rule**: S feels grateful or appreciative for A.
> **Essential rule**: counts as an expression of gratitude or appreciation.

The feeling of gratitude is the core function of thanks, but in modern English it has developed other functions as the short forms *thank you* and *thanks* are used in marking segments of interaction. In such exchanges, the semantic meaning of gratitude has given way to pragmatic meaning (e.g. of closing a phone conversation or finishing a transaction at a service counter). The subjective meaning of expressing the feeling of gratitude has developed into an interpersonal meaning in these discourse locations.[5] These modern functions, like *thanks* as a discourse marker and signal in closing sequences, compliment-thanking, well-wish-thanking and proposal-acceptance, have been studied by Aijmer (1996), and her study

---

[5] Thus, the development is in line with the order of language change from subjective to intersubjective meanings as verified in processes like discoursisation, pragmaticalisation and grammaticalisation (see Brinton 2007).

provides an excellent reference point for diachronic developments. In a historical study using the Corpus of Early Modern Dialogues 1560–1760 (CED), the complexity observed in modern English could not be found: the function of thanking was more or less restricted to expressing gratitude (Jacobsson 2002). Likewise, in our eighteenth-century material the speech act of thanking is mostly connected to the feeling of gratitude, sometimes overlapping with the feeling of obligation. Manifestations of the speech act generally occur as longer turns (see below). The motivation or 'object' of thanks is most often a benefit that one has already received, and thanks serve as an acknowledgement thereof.

The norms of behaviour demanded thanking for appropriate reasons, and such speech acts were essential in polite society. It was important to observe these rules and dress the acknowledgement in appropriate terms. Thanking may have been required in different contexts from today, but the handbooks do not give explicit advice on when to use it; it must have been common knowledge, learned by observation and imitation (cf. Lord Chesterfield's advice above). In modern English, in the category of 'immaterial things', 'a proposal to do something (e.g. to close the conversation)' provides the most common context for thanking (Aijmer 1996: 68); in the CED such examples are not found (Jacobsson 2002). In contrast, our material provides evidence of this motivation (see below). Like compliments, thanks require a second part. Modern conventions differ from earlier practices, and on this point my observations are in line with those of Jacobsson.

Alternative phrases for thanking can also be found, and even indirect and ornate ways to express gratitude and appreciation are frequent in our eighteenth-century materials. Expressions with 'oblige' are often intertwined with thanks, and this mode of expressing gratitude requires some further consideration. The *Oxford English Dictionary* gives the following definitions and examples: *Obliged (adj)* has the meaning 'bound by law, duty, or any moral tie, esp. one of gratitude; Oblige (v. 10. a. *trans.* (in *pass.*)). To be indebted or grateful *to* a person or (occas.) a thing'. Some relevant examples from the eighteenth century are:

(15)   1726 G. ROBERTS *Four Years Voy.* 53, I told them, I was very much obliged to them for their Good-will.

(16)   1791 *Gentleman's Mag.* 32/2 The republick of letters is infinitely obliged to M. Coste for the pains he has taken.

The phrase b. *much obliged*: 'I am very grateful', 'thank you very much', is also found in the eighteenth century:

(17)   1788 J. O'KEEFFE *Farmer* II. ii. 35 *Col. Dor.*: Well, I'll speak to him. *Jem.*: Much obliged – here he is!

We do not encounter the short form in our material, but there are several elaborate phrasings of thanks and indebtedness, quoted in the examples below. It seems that these passages with 'oblige' serve mostly as acknowl-edgements of material favours, and meeting the requirements of appropriate phrasing. The speech acts of thanking and acknowledging an obligation seem to overlap in these contexts, but the overlap is only partial and separate mean-ings are more common; the boundary to these neighbouring speech acts is fuzzy (cf. Jucker and Taavitsainen 2000).

A collection of thanking phrases with expressions of gratitude and other compliments of varying strengths are found in *The New Academy of Compliments* (1781). The influence of French court culture is obvious in these witty turns as mediated, for example, in Molière's plays, which at that time were in great demand.[6] Thanks are expressed in elaborate terms like, 'Sir, should I not render you thanks for your many favours, I should die of a deep impatience', 'Sir, your goodness hath forced me to a silence that I am not able to render you sufficient thanks for so great a favour' and 'Sir, you are so highly generous, that I am altogether senceless'. The compliments contain acknowl-edgements of favours and obligations, and many of the more indirect ones would count as thanks in the modern sense as well (e.g. 'Sir, your bounties have been shour'd upon me with such excess, that I am uncapable of a Complement', 'Sir, the Ocean's not so boundless as the Obligations you daily heap on me', 'You overcharge me with too great a Favour, in your condescending to pay me a Visit' or 'Farewell, fair Regent of my Soul, you still oblige my Gratitude'). The transactional aspects are very strongly present, and these turns are always addressed to someone superior in the social hierarchy; an inferior can never 'oblige' a superior (Bryson 1998: 168). Terms of address are prefixed to these phrases, to enhance the appropriate level of politeness.

Handbooks such as *A New Academy of Compliments* (1784) contain model letters for various occasions, including letters of thanks. They are fairly general in nature, and thus flexible to be adapted to various occasions. Example (18) is interesting for the present purposes as it directly ascribes thanks to the category of compliments and upgrades the contents by assuring that the expression of gratitude is coming directly from the heart:

(18)   Sir,
        Confessing you have obliged me with a very good Grace, and so perfectly, that I shall remain indebted to you all my life, I would to GOD some occasion would offer itself, which I might employ in your Service, thereby to witness, that as your Favours been extreme, I will attempt all Extremities to revenge myself. These are no Discourses of Compliment, my Heart dictates to my Pen

---

[6] Adaptations of Molière's (1622–73) plays appeared in English at the beginning of the eighteenth century. For instance, *The Amorous Widow*, based on Molière's *George Dandin*, was printed at least seventeen times between 1706 and 1790 under slightly different names. Adaptations and translations of other plays were also frequent. *Eighteenth Century Collections Online* (ECCO) gives 174 hits for items connected to Molière.

all that my Pen writes to you, with Assurance that I will not long unprofitably bear the Quality of, Sir, *Your most humble Servant.* (*A New Academy of Compliments* 1784: 41)

The following example of a model letter of thanks shows how humiliative discourse is intertwined in the above-mentioned 'Discourses of Compliment'. This passage is very much in line with the genre of prefaces and dedications of early printed books, where the virtues of the patron are enhanced and the author downplays his own merits with eloquent diction. The pattern is exactly the same in this letter and shows that the social practice had wider applications in the period:

(19)   Sir,
        I Know not in what Terms to give you Thanks for the Favours which your generous disposition has been pleased to bestow upon me. I am so unfortunate an Orator, that I am out of all hope to acquit myself that Way. It sufficeth me to put you in Mind of the Passion which I have to your Service, persuading myself, that the Remembrance it will excite in you, shall supplicate for the Fault of Incapacity; and that, considering the Ardor of my Zeal, rather than the Beauty of my Discourse, you will content yourself with my Disability, and that I assure you once again how perfectly I am, Sir, *Your most humble Servant.* (*A New Academy of Compliments* 1784: 41–2)

Answers to letters of thanks provide the required second turn and continue in the same vein. Here, again, the word *compliment* is used, and the passage displays a dexterous use of the first and second person pronouns:

(20)   Sir,
        Your Compliments have put me in a very ill Humour; I cannot write to you but in Choler, since you sue me as a Stranger, as appears by the Superfluity of your Ceremonies and unprofitable Thanks. It seems you have wholly forgot the absolute Power that your Merit has obtained over me. (*A New Academy of Compliments* 1784: 43)

The style of writing was neither peculiar nor new to the eighteenth century. A handbook of the previous century, called *The Wits Academy* (1677), contains an even more elaborate formulation for a letter of thanks, entitled 'A Letter full of Complements':

(21)   *Most worthy Friend,*
        I Being so infinitely obliged to you for those innumerable favours which you from time to time have been pleased to confer upon me, in common gratitude can do no less but make an humble acknowledgement in token of my great thankfulness for those unmerited kindnesses; having no other way to retaliate them at present but by telling you, that your unworthy Servant will be always ready at your command to obey and serve you to the very utmost of my poor power and ability, my daily prayers ... (1677: 80)

In a similar way, expressions of gratitude are intertwined with other polite turns of interaction in early newspaper materials. The ceremonious nature of the transactions is obvious. The titles (which also served as correct terms of address with deference) are carefully recorded in their appropriate forms. The earliest example comes from 1669 and contains an expression of gratitude in elaborate terms:

(22)   The Lord Commissioner brought into Parliament a Letter from his MAJESTY, signifying the great satisfaction his MAJESTY had taken at their Proceedings and how sensible he was of their good affections in so clear an asserting of his Prerogative; wherein also his MAJESTY calls upon them, that a General Act of Oblivion and Free Pardon may pass upon all, except such as the Parliament shall except, for which they all desired their most humble and hearty thanks should be returned to His MAJESTY. (1661kin00010)[7]

Examples from the eighteenth century are similar. They refer to the speech act of thanking (e.g. how subjects expressed their gratitude to the sovereign in a hierarchical society), but no exact wordings are given:

(23)   May it please your Grace, WE Her Majesty's most Dutiful and Loyal Subjects the Commons of Ireland in Parliament assembled, return our humble and hearty thanks to your Grace, for your Excellent Administration in this Government, and for your being the happy Instrument of obtaining so many good Laws for the Ease, Benefit, and Satisfaction of the Subjects of this Kingdom. (1711pmn02070)

'Address of thanks' seems to have been a formalised part of a ceremonial compliment, a speech act required at certain occasions. There are several occurrences:

(24)   Mr Speaker Reported also, That at the same time he presented the Address of thanks of this House to his Grace the Lord Lieutenant for his Excellent Administration, and particularly for his being instrumental in obtaining so many good Bills for this Kingdom; which Address is as followeth. (1711pmn02070)

(25)   At the same time the Speaker of the House of Commons presented their Address of thanks to his Grace, for his most Excellent Speech to both Houses; and this Day the House of Lords ordered their Address to his Grace on the same Occasion, to be printed. (1721fpt04480)

A more elaborate phrasing is found in an extract from 1761, asking for permission to present thanks, with an acknowledgement of gratitude:

---

[7] References for the extracts from the ZEN corpus follow the codes given by the retrieval software at http://es-corp.uzh.ch/.

(26)   Having had the Honour of being unanimously approved of at a General
        Meeting held here this Day to represent this County in the ensuing
        Parliament, We beg leave to return our sincere thanks for that Approbation;
        and entreat the Favour of your Votes and Interest on the Day of Election,
        which shall be ever most gratefully acknowledged, by GENTLEMEN, your
        most obliged, And obedient humble Servants, CHARLES GORE, JACOB
        HOUBLON. (1761lcr00667)

The subscription is the same as that commonly found in letters and seems to
have spread to oral use as well, as Jacobsson (2002: 68) recorded it among
responses to thanks in the dialogue corpus. His material includes instances in
which the expression of gratitude is boosted by an expression of deference.
Similar elaborations are found from the last decade of the century, here in an
advertisement from a fan manufacturer:

(27)   E. SUDLOW returns his sincere thanks to the Nobility, Merchants, and the
        Public in general, for the very liberal support he has received; and begs leave
        to inform them that they will always find a great Assortment of Fans,
        Fansticks, Mounts, c. wholesale, retail, and for exportation. (1791mcr06730)

The verb 'oblige' occurs frequently in these formal and ceremonious accounts
of interactions. Examples of the type 'I am, Sir, your obliged humble Servant'
or 'Which will much oblige Your most humble Servants' are common (cf. letter
subscriptions above):

(28)   Gentlemen, AT the earnest Request of our Friends, we have determined to join
        our Interest at the ensuing Election, and therefore jointly request the Favour of
        your Votes and Interest, which will greatly oblige, GENTLEMEN, Your most
        obedient, and most devoted humble Servants, JAMES CREED, WILLIAM
        MAYNE. (ex 206) (1761lep00559)

(29)   The inhabitants of Lambeth-Hill present their compliments to said gentlemen,
        and would have been much obliged to them had they ordered the Hill to have
        been repaved, instead of patching it up in places; and they apprehend they
        have the greater right to expect it, as many of the bye lanes leading from
        Thames-Street have been long since done. (1771lev06825)

A lexical search of *thank* in *The Monk* reveals that the word occurs in expressions of gratitude but is not used in any of the modern discourse functions (cf.
above). In addition to the core meaning, phrases like *Thank Heaven!* and *God
be thanked!* occur in emphatic, affective language use in exclamations, with
mild swearing functions, in accordance with other religious expressions of
oaths and swearing in the early periods (see Hughes 1991). The reasons for
gratitude are mostly favours, but an example of a new kind is found in the
passage quoted below, where the speech act of thanking provides a response to
an offer of a future action. According to Aijmer (1996), such offers are
commonly responded to with thanks in modern English:

(30)   'I know him intimately well. He is not at present in Madrid, but is expected
         here daily. He is one of the best of men; and if the lovely Antonia will permit
         me to be her advocate with him, I doubt not my being able to make
         a favourable report of her cause.'

         Antonia raised her blue eyes, and silently thanked him for the offer by
         a smile of inexpressible sweetness. Leonella's satisfaction was much more
         loud and audible. Indeed, as her niece was generally silent in her company,
         she thought it incumbent upon her to talk enough for both: this she managed
         without difficulty, for she very seldom found herself deficient in words.

         'Oh, Segnor!' she cried; 'you will lay our whole family under the most
         signal obligations! I accept your offer with all possible gratitude, and return
         you a thousand thanks for the generosity of your proposal. Antonia, why do
         you not speak, child? While the cavalier says all sorts of civil things to you,
         you sit like a statue, and never utter a syllable of thanks, either bad, good, or
         indifferent! –' (*The Monk* 1796: 18)

The turn is complicated. The feeling of gratitude is expressed several times in
repetitive phrases with somewhat different wordings, and the scolding for the
lack of thanks with an everyday stereotypical phrase, 'bad, good, or indiffer-
ent', further enhances the eloquence of the thanks. The examples in *The Monk*
indicate that thanking in the eighteenth century was performed with perhaps
common stock phrases but in longer and more elaborate turns. The short forms
consisting of an illocutionary force indicating device on its own are not found
in our material; nor does the CED contain them.

Address terms are found in connection with the speech act of thanking; here
the thanks are given in the minimum appropriate form of the period, which is
a full sentence, as in extract (31):

(31)   But before I take this step, Ambrosio, give me your solemn oath never to
         enquire by what means I shall preserve myself.'

         He did so, in a manner the most binding.

         'I thank you, my beloved. This precaution is necessary; for, though you know
         it not, you are under the command of vulgar prejudices. The business on
         which I must be employed this night might startle you, from its singularity,
         and lower me in your opinion. Tell me, are you possessed of the key of the low
         door on the western side of the garden?' (*The Monk* 1796: 183–4)

Most often the passages give indirect evidence of the formulations without the
actual wording of the thanks, but there are clear indications in the descriptions
that are given that the formulations must have been relatively elaborate, as in
extract (32):

(32)   Pursue, then, your design. I will accompany you to-morrow night, and
         conduct her myself to the house of the cardinal. My presence will be
         a sanction for her conduct, and prevent her incurring blame by her flight
         from the convent.'

> The marquis thanked him in terms by no means deficient in gratitude. Lorenzo then informed him, that he had nothing more to apprehend from Donna Rodolpha's enmity. (*The Monk* 1796: 124)

Other examples that indicate elaborate formulations in *The Monk* include: 'The petitioner returned him thanks with every mark of gratitude' (214) and 'She thanked him with respect and gratitude for his former visits' (101).

7.6   Conclusion

Inherently polite speech acts were important in interaction between members of polite society. Handbooks give first-hand evidence of the norms and highlight the eloquent phrasings of these speech acts. The accompanying behaviour, with the right gestures and facial expressions, is also explained in them. Newspapers of the period mostly report what took place in the public world among diplomats and the highest classes of society. In contrast, novels give us glimpses of more private spheres of interaction, even if my examples are fictional accounts in the Gothic vein. More comprehensive studies including other genres and other private domains of language use are needed for a more complete account of the topic. Both compliments and thanks have developed over the course of centuries. Compliments have become more private and personal. Thanks have acquired more interpersonal functions besides the core meaning of expressing the subjective feeling of gratitude.

We can conclude with a reference to Lord Chesterfield, a leading figure of politeness education in the eighteenth century. The main points of his teachings were posthumously versified by an anonymous Lady, which testifies to the wide appeal and popularity of his works. The framework of the teaching is in accordance with the long tradition of wisdom literature, handed down from father to son, and shows how norms and rules of behaviour are passed on from one generation to another. The following passage takes the form of a confession: the author of the most influential etiquette books of the eighteenth century was striving for honour and fame in his life, and he achieved them. He was successful, as he knew how to live up to the expectations of polite society. This verse deals with the power of appropriate and polished behaviour, including the application of inherently polite speech acts, as a confirmation of the efficacy of politeness as contained in Chesterfield's rules:

> These maxims, thro' life, I wou'd have you pursue,
> I practis'd them once, and now hand them to you;
> Successful they were, they brought honours and fame,
> For still I had art to preserve my good name.
>
> (*The Fine Gentleman's Etiquette* 1776: 7)

8   The Eighteenth Century: Educational Literature

8.1   Introduction

The eighteenth century is rich in didactic literature, from grammar books and dictionaries to conduct books, educational literature and didactic works of fiction (Watts 1999, 2002, 2011). Authors were concerned with all aspects of good and appropriate behaviour, and audiences were eager to learn from them. It was the age of codification of English in dictionaries and grammar books. It was the age of the so-called 'compliment culture', where even introductions and greetings were carried out as compliments in a very formal and ceremonious way. Conduct literature with advice on how to behave properly in a class system was highly popular, and there was an increased demand for dictionaries and grammar books giving advice on the correct use of language (see, for instance, Locher 2008 or Tieken-Boon van Ostade 2014). Theatre plays and fictional books were intended both to amuse and to instruct. Plays showed examples of good or bad behaviour and distanced themselves from the earlier licentiousness of Restoration comedy (see Jucker 2016), and in novels, in particular epistolary novels, class differences and appropriate behaviour were important topics.

In this chapter, therefore, I want to have a closer look at both the notion of politeness and the term *politeness* itself and how they were used in the eighteenth century, and by doing so, I want to avoid the danger of imposing a present-day understanding of what politeness is, or indeed should be, and focus instead on the contemporary use and perception of both term and concept (see also Fitzmaurice 2010: 88–9). Scholars of eighteenth-century politeness often distinguish between two different types of politeness, the Spectator mode and the Shaftesbury mode (Langford 2002: 312; see also Fitzmaurice 2010, 2016). The Spectator mode takes its name from the *Spectator* periodical, a daily paper produced by Richard Steele and Joseph Addison. This mode was dissociated from aristocratic birth or formal education. It could be achieved by a much broader segment of the population given the right behaviour:

The appeal of politeness thus paraded, described, characterised, applauded but rarely very precisely defined was its enabling capacity, permitting people who lacked the traditional components of social status – inherited rank, formal education and a place in the political hierarchy – to achieve it by adopting a looser, supposedly more 'natural' code of behaviour. (Langford 2002: 312)

The Shaftesbury mode, on the other hand, takes its name from Anthony Ashley Cooper, the third earl of Shaftsbury and his writings, which are directed at a more gentlemanly audience and advocate a show of manners and civility even if the surface may be deceptive.

My own investigation will focus on the discourse of politeness mainly in fictional texts. I will start with a bird's-eye view of the development of the term *politeness* as it can be ascertained in large historical corpora, in terms of both its frequency and its collocational patterns. In a next step, I will move on to a more detailed analysis of a small corpus of three epistolary novels. Epistolary novels are particularly suitable for such an analysis because they are not action-based. They consist of letters written by the characters of the novels, which leaves ample room for reflections and feelings on how to behave in society. I will show that even though the term *politeness* itself was not particularly frequent, it was part of an extensive politeness and impoliteness vocabulary that is significantly more frequent in my sample corpus of epistolary novels than in an alternative corpus of eighteenth-century novels of different literary genres.

In the last two sections of this chapter, I present case studies of the discourse of politeness in two types of fictional text of the eighteenth century: epistolary novels and theatre plays. They have in common that their authors wanted to both entertain and instruct their audiences. The educational intent reveals itself not just in the morality of the events depicted but also in the prefatory material that regularly accompanies both epistolary novels and plays. A close reading of selected extracts shows how the authors shaped the discourse of politeness, and how they described their characters' concern for proper behaviour. Politeness is seen in its intricate complexity. It describes an inherent property of the aristocracy, often in contrast to their actual behaviour. It also describes the shallow formalities of etiquette in words and gestures. And, above all, it describes the moral goodness of a person irrespective of their social class. These aspects are often in conflict with each other, but it is evident that the authors put their emphasis squarely on the morality of their characters.

8.2   Terms of Politeness: A Large-Scale Perspective

In recent years, the number of large-scale electronic resources for the analysis of historical data has grown at an unprecedented rate. These resources allow for some generalisations across vast sets of data, and they offer a first approach to explore the vocabulary of politeness at specific points in the history of the English language. The biggest such tool is the GoogleBooks project with the Ngram Viewer, which gives access to a corpus of five million books and a total of 361 billion words from around 1500 to 2000 (see Michel et al. 2010; Jucker et al. 2012; Aiden and Michel 2013). Figure 8.1 plots the term *politeness* and two related terms, *civility* and *courtesy*, from the eighteenth to the twentieth century.

It appears that around the middle of the eighteenth century, there was a marked increase in the frequency of the words *politeness* and *civility*, which is considerably later than suggested by Klein (1994a: 3, 4), who claims that the term *politeness* came to prominence in the later seventeenth and early eighteenth century. Or, if he is right, at least the prominence did not manifest itself in a high frequency. Its frequency rose from fewer than two instances per million words to between ten and twelve. But the frequency of both *politeness* and *civility* started to decline significantly towards the middle of the nineteenth century. The term *courtesy*, on the other hand, increased on a more modest level in the eighteenth century but continued on a relatively high level until the second half of the twentieth century. The database underlying this figure is, of course, somewhat problematic. It is an unsystematic set of texts, and it consists entirely of decontextualised ngrams, which means that no individual hits can be traced back to their original context of use. But the figure gives a first indication of the importance of the terms *politeness* and *civility* in the second half of the eighteenth century (see Jucker et al. 2012 for a more comprehensive diachronic view of the vocabulary of courtesy and politeness in the history of English).

In contrast to the GoogleBooks Ngram Viewer database, the Corpus of Late Modern English Texts (CLMET3.0) is a principled corpus of texts covering the period 1710 to 1920. It comprises some thirty-four million words of running texts. Its texts are classified into a range of different genres, and they were all written by British authors whose native language was English. In this case, the searches were extended. They included not only the nouns *politeness*, *civility* and *courtesy* but also – wherever attested – the plural forms and the related adjectives and adverbs (*polite, politely, politer, politest; civil, civilities, civiller; courteous, courtesies,* and *courteously*). Despite the differences of the Ngram Viewer and CLMET, they show a roughly similar development (see Figure 8.2).

Both the *politeness* and *civility* sets show an increase in the eighteenth century with a marked peak and a steady decrease thereafter. The *politeness* set peaks in the third quarter of the century while the *civility* set peaks in the last quarter and at a much higher level. The *courtesy* set, on the other hand, remains relatively steady at a low level.

Nevalainen and Tissari (2010) investigated the same set of politeness terms in a more specialised corpus, the 2.2 million-word eighteenth-century Extension of the Corpus of Early English Correspondence. They do not report normalised figures but relative frequencies of the three sets of

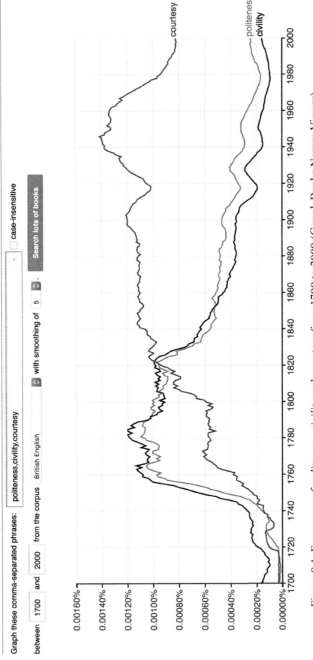

Figure 8.1 Frequency of *politeness*, *civility* and *courtesy* from 1700 to 2000 (GoogleBooks Ngram Viewer)

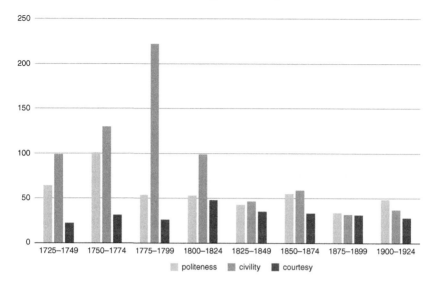

Figure 8.2 Frequency of three sets of politeness terms (per million words) across eight quarter centuries from 1725 to 1924 (CLMET)[1]

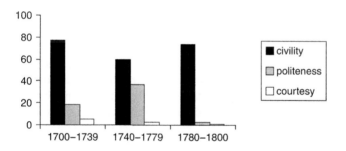

Figure 8.3 Relative frequencies (%) of the three sets of politeness terms (Nevalainen and Tissari 2010: 139)

politeness terms, which they plotted (reproduced in Figure 8.3; see also Nevala and Sairio 2017: 116 for a similar figure).

---

[1] The corpus is split into three seventy-year periods, but these periods proved to be too long to plot the frequency development of these terms. I therefore distributed the source files into quarter centuries according to the meta-information provided by CLMET3.0 (see Diller, de Smet and Tyrkkö 2010). The first quarter century is left out in this figure because it contains only four files and less than 150,000 words.

Figure 8.3 does not provide any information about the frequency of the individual sets independently, but it supports the findings given in Figure 8.2 to the extent that in the early eighteenth century, the *civility* set was somewhat more prominent than the others and significantly so towards the end of the century, because the frequency of the *politeness* set had already fallen again. The *courtesy* set played a marginal role throughout the century.

8.3   A More Focused Perspective: Epistolary Novels

From the large-scale perspective of the previous section, I now turn to a more detailed analysis focusing on epistolary novels. Epistolary novels were typical of the eighteenth century and were written and read in great numbers. They consisted of sequences of fictitious letters with variable numbers of different letter writers and different perspectives. In general, they focus more on psychological processes and descriptions of characters than on events and action, and thus provide direct access to the immediate emotions of the fictitious letter writer (see for instance Nünning and Nünning 1998: 131–8). As a genre, epistolary novels are closely connected to conduct books and letter-writing guides. In fact, some were intended to offer both model letters and a coherent narrative (for instance, Samuel Richardson's *Clarissa*; see Marks 1986). They are a particularly rich source of data for an investigation of politeness issues because of their preoccupation with character description and careful assessments of people's behaviours. They often contrast what they see as middle-class virtues with aristocratic licentiousness.

Newton (1990: 140), who looks at early American literature, uses the term 'conduct fiction' for such fictional texts with a close relationship to conduct literature. Code-of-conduct books give straightforward instructions to their readers with prescriptive injunctions, such as 'do not learn to romp' and 'obey your husband' (Newton 1990: 140), while conduct fiction presents the principles and ideals of good and appropriate behaviour in the developing fictional narrative: 'Written for a predominantly female audience, these hybrid texts suggest a trial/initiation motif by which female characters are tested, judged, rewarded, or punished by conduct book standards of virtue and right behavior' (Newton 1990: 140).

The main corpus of this investigation is made up of three epistolary novels and is supplemented by a comparison corpus which contains four novels of different genres.[2] Two of the epistolary novels of the main corpus were written by Samuel Richardson (1689–1761). They are *Pamela; or, Virtue Rewarded*,

---

[2] The novels for this project have been selected on the basis of their popularity and personal preferences. They are not meant to be representative of their respective genres in any strict sense. The texts for the corpus analyses were retrieved from the Project Gutenberg website.

first published in 1740 and *Clarissa, or, the History of a Young Lady*, first published in 1748. The third novel was written by Fanny Burney (1752–1840): *Evelina, or The History of a Young Lady's Entrance into the World*, first published in 1778. In all three novels a young and beautiful heroine tries to come to terms with the demands of a complex world of sometimes well-meaning but often less well-meaning characters who put their virtues to the test. Richardson's Pamela is a fifteen-year-old maidservant whose master, Mr B., unsuccessfully tries to seduce and rape her. Her unshakable virtue does not give in to the unwanted advances until his proposal of an equitable marriage across the dividing class boundaries. The quest for virtue of Richardson's Clarissa ends tragically. She fails to overcome the odds against her set up not only by a ruthless pursuer, Mr Lovelace, but also by her own family who aspire to social advancement through her. Fanny Burney's young heroine Evelina, finally, is the unacknowledged but legitimate daughter of an English aristocrat. She is brought up by a guardian in rural seclusion until she comes of age and is gradually introduced to the complex world of upper-class London society.

The educational intention of all three novels is evident not only in the obvious morality of the events depicted but also in the prefatory material of the three novels, for instance, in the subtitle of *Pamela*, 'Virtue Rewarded', or in the lengthy description on the title page of *Clarissa*: 'Clarissa. Or, the History of a Young Lady: Comprehending the most Important Concerns of Private Life. And particularly shewing, The Distresses that may attend the Misconduct Both of Parents and Children In Relation to Marriage.' Together, the three epistolary novels of the main corpus amount to a little more than 400,000 words.

The comparison corpus is made up of four eighteenth-century novels that do not belong to the genre of epistolary novels. They are *Robinson Crusoe*, an early adventure novel by Daniel Defoe, first published in 1719; *Tom Jones*, a comic novel by Henry Fielding first published in 1749; the first two volumes of *Tristram Shandy*, a sentimental novel by Laurence Sterne, first published in 1759; and *The Monk*, a Gothic novel by Matthew Lewis, first published in 1796. The four novels of the comparison corpus amount to just over 700,000 words.

In a first step, I tried to isolate the range of polite and impolite vocabulary in the three epistolary novels on the assumption that issues of behaviour were essential for the fictitious letter writers and required appropriate lexical means to talk about them. I also assumed that this kind of lexicon would be relatively more frequent in the epistolary novels than in other eighteenth-century novels. The search for polite and impolite vocabulary proceeded in an iterative fashion. I started out with a range of obvious terms gleaned from a close reading of the novels. For the politeness vocabulary these were, for instance, *civil, graceful* and *gentle*, and for the impoliteness vocabulary *disgraceful, wicked* and *impertinent*. I then searched for these terms and their derivational variants

Table 8.1 *Distribution of polite and impolite terms in eighteenth-century fiction (epistolary novels and a comparison corpus)*

	No. of words	Polite terms	Per 10,000 words	Impolite terms	Per 10,000 words
Epistolary novels					
Clarissa	85,986	190	22.1	185	21.5
Evelina	155,908	327	21.0	276	17.7
Pamela	170,606	372	21.8	481	28.2
Total	412,500	889	21.6	942	22.8
Comparison corpus					
Robinson Crusoe	234,903	133	5.7	143	6.1
Tom Jones	167,791	241	14.4	196	11.7
The Monk	137,082	218	15.9	82	6.0
Tristram Shandy	187,544	229	12.2	79	4.2
Total	727,320	821	11.3	500	6.9

(*gracefully, gentlest* and so on) in the seven novels of the two corpora. A careful inspection of the relevant hits revealed additional terms that regularly occurred in their vicinity and could be added to the list. This step was essential because it revealed whether individual terms had positive or negative default values. As I will show in more detail below, it turned out, for instance, that *artless* was very much a positive term that belongs to the list of polite vocabulary, while *artful* belongs to the list of impolite vocabulary. These figures obviously ignore the fact that these terms are not always used with their default values, and that they are sometimes used in contexts in which they are negated. They provide no more than a preliminary generalisation.

Table 8.1 gives the combined frequencies of all the polite and impolite terms together with normalised frequencies per million words. Figure 8.4 presents these figures in the form of a clustered bar diagram, and Figure 8.5 in a stacked bar diagram. Table 8.1 and Figures 8.4 and 8.5 reveal that there are very noticeable differences between the three epistolary novels and the comparison corpus. The combined frequency of polite and impolite terms is about forty to fifty per 10,000 words in the former versus something between just over ten and just over twenty-five in the latter. It is perhaps not very surprising that *Robinson Crusoe* shows by far the lowest combined frequency of polite and impolite vocabulary. Robinson is a castaway with little social interaction and no interaction with aristocratic society. He has little need to evaluate behaviour as either polite or impolite. The highest frequency of polite and impolite vocabulary in the comparison corpus is reached by *Tom Jones*, which is perhaps also not very surprising as it shares the setting of a wealthy country

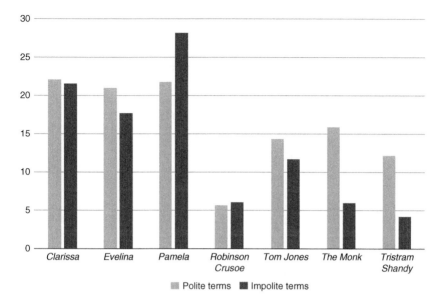

Figure 8.4 Distribution of polite and impolite terms in eighteenth-century fiction (per 10,000 words)

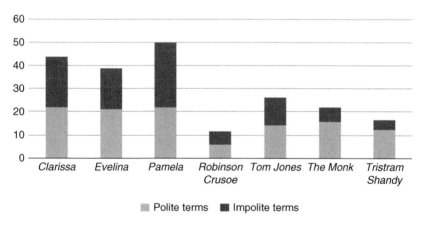

Figure 8.5 Combined frequency of im/politeness vocabulary in eighteenth-century fiction (per 10,000 words)

house and a range of moral issues with the three specimens in the main corpus. *The Monk* and *Tristram Shandy* stand out not so much because of the combined frequency of their polite and impolite vocabulary but because of the way in which the polite terms outnumber the impolite

Table 8.2 *Polite and impolite terms in three eighteenth-century epistolary novels (actual number of occurrences)*[3]

Polite terms		Impolite terms	
Fine	167	wicked*	173
respect*	160	wretch*	125
compliment*	98	disgrace*	90
grace*	87	impertinen*	82
natural*	87	disagreeable*	64
civil*	86	vile	61
polite*	68	saucy	34
Flatter	59	rude*	34
gentle/er/est	37	artful	32
courtes*	34	jest*	30
modest*	29	improp*	27
propriet*	28	horrid	24
elegan*	18	cunning	22
artless*	9	awkward	21
deference	8	pert*	19
good-breeding	7	odious	19
courteous	3	vulgar	16
well-bred	3	ill-bre(e)d*	12
unassuming	2	slut	11
		disrespect*	11
		unnatural*	9
		low-bred	6
		unpolite*	5
		unwomanly	4
		illiterate	3
		illiberal	3
		ill-manners	3
		incivil	3
		inelegant	2
		unruly	1
		unmannered	1
		ungentlemanly	1
		ungentle	1
		ungenteel	1
		ill-politeness	1
		uncivil	1

ones. In these two novels there are almost three times as many polite terms as impolite ones, while for all the other novels the relationship is

[3] An asterisk indicates possible derivational suffixes or other variations in the endings of these forms.

much more balanced, with impolite terms making up between about 45 and 55 per cent of the combined frequency. Table 8.2 gives an overview of the polite and impolite terms that occur in the three epistolary novels under investigation.

In the following I want to have a look at a few selected terms from both lists and demonstrate how they are actually used in the three epistolary novels of the main corpus. The term *polite** is not the most frequent. It occurs sixty-nine times in the three novels: *politeness* (40), *polite* (19), *politely* (6), *politer* (2) and *politest* (2). This term co-occurs regularly with terms such as *civility, considera-tion, gallantry, sweetness* or *diffidence*. Extracts (1) to (5) are typical examples:[4]

(1)   for a gentleman of your politeness would not say any thing that would make ladies blush. (*Pamela*)

(2)   but every day abounds in fresh instances of his condescending politeness. (*Evelina*)

(3)   and that elegant politeness, that flattering attention, that high-bred delicacy. (*Evelina*)

(4)   since that politeness which is acquired by an acquaintance with high life. (*Evelina*)

(5)   I would have you learn to be more politer, Sir, and not to talk to ladies in such a rude, old-fashioned way. (*Evelina*)

As can be seen from these and similar examples from the three novels, the term *polite* and its derivatives are generally ascribed to people or, more specifically, to people described as a gentleman or lady. It is put on the same level as 'flattering attention' and 'high-bred delicacy', and it is acquired 'by an acquain-tance with high life', which reinforces the connection between politeness and the higher social classes. It is also ascribed to behaviour, in particular to ways in which people are attended to, how they are received, addressed, invited, congratulated, thanked and so on. The opposite of politeness is not impoliteness but 'rude' and 'old-fashioned' behaviour. The term *impolite* is not attested in the three novels. It occurs five times in the form of *unpolite* or its derivatives.

The term *fine* is the most frequent one in the list of politeness terms in Table 8.2, but its meaning is much wider. It is not only used to describe people and their behaviour but also the quality of clothes, linen, silk and 'things' in general. In fact, the four most common nouns immediately following the adjective *fine* are *gentleman* with fifteen occurrences, *things* with ten, and *lady* and *clothes* with five each. When it is used to describe

---

[4] No page numbers are given as the passages can easily be retrieved electronically. See References for details.

people and their behaviour, its meaning is closely related to the designation *polite*, as the following examples show:

(6)   And he took my hand, and ran on, saying such fine speeches, and compliments. (*Evelina*)

(7)   for she had known many girls much worse than me, who had become very fine ladies after a few years residence abroad. (*Evelina*)

(8)   And yet, my dear father and mother, why should I, with such a fine gentleman? And whom I so dearly love? And so much to my honour too? (*Pamela*)

(9)   The hourly threatenings of your fine fellow, as well as your own unheard-of obstinacy, will account to you for all this. (*Clarissa*)

Occasionally, *fine* is used ironically, as in (9), but its general meaning is one of high praise.

The term *compliment** is also very high up in the list of politeness terms in Table 8.2 with ninety-eight occurrences in the three novels. It occurs in the forms *compliment* (45 times), *compliments* (44), *complimented* (6), *complimental*, *complimentary* and *complimenting* (1 each). Extracts (10) to (13) show that both ceremonious and personal compliments are attested:

(10)   Several of the neighbouring gentry sent their compliments to him on his return, but not a word about his marriage. (*Pamela*)

(11)   Nor will I, but by distant civilities, return the compliments of any of my acquaintances. (*Clarissa*)

(12)   And Miss Darnford was pleased to compliment me, that I had all the accomplishments of my sex. (*Pamela*)

(13)   He paid me the most high-flown compliments; and frequently and forcibly seized my hand. (*Evelina*)

Extracts (10) and (11) are most clearly instances of ceremonious compliments (see Section 7.4). Neighbours send their compliments on Mr B.'s return, which presumably means that they sent letters or cards to welcome Mr B. home after a longish absence. And Clarissa tries to avoid visits and, therefore, refrains from returning compliments to her acquaintances except in the form of 'distant civilities'. Such ceremonious compliments are quite different from Miss Darnford's compliment to Pamela in extract (12) regarding Pamela's accomplishments, or Lord Merton's compliments to Evelina in extract (13). These are personal compliments that in these examples are appreciated by Pamela but not by Evelina because she objects to Lord Merton's importunate and over-familiar behaviour.

The term *civility* and its derivatives together with the set of *politeness* terms are key terms for the entire eighteenth century (see Nevalainen and Tissari 2010; Bryson 1998; Thomas 2018). In the three novels, *civil** occurs eighty-two times, in the forms *civility* (28 times), *civil* (26), *civilities* (19), *civilly* (6), *civiller* (2), *civilized* (1). It is generally ascribed to gentlemen but also to people more generally and their behaviour:

(14)   Mr. Lovelace received from every one those civilities which were due to his birth. (*Clarissa*)

(15)   and then saying, with his usual politeness, something civil to each of us, with a very grave air he quitted us. (*Evelina*)

(16)   Mrs. Jervis, the housekeeper, too, is very civil to me, and I have the love of every body. (*Pamela*)

(17)   Du Bois was the only man of the party to whom, voluntarily, I ever addressed myself. He is civil and respectful, and I have found nobody else so since I left Howard Grove. (*Evelina*)

The examples show that this term, too, is used to distinguish between social classes. Mr Lovelace, in extract (14), deserves to be treated with a certain kind of civility because of his aristocratic birth. The examples also show the close connection to politeness. Lord Orville, in (15), is described as being polite as usual when he says something civil to the group of people he is leaving. And in (17), *civil* is combined with *respectful* to describe Du Bois, the French gentlemen who actually only speaks French and a little broken English in *Evelina*. The data contain some additional such combinations, for instance, 'civility and good manners' (*Clarissa*), 'civilly and kindly' (*Pamela*) or 'civility and kindness' (*Evelina*).

The term *artless** is not particularly frequent with only nine occurrences in the three novels (*artless*, 7; *artlessness*, 2) but it is interesting because of its specific usage, which shows that it was very much a positive term with a specific application. It co-occurs with *young, inexperienced, innocent, noble simplicity, honest, sweet humility,* and it is exclusively ascribed to young women (*heroine, young creature, angel, girl*):

(18)   There is such a noble simplicity in thy story, such an honest artlessness in thy mind, and such a sweet humility in thy deportment. (*Pamela*)

(19)   I send her to you innocent as an angel, and artless as purity itself. (*Evelina*)

(20)   but she is too young for suspicion, and has an artlessness of disposition I never saw equalled. (*Evelina*)

Impolite terms are somewhat more frequent and also more diverse than the polite terms in the three epistolary novels of the main corpus. The term *unpolite**, however, is remarkably rare. As pointed out above, the present-day English form *impolite* does not occur at all. It has only six occurrences (*unpolite*, 3; *unpoliteness, unpolitenesses, ill-politeness*, 1 each):

(21)   Put the case, that I were to marry the man you dislike: and that he were not to make a polite or tender husband, Is that a reason for you to be an unpolite and disobliging brother? (*Clarissa*)

(22)   You have always joined with me in remarking, that he will speak his mind with freedom, even to a degree of unpoliteness sometimes. (*Clarissa*)

(23)   there's no nation under the sun can beat the English for ill-politeness: for my part, I hate the very sight of them. (*Evelina*)

Extract (21) is taken from a letter that Clarissa writes to her brother, who does not approve of the man she says she wants to marry. But even if Mr Lovelace should turn out not to be a polite and tender husband, she argues, that does not justify her brother's impolite behaviour towards her. In (22), Clarissa describes Robert Lovelace to her best friend, Anne Howe. Too much openness and directness, apparently, can come across as somewhat impolite. The term *ill-politeness* is used in (23) the describe the entire English nation. The speaker is a French visitor recently arrived in London who lost her companions and has just been saved by Evelina and her friends but has also been addressed very rudely by the Captain, who dislikes everything foreign.

The most frequent impolite term in Table 8.2 is *wicked** It occurs in the forms *wicked* (142), *wickedness* (25), *wickedly* (5), *wickedest* (1) and co-occurs regularly with such terms as *base, treacherous, stratagems, cunning, merciless, dishonest,* and is ascribed to specific people (*woman*, 16; *master*, 11; *wretch*, 9; *creature*, 6; *gentleman, man, people, ravisher, violator, coachman, brute*) but also to *words, things, views, attempts, love, closet,* or *letter.* However, it must be noted that in this case the occurrences are very unevenly distributed across the three novels. Richardson's *Pamela* clearly stands out with a frequency of 18.3 per 10,000 words in comparison to only 0.6 in *Clarissa* by the same author and 0.4 in Burney's *Evelina.*

(24)   let not my affliction be added to by thy inexorable cruelty, and unwomanly wickedness. (*Pamela*)

(25)   But, oh! little did I think it was my wicked, wicked master, in a gown and petticoat of hers, and her apron over his face. (*Pamela*)

(26)   cried Lady Louisa; and then, turning to Lord Merton, 'why now, you wicked creature you, did you not tell me it was but one?' (*Evelina*)

(27)   Surely, said I, I am the wickedest creature that ever breathed! Well, said the impertinent. (*Pamela*)

The term *disagreeable** occurs sixty-four times (*disagreeable*, 62; *disagreeableness*, 2). It has a very wide applicability, it co-occurs with *awkward*, *ill-bred*, *improper*, *embarrassing* and is ascribed not only to people but also to *manners*, *intelligence*, *conclusion*, *altercation*, *situation*, *dialogue*, *scene*, *adventure*, *conversation*, *affair* and *reflections*. It also shows a rather skewed distribution across the three novels. In this case it is Richardson's *Clarissa* which stands out with 3.0 occurrences per 10,000 words, while *Pamela* has half that number and *Evelina* a mere 0.3 per 10,000 words.

(28)   And then Mr. Solmes's disagreeable person; his still more disagreeable manners; his low understanding. (*Clarissa*)

(29)   Notwithstanding my vexation at having been forced into a party so very disagreeable, and that, too, from one so much. (*Evelina*)

(30)   and was a tacit confession of the disagreeableness of the person they had to propose. (*Clarissa*)

The term *artful**, finally, occurs thirty-two times in the three novels (*artful*, 29; *artfulness*, *artfullest* and *artfully*, 1 each). Its negative impact can be seen in the terms it co-occurs with (*violent*, *vindictive*, *spiteful*, *subtle*, *perverse*, *forward*, *foolish*, *sly*). It is ascribed to people (*servant*, *creature*, *man*, *woman*, *wretch*) and to the more abstract *wiles*.

(31)   Sir Clement Willoughby must be an artful designing man: I am extremely irritated at his conduct. (*Evelina*)

(32)   and how much it behoves the fair sex to stand upon their guard against artful contrivances, especially when riches and power conspire against ... (*Pamela*)

(33)   if I can secure my innocence, and escape the artful wiles of this wicked master! For, if he comes hither, I am undone. (*Pamela*)

Two further terms need to be mentioned because they often occur with modifiers that turn them into terms describing polite or impolite behaviour without themselves being either polite or impolite in their default meanings. The first of these is *conduct*, which occurs 137 times in the three novels. The list of modifiers shows positive, negative and fairly neutral terms: *bad*, *comfortable*, *contrary* (4 each), *different*, *dissipated*, *former*, *future*, *generous*, *ill*, *past*, *present*, *regular*, *ridiculous*, *savage*, *spirited*, *unblemished* and *vindictive*. Extracts (34) to (39) give an indication of its breadth of usage:

(34)   Doubtless he must be greatly discontented at the dissipated conduct and extravagance of a man, with whom ... (*Pamela*)

(35)   how disinterested his conduct! how delicate his whole behaviour! (*Pamela*)

(36)   And pray, let me ask my dearest Mamma, in what has my conduct. been faulty. (*Clarissa*)

(37)   I know not how to express my indignation at his conduct. Insolence so insufferable. (*Clarissa*)

(38)   As I ask for your approbation or disapprobation of my conduct, upon the facts I lay before you. (*Clarissa*)

(39)   and if your conduct be such, that I have reason to be satisfied with it. (*Pamela*)

The second term to briefly consider is *manners*. It occurs sixty-one times in the three novels, and – like *conduct* – it can be modified by positive or negative adjectives but it seems to lack the neutral terms that are in evidence for *conduct*: *better, deficient, disagreeable, elegant, engaging, fashionable, faulty, French, good* (5 each), *ill-* (3):

(40)   pay the grateful debt of civility and good manners. (*Clarissa*)

(41)   ungentle in temper, and unamiable in her manners. (*Evelina*)

(42)   his air, and address were open and noble; his manners gentle, attentive, and infinitely engaging. (*Evelina*)

(43)   I am not totally despicable as a judge of good or ill-manners. (*Evelina*)

(44)   and as to his being a gentleman, he has no more manners than a bear. (*Evelina*)

(45)   one whose elegance surpassed all description, whose sweetness of manners disgraced all comparison. (*Evelina*)

(46)   her ignorance of the forms, and inexperience in the manners of the world. (*Evelina*)

From all these examples, a clear picture emerges of epistolary novels as a genre that takes manners as essential human qualities. The narrators and characters are likewise preoccupied by an assessment and evaluation of good and appropriate behaviour, and there is a rich vocabulary to talk about both those who succeed and those who fail to behave in this way. The term *politeness*, however, turns out to be less central than might have been assumed. For the middle-class authors of the three novels analysed above, the key was moral integrity and virtuous living rather than the mere etiquette of polite behaviour. In fact, politeness was seen as double-edged. It could be empty formalities that the higher social classes used to distinguish themselves and that were often not enough to hide their licentiousness and morally questionable behaviour. Politeness was only a worthy goal for everyday behaviour if it stood for virtuous morality.

The analysis so far has focused on the vocabulary of politeness and impoliteness in the eighteenth century. It has focused on the conventionalised meanings of individual terms which describe polite or impolite types of behaviour, but the more detailed and contextualised analyses have shown that actual uses occasionally deviate from the default values. In the following section, therefore, I zoom in even further and focus on a small number of selected passages taken from theatre plays in which fictitious characters discursively negotiate what they consider to be polite and impolite.

8.4   A Discursive Perspective: Educational Theatre[5]

At the very end of the seventeenth century, Jeremy Collier (1650–1726) published a pamphlet entitled 'A Short View of the Immorality and Profaneness of the English Stage', in which he attacked the profanity and moral degeneracy in the stage productions of Restoration comedy, which in themselves had been a reaction against the Puritan ban on theatre (Nünning and Nünning 1998: 90). It is in this context that new dramatic genres emerged, and two particularly prominent genres were the sentimental comedy and the domestic tragedy, their most prominent representatives being Richard Steele's *The Conscious Lovers* and George Lillo's *The London Merchant, or The History of George Barnwell*, respectively. Steele's *The Conscious Lovers* was first performed in 1722 (see Novak 1979; Hynes 2004). Steele wanted to set an example of a comedy that did not rely on lewd jokes or dubious characters. He wanted to show exemplary characters to imitate, and in the introduction to the play he states his aim to improve drama: 'and sure it must be an Improvement of it, to introduce a Joy too exquisite for Laughter' (Steele 1993: 68). Hynes (2004) has argued that although the play is not what might be called a 'living classic', it is important because of its innovations and departures from the traditional comic forms of the day. Steele introduced a new kind of virtuous hero and characters who were too good for the traditional comedy of the day. This new type of play avoids satire and emphasises good characters as models of behaviour (Hynes 2004: 148). In fact, in *The Conscious Lovers*, Mr Sealand, a rich merchant, says to Sir John Bevil: 'We merchants are a species of gentry, that have grown into the world this last century, and are as honourable, and almost as useful, as you landed folks, that have always thought your selves so much above us' (4.2, p. 124).

Richard Steele (1672–1729) was the co-founder together with Joseph Addison of *The Spectator*. He was a Member of Parliament and a strong supporter of the Hanoverian succession and of George I. For this support he was knighted and became manager of the Drury Lane Theatre in London. It was there that he wrote and staged *The Conscious Lovers*, and in his dedication to the king, Steele thanks him for the appointment.

---

[5] Section 8.4 is largely based on Jucker (2016).

In the play, Sir John Bevil wants his son to marry Lucinda, the daughter of a rich merchant, Mr Sealand. But Bevil Jr is in love with the orphan Indiana, and he faces the dilemma that he cannot marry her without disobeying the wishes of his father. So, he initially pretends to be willing to marry Lucinda, which in turn confuses and enrages his friend Myrtle, who is in love with Lucinda. To complicate matters, Mrs Sealand has different plans for her daughter Lucinda and wants to marry her to Cimberton, a coxcomb; and Bevil Jr's manservant, Tom, is in love with Lucinda's maid Phillis. The core scene of the play takes place in the fourth act, when Myrtle challenges his friend Bevil Jr to a duel. Bevil Jr refuses but Myrtle's insults bring him almost to accepting the challenge, before finally refusing and maintaining the civility. Hynes writes that:

> The movement of this scene is most significant. It was not enough for Steele simply to assert his hero's rejection of dueling, for a straightforward refusal to fight could always be attributed to cowardice. The 'patience of a man' must, on the contrary, be a manly patience, a principled calm backed up by a fully masculine power of action. In this sense it was essential for Steele to show Bevil's vacillations in the face of Myrtle's challenge. To be a virtuous man he must be peaceable, but not tame; not violent, but firm. (2004: 150)

In the sense of Sell (1991), Steele wanted to maintain a high level of politeness both on the extradiegetic and on the intradiegetic level. He was extremely polite to his audience in the theatre by presenting characters that are extremely polite to each other. The extradiegetic level between him and his audience was of central importance. He wanted to educate by presenting exemplary characters to his audience. The play was used to advance a social and cultural ideal, 'even the back-chat among the servants is governed by notions of loyalty and propriety' (Lindsay 1993: xxiv). Ozoux describes the politeness of the play with the term 'gentility': 'C'est par le biais de cette nouvelle méthode que Steele revient sur le concept de "gentility", en offrant au spectateur l'image d'un gentleman exemplaire' (2002: 160).

In extract (47), Humphrey, an old servant to Sir John Bevil, is given the task of sounding out Bevil Jr's true feelings for his intended bride, Lucinda, by approaching Tom, Bevil Jr's manservant. The ensuing conversation between the two servants is full of explicit talk about proper behaviour. It is also fashioned as a contrast between the old world and the new:

(47)   HUMPHREY ... Oh, here's the prince of poor coxcombs, the representative of all the better fed than taught. – Ho! ho! Tom, whither so gay and so airy this morning?

Enter Tom, singing.

TOM Sir, we servants of single gentlemen are another kind of people than you domestick ordinary drudges that do business: we are rais'd above you:

The pleasures of board-wages, tavern-dinners, and many a clear gain; vails, alas! You never heard or dreamt of.

HUMPHREY Thou hast follies and vices enough for a man of ten thousand a year, tho' 'tis but as t'other day that I sent for you to town, to put you into Mr Sealand's family, that you might learn a little before I put you to my young master, who is too gentle for such a rude thing as you were into proper obedience ...

TOM ... You talk as if the world was now, just as it was when my old master and you were in your youth – when you went to dinner because it was so much a clock, when the great blow was given in the hall at the pantrey-door, and all the family came out of their holes in such strange dresses and formal faces as you see in the pictures in our long gallery in the country.

HUMPHREY Why, you wild rogue!

TOM You could not fall to your dinner till a formal fellow in a black gown said something over the meat, as if the cook had not make it ready enough.

HUMPHREY Sirrah, who do you prate after? – Despising men of sacred characters! I hope you never heard my good young master talk so like a profligate.

...

HUMPHREY I hope the fashion of being lewd and extravagant, despising of decency and order, is almost at an end, since it is arrived at persons of your quality. (*The Conscious Lovers* 1.1, p. 78–9)[6]

The two servants here discuss the nature of proper behaviour. Tom believes that he has a much better life because he does not have to follow the old-fashioned formalities of earlier times, when Humphrey and Sir John Bevil were still young. Humphrey, on the other hand deplores the lack of good manners and decency in the younger generation. He compares Tom's behaviour to those of a rich person, 'Thou hast follies and vices enough for a man of ten thousand a year', and then expresses his hope that such bad manners are no longer fashionable because they have already percolated down the social ladder to the likes of Tom. For Humphrey, good manners are a sign of a good character. He considers Tom's tirade against the formalities surrounding dinners to be an attack against the good character of the people who observe these formalities. He believes that Bevil Jr, the young master, has a gentle disposition which would not be able to cope with Tom's rude behaviour, and and he should have been educated before he was brought into contact with Bevil Jr. Thus, we learn a lot about the importance of proper behaviour, which in this passage mainly concerns non-verbal aspects, such as the way to call people to dinner, the formal dress, the facial expressions and grace being said at the beginning of the meal.

---

[6] Quotations of *The Conscious Lovers* follow Lindsay's (1993) edition.

In extract (48), the main character of the play, Bevil Jr, visits the orphan Indiana, the woman he loves. The topic of their conversation also focuses on proper behaviour:

(48)   Enter Bevil junior

BEVIL JUNIOR   Madam, your most obedient – I am afraid I broke in upon your rest last night – d'twas very late before we parted; but d'twas your own fault: I never saw you in such agreeable humour.

INDIANA   I am extremely glad we were both pleas'd; so I thought I never saw you better company.

BEVIL JUNIOR   Me, Madam! You rally; I said very little.

INDIANA   But, I am afraid, you heard me say a great deal; and when a woman is in the talking vein, the most agreeable thing a man can do, you know, is to have patience, to hear her.

BEVIL JUNIOR   Then it's pity, Madam, you should ever be silent, that we might be always agreeable to one another.

INDIANA   If I had your talent, or power, to make my actions speak for me, I might indeed be silent, and yet pretend to something more than the agreeable.

BEVIL JUNIOR   If I might be vain of any thing, in my power, Madam, d'tis that my understanding, from all your sex, has mark'd you out, as the most deserving object of my esteem.

INDIANA   Should I think I deserve this, d'twere enough to make my vanity forfeit the very esteem you offer me. (*The Conscious Lovers* 2.2, p. 99)

Bevil Jr apologises for staying too long on his previous visit the night before and Indiana compliments him for having been such an attentive interlocutor. They flatter each other and artfully refuse the praise they receive because accepting it would show a lack of modesty. It is part of good manners to be a good listener. Bevil Jr, therefore, suggests that Indiana should talk all the time to give him the chance to be a good listener, which would be agreeable to both of them, and Indiana immediately returns the compliment by suggesting that he doesn't even need words. He can make his actions speak for him and make him agreeable. He then singles her out as 'the most deserving object of my esteem', to which she replies by explicitly stating the dilemma of the compliment. If she accepts the compliment, she no longer deserves it, because it would be a sign of vanity and reduce the esteem that she deserves.

In extract (49), Mr Sealand, the father of Lucinda, talks to a servant who opens the door when he wants to talk to Indiana. He wants to find out whether her relationship to Bevil Jr might be a threat to his own plans of a marriage between his daughter and Bevil Jr;

(49)   MR SEALAND   I think this is the door – *(Knocks.)* I'll carry this matter with an air of authority, to enquire, tho' I make an errand, to begin discourse. *(Knocks again, and enter a Foot-Boy.)* So, young man! is your lady within?

BOY   Alack, Sir! I am but a country boy – I dant know whether she is, or noa: but an you'll stay a bit, I'll goa, and ask the gentlewoman that's with her.

MR SEALAND   Why, Sirrah, tho' you are a country boy, you can see, can't you? you know whether she is it at home when you see her, don't you?

BOY   Nay, nay, I'm not such a country lad neither, Master, to think she's at home, because I see her: I have been in town but a month, and I lost one place already, for believing my own eyes.

MR SEALAND   Why, Sirrah! Have you learnt to lie already?

BOY   Ah! Master! Things that are lies in the country, are not lies at London – I begin to know my business a little better than so – but an you please to walk in, I'll call a gentlewoman to you, that can tell you for certain – she can make bold to ask my lady her self.

MR SEALAND   O! then, she is within, I find, tho' you dare not say so.
BOY Nay, nay! That neither her, nor there: what's matter, whether she is within or no, if she has not a mind to see any body? (*The Conscious Lovers* 5.2, p. 134)

In this amusing little interaction Mr Sealand wants to find out whether Indiana is at home but the servant does not want to give a clear answer to what seems to be a simple question. In fact, he spells out the dilemma in his last turn in this interaction. It does not matter whether she is actually at home or not, but only whether she wants to receive visitors.

In the end, Mr Sealand finds out that Indiana is his long lost first daughter, and everything turns out well. Bevil Jr can marry Indiana, Lucinda marries Myrtle, and Cimberton is no longer interested since the dowry has now been halved. Thus, all the main characters stay true to their noble and virtuous self. And even though some dressing up has been necessary to bring about the happy ending (Myrtle and Tom disguised as lawyers to delay the unwanted marriage procedures), the play is remarkably free of deception and intrigue. The play, it seems, is exceedingly polite on all levels. It is only the servant Tom, and to some extent the unwanted lover Cimberton, who deviates a little from the ideal of a perfectly polite character.

George Lillo (1691–1739) was an English playwright who wrote several plays including *The London Merchant, or The History of George Barnwell*, which was first performed in London in 1731. It is an important play because it created a new genre, the domestic tragedy, in which everyday, non-aristocratic people interact in a contemporary British context, mostly in intimate private settings. The focus is on the subjective experiences, sufferings and sentiments of the protagonists, and the domestic tragedy aims to propagate middle-class virtues and moral values (Nünning and Nünning 1998: 99). Neumann (2011: 160–1) even argues that the genre is defined by its didactic intention. There is a direct link between the standards of judgements applied to the characters of the play and the standards of the real world (see also Wallace 1992: 129). The intention is to elicit a sympathetic and emotional response in the audience.

In the dedication to his patron, Sir John Eyles, a Member of Parliament and Alderman of the City of London, Lillo argues that princes are not alone in suffering misfortunes and, therefore, tragedy should not confine its characters to princes:

> Plays founded on moral tales in private life may be of admirable use, by carrying conviction to the mind with such irresistible force as to engage all the faculties and powers of the soul in the cause of virtue, by stifling vice in its first principles. They who imagine this to be too much to be attributed to tragedy, must be strangers to the energy of that noble species of poetry. (1993: 262)

In the prologue, spoken by the actor who plays George Barnwell, the play to be performed is called a 'tale of private woe', and is set in contrast to the tragic muse which 'delights to show Princes distressed, and scenes of royal woe' (Lillo 1993: 265). The play is a 'moral tale'

> Which, for a century of rolling years,
> Has filled a thousand, thousand eyes with tears.
> If thoughtless youth to warn, and shame the age
> From vice destructive, well becomes the stage. (Lillo 1993: 265)

In the play, the apprentice George Barnwell is seduced by Sarah Millwood, a London prostitute, but he immediately feels guilty for having disobeyed his master, Thorowgood, a London merchant. He is prompted by Millwood to steal a large sum of money from his master, and later she even convinces him to murder and rob his rich uncle. After the murder, George returns to Millwood with bloody hands but without the money. George and Millwood are arrested. In his prison cell, George is visited by Thorowgood, by Trueman, his fellow apprentice, and by Maria, Thorowgood's daughter, who all forgive him. George is truly repentant and awaits his execution.

The double title of this play refers to the two male protagonists. The first part refers to the exemplary London merchant and the second to George Barnwell, his apprentice, who can be interpreted as a fatal deviation from the ideal of a good merchant (Neumann 2011: 165). In extract (50), which is taken from the very first scene of the play, Thorowgood talks to Trueman, and instructs him about the true nature of an honest merchant. Merchants are stylised as pillars of society. They contribute to both its safety and happiness, which gives them a dignity and honour that comes with the highest expectation of virtuous behaviour. Trueman wholeheartedly embraces these ideals and condemns the mere thought of a deviation from the path of virtue, and with these words already condemns the actions of his fellow apprentice that will unfold in the course of the play:

(50)   TRUEMAN   He must be insensible indeed, who is not affected when the safety
of his country is concerned. Sir, may I know by what means? If I am too bold —

THOROWGOOD   Your curiosity is laudable; and I gratify it with the greater
pleasure, because from thence you may learn how honest merchants, as such,
may sometimes contribute to the safety of their country, as they do at all times
to its happiness; that if hereafter you should be tempted to any action that has
the appearance of vice or meanness in it, upon reflecting on the dignity of our
profession, you may, with honest scorn, reject whatever is unworthy of it.

TRUEMAN   Should Barnwell, or I, who have the benefit of your example, by
our ill-conduct bring any imputation on that honourable name, we must be left
without excuse. (*The London Merchant* 1.1, p. 269)[7]

In the eighteenth-century context of the rising middle class, the ideology of
politeness and educational theatre, this must have been meant as an instruction
to the theatre audience as well. The values that Thorowgood and Trueman
ascribe to the exemplary merchant are communicated on both the intradiegetic
and extradiegetic levels.

In the second scene of the play, the merchant talks to his daughter, Maria, and
continues on the theme of the good merchant. He instructs her to prepare a feast
for guests he wants to entertain. No costs are to be spared to provide the best
possible food and entertainment:

(51)   THOROWGOOD   Well, Maria, have you given orders for the entertainment?
I would have it in some measure worthy the guests. Let there be plenty, and of
the best, that the courtiers, though they should deny us citizens politeness,
may at least commend our hospitality.

MARIA   Sir, I have endeavoured not to wrong your well-known generosity by
an ill-timed parsimony. (*The London Merchant* 1.2, pp. 270–1)

Thorowgood sets up a contrast between his courtier guests, members of the
aristocracy, and the middle class he belongs to as a merchant. The notion
'politeness' is clearly used as an ideology by the aristocracy to distinguish
themselves from the lower social classes (Watts 1999, 2002). Thorowgood
appears to accept the class division but he aspires to a type of behaviour that is
as close as possible to the polite behaviour of the aristocracy. The term
'hospitality' seems to capture much of what would be 'polite' except for the
ideological overtones of the upper classes. The term 'citizen' was loaded in the
eighteenth century. In the same way that 'polite' could be used by the upper
classes as an attribute of inclusion into their own ranks, the term 'citizen' was
used to keep the middle class out.[8]

In the middle of the play, Trueman and Mary explicitly discuss good and
appropriate behaviour. George Barnwell has stolen a considerable amount of

---

[7] Quotations of *The London Merchant* follow Lindsay's (1993) edition.
[8] I am grateful to Laura Wright for this insight.

money from his master, and he has failed to return home. Trueman and Mary are convinced that there must be a reasonable explanation for this behaviour and want to cover for him in front of Thorowgood. Mary proposes to replace the stolen money from her own funds and Trueman wants to invent a reason for Barnwell's absence:

(52)   TRUEMAN   Trust to my diligence for that. In the meantime, I'll conceal his absence from your father, or find such excuses for it that the real cause shall never be suspected.

MARIA   In attempting to save from shame one whom we hope may yet return to virtue, to Heaven and you, the judges of this action, I appeal, whether I have done anything misbecoming my sex and character.

TRUEMAN   Earth must approve the deed, and Heaven, I doubt not, will reward it.

MARIA   If Heaven succeed it, I am well rewarded. A virgin's fame is sullied by suspicion's lightest breath; and therefore, as this must be a secret from my father and the world for Barnwell's sake, for mine, let it be so to him. (*The London Merchant* 3.3, p. 295)

Maria is concerned about whether her action of covering up for Barnwell's theft is appropriate for her social position. Her reputation must remain pure. They agree that her actions will be judged by heaven. What they plan to do must be right because they do it in Barnwell's interests. They still believe in his moral integrity, despite the facts, or at least in the possibility that he will return to the path of virtue. Once again, the moral values that are discussed between the characters are projected beyond the intradiagetic level. They are directly relevant to the theatre audience, who are expected to learn from the examples on the stage.

The heavy morality of this play, however, makes it difficult for a modern audience. Collins is probably still typical of current opinions when he compares Restoration drama with what came afterwards: 'Restoration drama sparkles by comparison with the virtual nullity which followed it' (1957: 156) and 'the plays which followed [after Restoration drama], though informed by higher moral intentions, were dull, un-lifelike, fundamentally insincere (Steele's are the typical example)' (1957: 171). It seems that excessively polite drama does not make for good entertainment. Culpeper argues that 'there are good reasons why drama in general thrives on verbal conflict. Impolite behaviour, either as a result of social disharmony or as the cause of it, does much to further the development of character and plot' (1996: 364).

8.5   Conclusion

The eighteenth century is called the age of politeness, but the concept of politeness was complex and multifaceted. In the eighteenth century, it could be used as an ideology to distinguish the 'polite' (i.e. higher social classes) from the rest. It could be used to describe the surface manners that were in accordance with prescribed etiquette, a mode that could be used to deceive and to hide darker motives. And it could be used to describe humanistic morality and religious piety. A corpus analysis of *politeness* and related terms confirms their importance in the eighteenth century with a marked increase in their frequency in the second half of the century. They testify to the importance of the discourse of appropriate behaviour and good manners.

This discourse of politeness can also be seen very clearly in some of the fictional writings of the eighteenth century. Fictional texts are complex communicative acts. On the one hand, they constitute communicative acts between an author and his or her reader, on the extradiegetic level. And, on the other hand, they depict communicative acts between characters of their narratives, on the intradiegetic level. The focus on three epistolary novels here has confirmed the multifaceted nature of politeness. The fictitious characters, and with them perhaps their middle-class authors, see politeness very much as an ambivalent phenomenon. It is seen as a feature that distinguishes aristocratic society, but also as a high ideal of good manners which cannot be attained through the mere observance of rules of etiquette. Such rules depend on an underlying virtuous morality and they need to be displayed in an entirely unconscious and unpretentious manner. In two early eighteenth-century plays, Steele's *The Conscious Lovers* and Lillo's *The London Merchant*, the characters are polite and virtuous as an example and for the edification of the audience. Even Barnwell, the protagonist who becomes a murderer, appears as a 'tragic middle-class hero who commits a fatal error *and* represents virtue' (Neumann 2011: 167; emphasis original). In the end he repents and takes full responsibility for his actions, and he accepts his punishment, the death sentence.

The educational intent of these novels and plays is clearly evident, and in many cases, it is explicitly spelled out by their authors in a dedication, preface or prologue. This attempt to instruct and improve reading audiences and theatregoers must be seen in the context of the socially aspiring middle classes, who had a desire to learn appropriate, and in particular polite, behaviour and needed advice not only from plays and novels but from conduct books, grammar books and dictionaries, which were published in ever-increasing numbers in the eighteenth century (see Michael 1987; Locher 2008). In fictional texts, it is often possible to contrast the outward behaviour of individual characters with their true intentions. In this respect, readers or theatregoers occupy a privileged position. Thus, fictional texts provide one excellent source of data for politeness theorists, and in return, the analysis of politeness and impoliteness in specific fictional texts may provide new insights for the literary scholar.

9   The Rise (and Fall) of Non-imposition Politeness

9.1   Introduction[1]

Brown and Levinson famously claimed that 'When we think of politeness in Western cultures, it is negative-politeness behaviour that springs to mind. In our culture, negative politeness is the most elaborate and the most conventionalized set of linguistic strategies for FTA [face-threatening act] redress; it is the stuff that fills the etiquette books' (1987: 129–30). And indeed, many forms of what they call 'negative politeness' can easily be retrieved, for instance from the Corpus of Contemporary American English (COCA), which provide some support for this claim:[2]

(1)   Miss Vivian, I wonder if you might come down to the front desk. There's someone here to see you. (COCA, FIC, 1990)

(2)   but there's just one small thing. Could you possibly contribute somewhere between $35,000 and $200,000 to buy your way onto the show? (COCA, SPOK, 1995)

(3)   Would you draw me a picture of what you saw? (COCA, SPOK, 1990)

(4)   Well then, while we wait for the map, perhaps you could pass on an enquiry to someone who deals with difficult problems. (COCA, FIC, 2011)

(5)   And I wonder if you could tell us a little bit about your process. (COCA, SPOK, 2010)

(6)   Sheila, can I ask you to read the poem by Linda Pastan on page 77? (COCA, SPOK, 2000)

(7)   Perhaps you might like to tell me the chief reason. (COCA, FIC, 2008)

(8)   A word of advice, if I may: in the future, you might consider keeping your own counsel on matters of which you know nothing about. (COCA, FIC, 2011)

---

[1] Nina Helg-Kurmann, Anja Leu and Lukas Zbinden deserve a special word of thanks for a lot of help with coding material for this chapter.

[2] In this chapter, the focus shifts to American English because the Corpus of Historical American English provides a unique and sufficiently large source for the development of English over the last two centuries.

In all these examples, the speakers use formulations that suggest that they do not want to impose on the addressee. They ask the addressee about his or her willingness or ability to carry out a certain action, they suggest the addressee's action as a mere possibility or they speculate tentatively on whether the addressee might be willing to do something. Wierzbicka (2006: 45–8) suggests that such forms are typical of present-day English. She lists what she calls 'whimperatives' such as *could you (do x), will you (do x), would you (do x)* or suggestory formulae such as *you might like to, you might consider, I would suggest, perhaps you could, I wonder if you could*. According to Wierzbicka, these forms are not typical of Western cultures in general, but they represent Anglo scripts. She stresses the fact that such strategies are not universal but very culture-specific:

Clearly, speakers of English are quite happy to identify some of their utterances as (mere) suggestions but are reluctant to identify any as attempts to put pressure on the addressee. For speakers of many other languages, for example, Russian or Italian, on the other hand, the opposite is true. (Wierzbicka 2006: 39)

Critics of Brown and Levinson, especially the politeness theorists of the second wave of politeness theory (see Chapter 1), have stressed that such formulations do not have inherent politeness values, and indeed in specific situations such formulations may come across as inappropriate, perhaps even insulting. They may be used in jest or ironically, in situations in which it is clear that the addressee is obliged to do the required action anyway, or alternatively in situations in which it is clear that the addressee will not even dream of carrying out the suggested action. However, such situational readings depend on the conventionalised default values of the forms. The default values suggest that the addressee might not be willing or able to carry out the action, and it is exactly this suggestion that might come across as inappropriate or even impolite.

It is therefore interesting to study such forms of non-imposition politeness even if on occasion they are used for purposes that cannot be described as polite, and it is interesting to investigate their origins. The available research suggests that such forms of non-imposition politeness are, in fact, relatively recent. Back in the 1990s, Kopytko (1995) already suggested that Shakespeare's Early Modern English was characterised by positive politeness rather than negative politeness typical of present-day English. Culpeper and Demmen (2011) maintain that non-imposition politeness in the form of ability-oriented conventional indirect requests (*could you, can you*) are not attested before 1760, and that there are very few before 1800. They note an increase in the nineteenth century, but the forms are still rare, and they surmise that a sharp rise must have occurred after 1900, and, therefore, later than the data they were investigating.

In this chapter, I will investigate the question of the rise of non-imposition politeness in more detail. I will first assess some of the claims that have been made about negative politeness, or more specifically, non-imposition politeness in present-day English. In Section 9.3, I am going to look at the available literature on the history of non-imposition politeness before I turn to my own case study of the development of a range of formulaic politeness expressions that are indicative of non-imposition politeness. I will trace their development over the last two centuries as recorded in the Corpus of Historical American English (COHA) and supplemented by the COCA, which, at the time of writing, records data from 1990 to 2017.

9.2   The Diachrony of Non-imposition Politeness: Previous Research

It has often been noted that today's forms of negative politeness illustrated in (1) to (8) above are relatively recent. In Early Modern English, and in particular in the works of William Shakespeare, they were not in evidence. Brown and Gilman (1989: 181), for instance, observe that requests in Shakespeare's plays use phrases such as *I do beseech you*, *I entreat you*, *I pray you*, *Pray you*, *Prithee*, *I do require that*, *So please your Majesty* or *If you will give me leave*, while the negatively polite forms *could you* and *would you* that are typical today cannot be found in their data. On the authority of Millward,[3] they claim that these new forms were not invented until the nineteenth century (see also Fennell 2001: 165 and Busse 2008: 95 for similar claims).

In Chapter 5, I mentioned Kopytko's observation that there may have been a shift from a preponderance of positive politeness strategies in Shakespeare's plays towards a negative politeness culture in present-day British society:

I tentatively assume that the high rate of occurrence of positive politeness strategies in Shakespeare's plays characterises the interactional style or 'ethos' of Elizabethan society . . . If both claims, i.e. about the Elizabethan society and modern British society, are at least to some degree true, it may be tentatively proposed that the interactional style or 'ethos' of British society has evolved from the dominating positive politeness culture in the 16th century towards the modern negative politeness culture. (Kopytko 1995: 531–2)

Kopytko's formulation is appropriately hedged and tentative. It is based, on the one hand, on a detailed analysis of the fictional worlds created in Shakespeare's plays and, on the other, on the stereotypes of present-day English society mentioned in the previous section. Generalisations are risky at both ends. Shakespeare's plays may bear little resemblance to other spoken and written genres of his time. And stereotypes may highlight features that are particularly

---

[3] Personal communication.

noticeable for one reason or another even if they are restricted to certain contexts only and are not as widespread as their stereotypical nature would have us believe. However, as the examples in the previous sections have shown, it is very easy to collect relevant examples from present-day English corpora. Such forms clearly do occur frequently in present-day English and, therefore, beg the question as to when they started to develop and how their frequency developed over time.

Wierzbicka also talks of the use of explicit performatives in earlier forms of English, such as *I pray you* in Shakespeare, and what she calls the 'triumph of suggestions in modern English' (2006: 45ff). She hypothesises that the development of requests in the history of English went through the following four (overlapping) stages:

Stage I   a free use of the imperative and of the performative verbs of 'requesting'

Stage II   growing restrictions on the use of the imperative, the rise of the whimperative, the decline of the performative use of verbs of 'requesting'

Stage III   the rise of 'suggestions' of various kinds

Stage IV   from *I would suggest* to *I was wondering if.* (Wierzbicka 2006: 53)

She provides the following schematic examples as illustrations for these four stages:

Stage I   *I pray thee, do it*

Stage II   *Could you/would you do it?*

Stage III   *I would suggest . . . /Perhaps you could . . . /You might like to . . .*

Stage IV   *I was wondering if you could . . . /I was wondering if you'd like to . . .* (Wierzbicka 2006: 53)

However, she does not provide any empirical evidence or a time scale for these stages. Intuitively it would appear that Stage I represents a form that is regularly attested in Shakespeare's plays while Stages II to IV encompass forms that are still current today.

Culpeper and Archer (2008) investigated requests in late Early Modern English with data drawn from the Sociopragmatic Corpus (SPC) consisting of play texts and trial proceedings covering the period of 1640–1760 (2008: 60). They found that requests in their corpus are overwhelmingly formulated as impositives, such as imperatives ('Take away her sword'), explicit performatives ('I demand to know', 'I charge you tell me'), locution derivable or obligation statement ('we must go to the city', 'I must speak to you') (Culpeper and Archer 2008: 71). Forms of conventional indirectness, on the other hand, are relatively rare. In fact, the impositives account for more than three quarters of all requests in both the trial proceedings and in the play texts of their corpus. This stands in marked contrast to the findings of Blum-Kulka and House (1989: 134), who identified conventional indirectness as the clearly dominating category of requests in several different cultures in their Cross-Cultural Speech Act Realization Project (CCSARP). Their (Australian) English informants used the highest number of conventionally indirect requests, representing over 80 per cent of all their requests, while the other cultures (German, Canadian French, Hebrew and Argentinian Spanish) had somewhat lower values, between about 60 and 75 per cent. Culpeper and Archer (2008: 76) stress that these results cannot be taken as an indication that early modern English society was less polite than present-day societies. Indirectness does not necessarily correlate in any direct way with politeness. To support this claim, they quote Wierzbicka, who states of modern Polish that:

the use of interrogative forms outside the domain of questions is very limited, and since the interrogative form is not culturally valued as a means of performing directives, there was, so to speak, no cultural need to develop special interrogative devices for performing speech acts other than questions, and in particular, for performing directives. (2006: 33)

Culpeper and Archer (2008: 77) even maintain that their findings for Early Modern English are consistent with Wierzbicka's description of the Polish situation.

Culpeper and Demmen (2011: 51) continue the argumentation that the politeness practices described by Brown and Levinson (1987) with their emphasis on individualistic face wants are not only cross-culturally but also diachronically specific to present-day English. They focus on the nineteenth-century culture of the Victorian period (1837–1901) and link the diachronic changes of these practices to dramatic social and ideological changes in the wake of industrialisation and urbanisation. It was the nineteenth century, according to Culpeper and Demmen (2011: 60), that provided the appropriate social and cultural background for an ideology of individualism and, therefore, for the rise of negative politeness and conventional indirectness.

In present-day English, claim Culpeper and Demmen with reference to Aijmer (1996: 157), 'the most common way of delivering a conventional indirect request is to use the structure *could you X*, and the next most common way is *can you X*' (2011: 51). For their investigation, they use A Corpus of Late Modern English Prose and A Corpus of Nineteenth-century English covering the nineteenth century and totalling one million words, but it turns out that ability-oriented conventional indirect requests are surprisingly rare in their data despite a modest increase over the course of the century. Their combined frequency rises from 0.7 instances per 10,000 words at the beginning of the century to 1.0 in the middle and 1.3 at the end (Culpeper and Demmen 2011: 69). They surmise that 'it may well be that the most substantial rise in such requests between the eighteenth century and the present day took place after 1900' (Culpeper and Demmen 2011: 75).

Shvanyukova builds on this idea of a paradigmatic change that took place in the nineteenth century and led to 'a previously unknown concern for the interlocutor's negative face and the wish to safeguard her/his freedom from imposition' (2019: 176). Her data consists of 139 model letters in four nine-teenth-century letter-writing manuals for business correspondence, including orders for goods, letters requesting payment for services provided, job applications, complaints and various other types. Shvanyukova surmises that these model letters were at the same time a prescriptive help for less experienced writers and a descriptive reflection of actual current letter-writing practices (2019: 186). The requests in these letters show a wide variety of different strategies with a noticeable preference for indirect and mitigating strategies, as for instance in (9) and (10):

(9)   I shall be greatly obliged by your remitting by return of post the amount of my account L.42.18.6. (CLW, L6, 13)

(10)   Will you therefore, dear sir, kindly try to help me in this matter? (SELW, L32, 87)

In both cases the request is formulated in a tentative way that – at least on the surface – tries to reduce the imposition on the recipient of the letter. However, it is interesting to note that in Shvanyukova's data, there are only two examples of ability-oriented indirect requests of the type *you can* plus verb (2019: 189). These commercial model letters show a great concern for the negative face of the recipient, but they do not yet employ the present-day English strategies *could you X* and *can you X*.

Today, as the opening quotes of this chapter have demonstrated, there seems to be a widespread agreement that forms of non-imposition politeness are frequently used in many contexts. In the words of Stewart, 'in certain circumstances at least, British English tends towards negative politeness and favours off-record strategies in carrying out certain face-threatening acts. It seems, at least, that to be British a healthy degree of paranoia can help' (2005: 128). Or, in Culpeper and Terkourafi's rather more sober words, it is a fact that 'at least in middle-class British English culture, indirectness, inexplicitness, circumlocution, incompleteness obliquity and so on are often associated with being polite' (2017: 27–8).

However, not much is known about the precise distribution of such strategies in present-day English. Is it restricted to British English or even to certain areas within Britain? Is it restricted to certain social classes or to certain genres? Or is it just the frequency that differs according to the different varieties? Culpeper and Gillings (2018) take the widespread stereotype of the friendly northerner as a starting point to investigate the distribution of positive and negative politeness features in present-day British English. Following Jucker (2012a), they distinguish between two types of negative politeness and propose labels that are more transparent and less misleading than Brown and Levinson's (1987) terms 'positive' and 'negative', which are sometimes misunderstood as implying 'good' and 'bad'. They propose the term 'solidarity' to capture Brown and Levinson's positive politeness, while the concept behind the term 'negative politeness' is split into the terms 'deference' and 'tentativeness'. The former refers to elements that emphasise the addressee's superior power and status, while the latter refers to elements that soften the impact of what is said.

Culpeper and Gillings (2018) suggested a number of diagnostics derived from non-academic commentaries that they had collected on the politeness differences between the north and the south. These diagnostics had to be searchable; they had to occur with reasonable frequency in their data and they had to be assignable to one of the three types of politeness. Table 9.1 gives an overview of the formulaic politeness expressions that they used as diagnostics.

Culpeper and Gillings note that *could you* and *please* date back to the nineteenth century, and they connect this to the 'emerging Victorian values of individualism, self-sufficiency and privacy, all of which meant an indirect approach was likely to be highly valued' (2018: 40; see also Culpeper and Demmen 2011). Both these elements, according to Culpeper and Gillings, fit the description of tentativeness or non-imposition. *Could you* clearly signals tentativeness. The speaker does not impose on the addressee but – at least on the surface – merely enquires about the addressee's ability to do something. *Please*, as I will show below, derives from *if you please* with the meaning 'if it is your wish' or 'if it is your pleasure'. In this sense, it clearly stresses

Table 9.1 *Formulaic politeness expressions and their corresponding politeness types (Culpeper and Gillings 2018: 39)*

Formulaic politeness expression	Politeness type
could you	Tentativeness
please	
sir, madam	Deference
thank you, thanks, ta	
love, mate	Solidarity
cheers	
hello, hi	
goodbye, bye	

tentativeness and non-imposition but, as Culpeper and Gillings (2018: 40) correctly point out, the original conditional meaning of *if you please* has largely been bleached away in present-day English's *please*. In fact, as I will also show below, there are reasons to be sceptical that *please* is still indicative of tentativeness or non-imposition in the same way that it might have been in the nineteenth century and perhaps well into the twentieth. It turns out that after a considerable rise in frequency, collocations of *could you* and *please* are now receding again, and one possible explanation for this could be that speakers who want to formulate an utterance as a mere and non-imposing suggestion shy away from using *please* because that would unambiguously mark their utterance as a request despite the tentativeness of the *could you* formulation.

The diagnostics for deference politeness consist of the honorifics *sir* and *madam* and the thanking expressions *thank you*, *thanks* and *ta*. The honorifics derived from earlier terms of address and today they are only used in relatively restricted situations, typically with asymmetrical speaker roles, as in service encounters or in school pupil-teacher interactions (Culpeper and Gillings 2018: 41). Thanking expressions have already been classified as negative politeness strategies by Brown and Levinson (1987: 210–11) because the speaker goes on record as incurring a debt. Culpeper and Gillings classify them as deference politeness because 'it fits the way that [Brown and Levinson] conceive of deference as the humbling of the self or the "raising" of the other' (2018: 43).

Solidarity politeness, finally, is identified through terms of endearment, *love* and *mate*, which illustrate Brown and Levinson's 'use in-group identity markers' output strategy, and through the salutation expressions *cheers*, *hello*, *hi*, *goodbye* and *bye*, which can all be used to establish and reinforce good relationships with the addressee and thus enhance the solidarity between speaker and addressee.

As a dataset Culpeper and Gillings used a sample of the Spoken British National Corpus 2014, which is demographically annotated and contains some 7.5 million words. They stress that their frequency counts are based on occurrences that were manually screened to remove any unwanted hits. In the end, their results show no significant difference between their northern and southern data in terms of tentativeness politeness, and – against their hypothesis – their southern data show higher levels of both deference politeness and solidarity politeness than their northern data. They conclude that their results 'do not provide evidence for the popularly assumed north-south England divide in terms of preferences for different types of politeness' (Culpeper and Gillings 2018: 54), but they are quick to point out that the reason for this could potentially be found in their choice of diagnostic politeness expressions or in the different composition of the two parts of their corpus. It appears that the northern data include fewer recordings of rather formal situations, for instance, and (in)formality is, of course, related to issues of politeness.

9.3   Data and Method

Much of the work reviewed above dealt with politeness expressions in British English. It is conceivable and in fact even likely that the situation in American English is different, at least in some of its details of preferred constructions and rates of development. However, the following case study is based on American English for the simple reason that the COHA offers a unique source of data for the last 200 years, which cannot be paralleled with British English data. The elements under investigation are not high frequency elements, at least not in the registers included in historical corpora. Corpora such as Archer or the LOB family contain only a fraction of the material in COHA and they do not cover both the nineteenth and the twentieth centuries with the same precision and detail.

The COHA contains data from 1810 to 2009 and with 400 million words offers a unique account of the recent development of American English. According to its compiler, Mark Davies, it covers a balanced selection of texts of the four registers fiction, magazines, newspapers and non-fiction books for all decades and, therefore, makes it possible to trace changes across time. However, the first decade of the COHA, the 1810s, turned out to be very problematic in all the searches reported in this case study. It is by far the smallest decade and contains only 1.6 million words (i.e. 0.3 per cent of the whole corpus). The second decade, the 1820s, is the second smallest but it already contains three times as many words. In practically all searches, the 1810s turned out to be a serious outlier with frequency figures that were between three and ten times as high as the neighbouring decades. The reasons for this are to some extent no more than speculations, but the composition appears to have a major influence because this decade – despite Mark Davies's claims – has a different composition. Drama is heavily over-represented and newspapers are missing. Therefore, it appears to be prudent to exclude this decade from the investigation and start with the 1820s. Moreover, it turned out that a grouping of decades into larger periods reduces some of the accidental ups and downs from one period to the next and highlights the overall trends in a clearer fashion. Therefore, the nineteen remaining decades were combined into four periods of forty years each and a last period of thirty years (the 1980s, 1990s and 2000s), except for a few searches where a more detailed perspective was necessary.

For the most recent developments, I turn to the COCA, which has data covering the period from 1990 to 2017 and a total of 560 million words. The composition of this corpus differs from the COHA because it also includes spoken language. The data website interface of the corpus offers the possibility of diachronic searches according to five-year periods. So far, six such sub-periods are available with roughly 100 million words each, except for the last sub-period, which, at the time of carrying out the research for this chapter (January to April 2019), contained only 60 million words for the years 2015 to 2017. These half decades were merged into two periods of ten years and a remaining period of seven years.

Many of the searches that I carried out for the following investigations returned too many hits because they included the search term in contexts that had nothing to do with the intended pragmatic meaning. The term *please*, for instance, can not only be used in the context of a polite request but also as a verb ('which would please me for silly sentimental reasons', COCA, ACAD, 2017). Culpeper and Gillings (2018: 51) managed to restrict some of their searches syntactically, by searching only for instances of *please* that were annotated in their corpus as adverbs. This procedure proved unreliable for searches in the COHA because the syntactic annotation, especially in the early decades, turned out to be somewhat erratic.

However, it was not possible to inspect all the hits manually, so the following procedure was used to determine an approximate number of occurrences of the search item for each decade of the COHA or each five-year period of the COCA. Two coders retrieved two independent random samples of 100 hits including the search term for each time period (i.e. twenty different samples for each search term in the case of the COHA). For each such sample they determined the number of politeness-related hits out of the 100 retrieved hits. It was necessary to do this for every single decade because earlier trials had made it clear that the ratio of relevant versus irrelevant hits can differ considerably across decades. In a next step the two coders compared their figures for each decade. If the difference was smaller or equal to fifteen, the two figures were accepted, and their average was used as the relevant factor together with the raw figure of all hits for the decade to establish an estimate of relevant hits for the decade. If the difference was greater than fifteen, new samples were drawn and the procedure repeated.

This procedure is a modification of a traditional inter-rater reliability test. The coders did not code the same sample of 100 hits but independently drawn random samples. There were only two codes to be assigned, politeness-relevant or false hit. In many inter-rater reliability tests, a level of 70 per cent agreement between coders is deemed to be sufficient. But here it was not the individual codes that were compared but the percentage of relevant hits in relation to all hits, and, therefore, a higher level of correspondence was imposed. Moreover, a traditional inter-rater reliability test is carried out to ascertain, on the one hand, that the established categories are sufficiently robust and, on the other, that the coders are sufficiently trained to return reliable results. Once the trials achieve the required agreement levels, the coders can then code additional material independently. Here, all the material was coded by two coders in order to get a more accurate estimate of the percentage of relevant hits for each single search term and each single decade.

9.4   Non-imposition Politeness in 200 Years of American English

The word *please* has a special status in everyday perceptions of politeness. Many parents even accord it the status of a 'magic word' that their children are encouraged to use, or perhaps even coerced into using, to perform successful requests (Culpeper 2011b: 394; Culpeper and Gillings 2018: 34). According to Biber et al. (1999: 1098), it is about twice as frequent in British English conversations than in American English conversations with roughly 400 and 200 occurrences per million words, respectively. Murphy and De Felice (2018: 84) confirm the difference with their data of requests in American English and British English corporate emails: 55 per cent of their British English requests include *please* while only 27 per cent of the American English requests do so. The *Oxford English Dictionary* speculates that it originates from *please you* (*your honour*, etc.) but that it was subsequently taken to be a short form of *if you please* (*OED* 3rd ed., please, *adv.* and *int.*). And indeed, the COHA records some early occurrences of *please you* in requests, such as (11) to (15):

(11)   't is so biting cold: may it please you to let me mend the fire? (COHA, FIC, 1818)

(12)   Wilt please you take refreshment ere we part? (COHA, FIC, 1819)

(13)   the old man interrupted him, 'you must, so please you, be guided for this once by your old servant. (COHA, FIC, 1847)

(14)   Our business ends! Will it please you, leave us now! (COHA, FIC, 1849)

(15)   And you, lady; will it please you to return to your carriage? (COHA, FIC, 1901)

These examples appear to differ in the urgency of the request but all of them are accompanied by phrases, such as *may it please you*, *will it please you* or *so it please you*, which – at least on the surface – make the fulfilment of the request contingent on the addressee's pleasure in doing so or their benevolence. In this sense they are clear instances of non-imposition politeness.

The form *if you please* occurs more regularly but like *please you*, it is more frequent in the earlier parts of the COHA. Extracts (16) to (22) provide some relevant examples:

(16)   Nay nay, be quiet if you please, and hear what I have to say. (COHA, FIC, 1830)

(17)   You have forgotten your own sister's name. Call me Adelaide, if you please, Sir. (COHA, FIC, 1845)

(18)   'Then just get something and open the box if you please,' she said, indicating her command to Winthrop. (COHA, FIC, 1852)

(19)   Then, if you please, mum, I think I'll go,' said Glory. (COHA, FIC, 1863)

(20)   I had rather not answer these questions, gentlemen, if you please. I'm an old servant of the family. (COHA, FIC, 1874)

(21)   And so, if you please, would you be so kind as not to think quite so badly of me?' (COHA, FIC, 1884)

(22)   'Come inside, if you please.' (COHA, FIC, 1900)

In some of these examples the phrase is used in contexts that are clearly marked as requests or even commands, such as (16), (18) or (21). Other examples look like requests for permission, (19) and (20), or like polite invitations, (17) and (22). But these categories cannot easily be distinguished. Whether the speaker invites the addressee to call her Adelaide, entreats her to do so or even commands her (17) is open to speculation. The larger context could perhaps give some indication, or the speakers in these extracts could be deliberately vague in an attempt to make their utterance maximally non-imposing. In present-day English, however, both *please you* and *if you please* occur only very rarely. Figure 9.1 plots the frequency of *please* and, as a subtype of *please*, *if you please* across the five sub-periods of the COHA that I have defined for this case study. The frequency of *please* as a politeness token has been estimated according to the method outlined in the previous section.

The pattern is very clear. This particular token of non-imposition politeness shows a steady increase throughout the eighteenth and early nineteenth century and a levelling in the second half of the twentieth century. In the first sub-period, *please* rarely occurred on its own, but in the course of time the full form disappeared almost entirely.

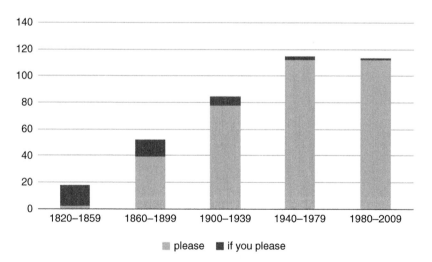

Figure 9.1 Frequency of *please* and *if you please* per million words in the COHA (manually adjusted to exclude false hits)

These figures are largely based on the fiction material. It is there that we find most of the occurrences of *if you please* and *please*. The frequencies of just over 100 occurrences per million words in the two most recent sub-periods compare with the frequencies reported by Biber et al. (1999: 1098) of about 200 occurrences per million words in American English conversations.

In the COCA, the levels are lower because it includes a much wider spread of different registers which presumably do not regularly include (representations of) spoken language. These frequencies, therefore, cannot be directly compared either with the frequencies for the COHA or with the frequencies reported by Biber et al. (1999). But interestingly they show a steady increase across the twenty-seven years included in the corpus (see Figure 9.2).

In the 1990s the frequency of *please*, which was again manually adjusted to include only politeness-relevant instances, amounts to seventy-two instances per million words. In the 2000s this figure rises to seventy-seven and in the 2010s (2010–2017) it already reaches ninety-eight instances per million words. Thus it appears that the levelling of the frequency of *please* that manifests itself in the COHA material is not confirmed by the COCA material, and there is certainly no evidence of an ongoing reduction of the frequency of *please*.

The most prototypical elements of non-imposition politeness, however, are the conventional indirect requests (*could you*, *can you*, etc.). Aijmer (1996: 157) lists twenty-eight different patterns that occur a total 104 times in the London-Lund Corpus, but only ten of them occur more than once. The most frequent patterns are *could you*, *can you*, *would you* and *will you*. Some

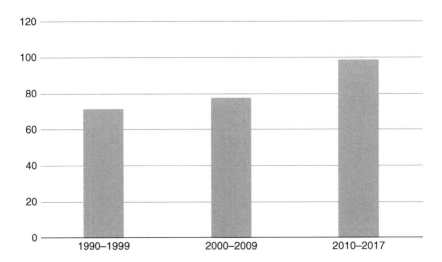

Figure 9.2 Frequency of *please* per million words in the COCA (manually adjusted to exclude false hits)

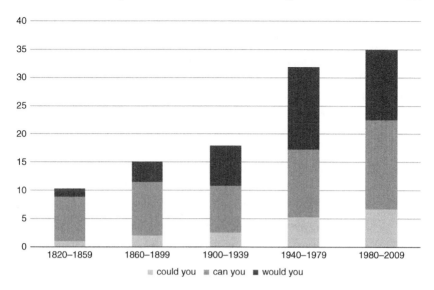

Figure 9.3 Cumulative frequency of three conventional indirect requests per million words in the COHA (manually adjusted to exclude false hits)

of the less frequent patterns are no more than elaborations of these main patterns, such as *could you possibly, could you kindly* or *could you perhaps*, which all occur just once. In fact, the twenty-eight patterns can be reduced to the following eight main patterns: *could you, can you, would you, will you, you could, couldn't you, can't you* and *won't you*. All these forms occur in both polite requests and other syntactic and pragmatic contexts where their occurrence is not related to non-imposition politeness. Figure 9.3 is based on the three most frequent forms, *could you, can you* and *would you*. The frequency figures are again estimates established on the basis of manual inspection for each item and each decade as described in the previous section.

Figure 9.3 provides empirical evidence for a slow growth of conventional indirect requests throughout the nineteenth and early twentieth century and a considerable increase towards the middle of the twentieth century which is followed by a further slight increase. The three constructions show rather different developments. *Could you* started on a very low level and steadily increased across the five sub-periods. *Can you* was by far the most important construction of the three in the first sub-period. It also shows a more or less steady increase except for a slight reduction in the third sub-period. And *would you* shows the most pronounced increase of the three throughout the first four sub-periods with an interesting decline from the fourth to the fifth sub-period. The following extracts provide relevant examples:

(23)   'Can you tell us, madam,' rejoined Mr. Kellond hastily, 'if the … (COHA, FIC, 1831)

(24)   Oh, Russell! can you give me this consolation, without which my future will be dark indeed? (COHA, FIC, 1864)

(25)   If neither of those days should suit you, could you kindly suggest another day? (COHA, 1879, FIC)

(26)   Would you be kind enough to tell me if the report be true? (COHA, FIC, 1900)

(27)   Well, in that case can you let me have ten until Monday? (COHA, FIC, 1911)

(28)   Could you tell me where I could get an aspirin. Please. (COHA, FIC, 1990)

(29)   'Would you like to close the door, Miss?' the bartender asked. (COHA, FIC, 1941)

(30)   Would you please read that back? (COHA, FIC, 1980)

(31)   Could you elaborate, please? (COHA, FIC, 1993)

(32)   Can you check the church's records and see if a Mr. Jamie Hathaway is – was. (COHA, FIC, 2001)

Again, these examples show a range of impositions that in themselves may vary in their severity, even though it is difficult, without more context, to gauge the precise amount of effort that would be required from the addressee. The formulations themselves differ in the level of non-imposition. Some use the *could you X, would you X* or *can you X* formula as the only mitigating element, and *X* indicates the actual action that is expected from the addressee, as in the cases of (23), (24), (27) and (32). Other formulations combine several elements that make the imposition appear less imposing, for instance by adding *kindly*, as in (25), or *please*, as in (28), (30) and (31). And in (26) and (29) *X* stands not for the action itself but for the addressee's kindness or willingness to do what is required, *would you be kind enough to tell* and *would you like to close*.

Figure 9.3 suggests an increase of conventional indirect requests that continues unabated into the present day. However, a more detailed look at each decade reveals that this may be misleading. Figure 9.4, therefore, plots the same frequency figures as Figure 9.3, but broken down to the individual decades. Figure 9.4 suggests a downward trend over the last four decades of the COHA that was disguised by the larger periods shown in Figure 9.3. However, this downward trend is mostly due to the reduction in frequency of *would you*. Both *could you* and *can you* show a slight increase over the first

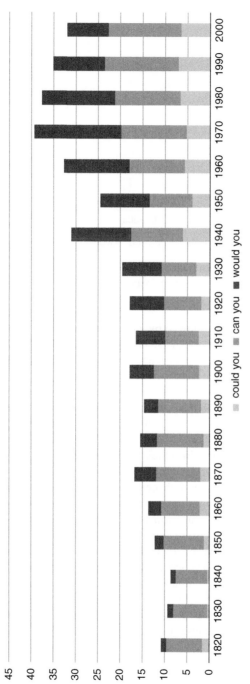

Figure 9.4 Cumulative frequency of three conventional indirect requests per million words in the COHA per decade (manually adjusted to exclude false hits)

■ could you ■ can you ■ would you

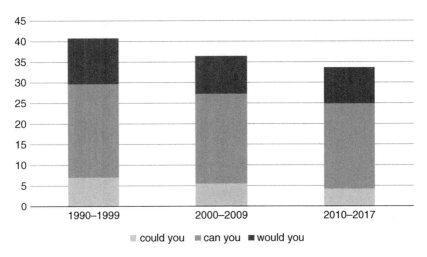

Figure 9.5 Cumulative frequency of three conventional indirect requests per million words in the COCA (manually adjusted to exclude false hits)

three of these four decades followed by a minimal decrease to the last decade. Figure 9.5, therefore, looks at the evidence in the COCA. This is again based on the much larger but more diverse database included in the COCA, with roughly 200 million words per decade. According to Figure 9.5, the COCA provides confirming evidence for the downward trend of the three conventional indirect requests investigated here, both individually and in combination. Individually, the differences are not very big, but they are consistent and cumulatively they provide a clear picture.

Thus, we have a situation in which *please* continues to increase, albeit at a very moderate rate, in contrast to its steep rate of increase throughout the nineteenth and early twentieth century. And at the same time, *could you* and *can you* in their function as non-imposition elements are levelling and *would you* in the same function has clearly been decreasing over the last few decades. It is, therefore, interesting to explore how *please* inter-acts with the three items of conventional indirect requests. For this purpose, collocation searches were carried out searching for one of the three indirect requests as a node and *please* as a collocate. Trial runs suggested that a span of three items to the left of the node and six items to the right provided the best results with only very few hits that did not consist of a polite request. Collocation searches with this particular span include the following examples, which all appear to be genuine requests:

(33)   she asked: 'Can you tell me, please, the way to Dr. Abbott's office?' (COHA, FIC 1909)

(34)   But could you name one, please? (COHA, FIC, 1930)

(35)   'Would you please put him on,' said Kroner's secretary. (COHA, FIC 1952)

(36)   Mr. Terle, could you please bring her in out of the weather? (COHA, FIC, 1957)

(37)   Please, would you tell me what you think I've done? (COHA, FIC 1982)

(38)   Please, could you tell me the best thing to do? (COCA, FIC, 2017)

(39)   Could you lower those signs please? (COCA, SPOK, 2016)

(40)   Excuse me, Miss, could you give us some change please? (COCA, SPOK, 2017)

(41)   Can you answer his question, please? (COCA, fic, 2000)

(42)   Please, can you lend me an office because I haven't got one. (COCA, SPOK, 1991)

(43)   Will you boys please shut your traps! (COCA, FIC, 2004)

The requestive force of these utterances differs considerably, despite the fact that the presence of *please* marks them all as requests rather than a genuine question, a suggestion or a piece of advice for instance. The precise politeness value is also difficult to assess, especially without more context. The non-imposing formulation on its own does not make the utterance automatically polite. But nonetheless the formulation in each case is a token acknowledgement that the addressee has some option of carrying out the action or not. The formulation may come across as gracious and polite or as sarcastic and rude depending on whether the nominally conceded choice is genuine or spurious, but in each case it plays on the option given to the addressee to either comply or not. In some cases, this option may be sincerely granted, and in others it may be ironically hinted at. Figure 9.6 plots the development of these collocations in the COHA and Figure 9.7 in the COCA. For Figure 9.6 it is again necessary to plot individual decades since the larger periods used elsewhere in this chapter would disguise the clear decrease over the last three decades.

Figure 9.6, with data from the COHA, shows a very clear trend. Non-imposition requests combining a conventional indirect formulation with *please* are very rare indeed throughout the nineteenth century and well into the twentieth. Their frequency rises dramatically from the 1940s to the 1980s, when they reach their highest level before they start to decline again. Figure 9.7, which plots the development since 1990, indicates that the trend shown in the COHA continues into the current decade. The figures retrieved from the two corpora can only be compared with some caution because of their different composition, but Figures 9.6 and 9.7 indicate that the frequencies of

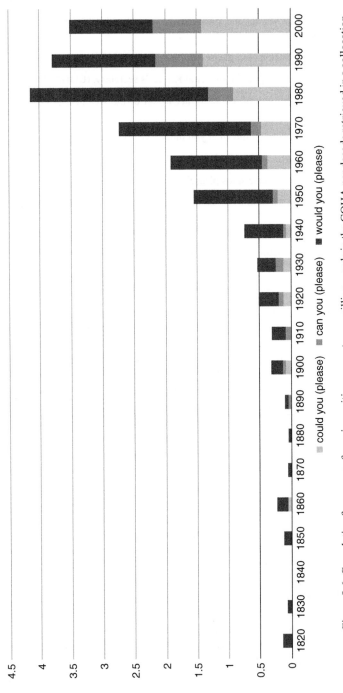

Figure 9.6 Cumulative frequency of non-imposition requests per million words in the COHA per decade retrieved in a collocation search with *please* occurring within a span of L3–R6.

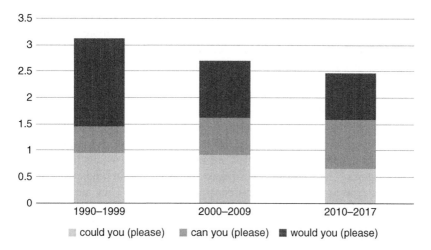

Figure 9.7 Cumulative frequency of non-imposition requests per million words in the COCA retrieved in a collocation search with *please* occurring within a span of L3–R6.

non-imposition requests are roughly proportional. The frequencies for the last two decades of the COHA, which overlap with the COCA, are 3.8 and 3.5 per million words while the figures for the COCA range between 3.1 and 2.7 per million words.

A more careful look at the figures reveals that the development of *would you* in collocation with *please* is more pronounced than the other two forms. Its increase, which seems to have started in the 1930s, is much bigger than the increase in frequency of the other two forms. It starts with 0.3 occurrences per million words and reaches almost ten times that figure by the 1980s (2.8 per million words), and by the 2000s it has already receded to 1.3 per million words again. *Could you* and *can you* in collocation with *please* continue to increase to the 1990s and then stay more or less level. In the COCA it is again *would you* that is mostly responsible for the overall reduction, while *could you* and *can you* stay more or less level.

9.5   Discussion

The frequency figures presented in the previous section provide some interesting results. Some of the most prototypical elements of non-imposition politeness, according to the evidence in the COHA, came to prominence much later than previously assumed. Their frequency only started to rise noticeably in the second half of the twentieth century. It appears that by the time that Brown and Levinson (1978, 1987) described them as typical features of (British) negative politeness, they had, at least in American English, only been in evidence for about a generation or so. What might be even more surprising is the fact that the available evidence for American English indicates that the frequency of these elements has already peaked and is now on a downward trend with *would you* taking the lead.

It must be stressed again that the quantitative development of these elements should not be mistaken as a quantification of politeness in general. The increase or decrease in the frequency of elements such as *please* or *would you* in certain contexts does not mean that people are becoming more or less polite, it only means that the elements themselves are becoming more or less important in these contexts. The elements investigated in this chapter are indicative of one particular type of politeness, non-imposition politeness. They are one option for speakers to indicate that they do not want to impose their wishes on their addressees. There does not appear to be any plausible way of measuring the overall politeness of a speech community and, therefore, it seems prudent to assume that there are no significant changes. But, as not only this but also the previous chapters of this book have shown, the means of expressing politeness in interpersonal relations keeps changing throughout the history of the English language.

Culpeper and Demmen (2011: 51) link the change in politeness practices in the nineteenth century directly to social and ideological changes at the time, and in particular the rise of the individual self and self-help. They mention social and geographical mobility, urbanisation and industrialisation as particularly important developments in the nineteenth century which created the conditions for an ideology of individualism:

Both social and geographical mobility, both of which were so dramatic in nineteenth-century Britain, did much to divide the self from society. Community ties were weakened; people had to become more independent. As social ties became weakened, the notion of privacy became stronger, and acquired positive value in the Victorian period. The notion of privacy, of one's private space, of freedom from imposition is of course related to negative face. (Culpeper and Demmen 2011: 60)

This might go some way to explain the rise of non-imposition politeness observed in the previous section, but it does not really account for the timing of these changes. Culpeper and Demmen talk about the situation in Great Britain. It is not plausible to suggest that these developments took place so much later in the United States. It appears then that the social and ideological conditions identified by Culpeper and Demmen are perhaps a necessary but not in themselves a sufficient criterion for the increase in popularity of the particular non-imposition elements investigated in this chapter. It would also be difficult to argue that the ideology of individualism is currently receding in order to explain the apparent downturn in the frequency of these elements within the last few decades. It is more plausible to assume that other forms are taking over. Perhaps speakers are turning away from non-imposition politeness to solidarity politeness, or opting for even more tentative forms of non-imposition politeness. Let us briefly explore these two possibilities, which, of course, do not exclude each other.

Lakoff (2005: 32) has already observed that camaraderie politeness is taking over in American English, while negative politeness is under threat. As evidence, she relates a story from a newspaper article published in 1994, which states that a San Francisco telephone company, Pacific Bell, required its directory assistance operators to shorten their greetings, 'Hi, this is Mary. What city, please?' by dropping the *please*. The move was intended to save half a second per call, which produces a substantial saving over the thousands of calls handled by the company. Lakoff (2005: 33) comments that it is significant that it is the marker of negative politeness *please*, which is deleted while *hi* and the self-identification with a bogus name, 'I'm Mary', both of which are markers of positive politeness or camaraderie, are kept. She views this as 'just another indication of the victory of the latter [i.e. positive politeness] in America' and as a 'clear instance of camaraderie outflanking formal distance politeness' (Lakoff 2005: 33). According to this view, the recent reduction of conventional polite requests in American English reported in the previous section would be part of this overall shift from negative to positive politeness.

Lakoff further suggests that this shift from negative to positive politeness is related to an increasing blurring of the line between the private and the public sphere. Traditionally, different forms of politeness were appropriate for the different spheres:

> As the Pacific Bell example suggests, America is becoming an increasingly conventionalized-camaraderie society. In a culture using conventional distance (such as the U.S. used to be), it was important to show non-intrusiveness: a speaker needed to present directives as mitigated requests, even when the illocutionary force of the speech act was an offer – to give the caller needed information. (Lakoff 2005: 34)

Alternatively, or perhaps in addition, speakers may also prefer to make their non-imposition requests even more tentative and non-imposing. That would help to explain the reduction of collocations of *would you*, for instance, with *please*. It is possible that speakers increasingly omit *please* in this context because *please* has a double function. It is both a mitigating device that weakens the illocutionary force of a request (e.g. Shvanyukova 2019: 178), but it also unambiguously flags the requestive force of an utterance and thus increases its illocutionary force, even if it is formulated tentatively as a non-imposition request. Without *please* its requestive force is further reduced, and it is up to the addressee to interpret it as a request. Its absence increases its non-imposing nature.

Breuer and Geluykens (2007), on the basis of their comparative DCT study, provide evidence that speakers, and in particular American English speakers, prefer to position mitigation outside of the requestive head act itself. And ultimately, speakers may prefer to desist entirely from using forms such as *could you, can you* or *would you* because of their conventionality as requests and resort to mere hints.

Grainger and Mills (2016: 82–3) provide an illustrative anecdote on indirectness and intercultural misunderstandings. Grainger had met two Zimbabwean friends for an evening out in town. At the end of the evening, Grainger got back to her car to drive home while one of her friends who lived near the town centre said, 'I think we will wait for a bus, I don't feel like walking home'. After they had parted ways and Grainger had driven home in her car, it occurred to her that her friend's utterance might have been a hint, perhaps even an indirect request for a lift. A subsequent exchange via short text messages confirmed this suspicion. The utterance had indeed been meant as a hint. In this case, Grainger recognised the hint for what it was, albeit much too late to offer the desired lift. But the example illustrates how difficult it may be to recognise a hint, even for conversationalists with the appropriate contextual knowledge. For the analyst, this is even more difficult. Extracts (44) to (47) provide some illustrations including the formulations *could you, can you* or *would you*:

(44)   When you talk to them, they're very convincing. But then I'd say, Well, could you come to Stanford and be studied? 'Oh, no, no, no. I'm too busy.' (COCA, SPOK, 1999)

(45)   'How soon can you be ready to leave for Los Angeles?' he asked without preamble once we were seated across from each other. I cocked my head. 'Are you inviting me or sending me?' That surely made him feel young. He smiled. 'Sending.' (COCA, FIC, 2017)

(46)   He lifted his guitar and strap from around his neck, placed the guitar on its stand, slid his chair over, and played an E blues scale on the piano. Can you play that? he said. It ain't but se'm notes. E blues. The Bleeder wore dark, loose clothes. Don't worry about no fingering, he said. Just hit the notes. (COCA, FIC, 2011)

(47)   'But it didn't last long, did it? Two years later, the school expelled you and sent you home. They couldn't deal with you.' He paused. 'Would you like to tell me why?' Her hands clenched into fists. She couldn't breathe. He knew. 'Shall I tell you?' he asked softly. (COCA, FIC, 2014)

In these cases, it is not straightforward to decide whether we are dealing with a question or a request. *Could you, can you* or *would you* seem to be part of a real question in which the speaker enquires about the ability of the addressee, but at the same time there is probably a hint that the addressee might, if possible, actually perform the action mentioned in the question. In (44), the doctor asks for the availability of patients to be examined in Stanford. In (45), the speaker asks the I-narrator when he would be ready to leave, and in this case the addressee even asks explicitly about the illocutionary force of the question. Was it an invitation or an order? In (46), the speaker asks about the addressee's ability to play an E blues scale on the guitar, and from the wider context of the extract it becomes clear that the addressee of the question tried after having been shown and succeeded. But here, too, the utterance remains ambiguously between a question that could have been answered by *yes* or *no*, and a request that requires some non-verbal action on the part of the addressee. In (47), finally, the interrogator asks his interviewee whether she would like to tell her story, which is again both a question and a request.

Such examples are difficult to classify because they are meant to be ambiguous. They are, at least on the surface, clearly more tentative than formulations that include *please*. In the actual situations, the addressees are, of course, fully aware of the interactional dynamics between themselves and the speakers, and this assessment will play an important part in the interpretation of *could you*, *can you* or *would you* as a genuine question, as an invitation, a request or as a straightforward command.

9.6   Conclusion

It appears to be difficult to provide an overall explanation that accounts for the frequency patterns of the non-imposition elements reported in this chapter. In the COHA, they came to prominence much later than previously assumed (i.e. sometime after the Second World War), and at present they seem to be declining again. However, they forcefully make the point that specific forms of politeness are not only culture-specific, they are also historically situated. These elements have to be seen within a larger context of other ways of not imposing on an addressee and other ways of being polite. Many of these elements do not lend themselves easily to corpus-based searches and therefore defy easy quantification. In any case, and despite what some social commentators would have us believe, the rise and fall of individual politeness-related elements does not provide any useful evidence for a rise or fall of the overall politeness levels of a society.

10　Conclusion: Politeness, Manners and Dissimulation

10.1　Introduction

The chapters of this book have highlighted selected aspects of what in a broad sense can be described as politeness in the history of English, from its Anglo-Saxon origins up to the present day. In the Preface I described the journey through the centuries as a road trip and the descriptions of different types of politeness as snapshots taken along the way, including long-shot panoramas and various close-ups of interesting details on the wayside. The pictures are selective and the result of personal preferences and choices. Nevertheless, taken together they also give an impression of the changing countryside along the way.

In this chapter, I will now try to summarise the journey into a more coherent narrative that focuses on the overall changes rather than the individual picture points themselves. How did the type of politeness that I described for the Anglo-Saxon period change into what we are familiar with today? Can we identify a point in the history of English at which a concern for good breeding and moral behaviour turned into a concern for superficial manners of outward appearance? Was there a point at which politeness turned into dissimulation, an attempt to deceive our interlocutors and give them a better opinion of us?

Table 10.1 gives a much-simplified overview of the important developments of politeness in the history of English. There is no claim that types of politeness identified for a particular period are exhaustive for that particular period. Other types are likely to have existed. This is particularly obvious for the more recent periods, for which we have much more data than for the early periods. And it has to be stressed once again that these periods are long and diverse. The Old English period lasted some seven centuries, and present-day English is spread out over the entire globe. Generalisations can only be coarse-grained and crude. But on my journey through the history of English, I found the types listed in Table 10.1 particularly striking and noteworthy.

Table 10.1 *Politeness in the history of English: A simplified overview*

Period	Society	Type of politeness	Key terms
Old English	Germanic tribes, early Christian	Discernment, humility and gentleness	*Þeawfæstnes* ('obedience'), *manþwærnesse* ('gentleness')
Middle English	French influence, court culture	From discernment to deference	*Curteisie* ('courtesy')
Early Modern English	Renaissance, Reformation	Deference, solidarity	*Civility, sprezzatura*
Eighteenth century	Social classes, 'polite' society	Compliment culture	*Politeness, manners*
Present-day English	Egalitarian, democratic and antiauthoritarian	Rise of non-imposition politeness	*Could you possibly . . . ?*

10.2   Discernment, Courtesy and Civility

For the Old English period, the evidence is particularly scanty. The analysis presented in Chapter 3 started with relevant lexical items derived from the *Thesaurus of Old English* under the heading 'Humanity, courtesy, civility', which suggested that the type of politeness found in the surviving texts in Old English were concerned, on the one hand, with adherence to rules and discipline and, on the other, with humility and gentleness. *Þeawfæstnes* ('obedience') and *manþwærnesse* ('gentleness') turned out to be key terms with occurrences in religious texts. I have used the terms 'discernment politeness' and 'politeness of humility and gentleness' to capture these aspects (see also Ridealgh and Jucker 2019). Additional evidence concerning the forms of requests and address presented by Kohnen (2008a, 2008b) further suggests that politeness in the modern sense did not play a significant role. In the society of Germanic tribes, mutual obligation and kin loyalty were paramount; personal face wants, in the sense of freedom from imposition, and a desire to be appreciated appear to have been much less significant: 'Politeness in early Britain has more to do with social indexing, with recognising one's place in the scheme of things' (Culpeper and Demmen 2011: 59).

French influence after the Norman Conquest of 1066 brought new concepts. The semantic field of courtesy and politeness as recorded in the *Historical Thesaurus of the Oxford English Dictionary* expanded considerably during the Middle English period, and the term *curteisie* ('courtesy') epitomises a new type of politeness. Careful readings of relevant passages in Chaucer's *Canterbury Tales* reveal that the term was used to refer to a virtue that aristocratic characters quite naturally strive for. In the case of members of the clergy, an invocation of *curteisie* is generally less appropriate, and descriptions are often ironic. But even characters of the lower social ranks occasionally invoke the concept (e.g. with the phrase *for your curteisie*), when they see that social decorum is in danger of being infringed. Thus, we have a new type of courtly politeness, as the etymology of the term suggests, but it essentially still describes a non-strategic use of politeness, and in this sense it can still be described as a form of discernment politeness. It describes an adherence to expected behaviour and a conformity to the necessary level of social decorum.

The French influence also introduced the distinction between the pronominal terms of address, *ye* and *thou*, for a single addressee. As I have shown in Chapter 4, once again based on evidence from Chaucer's *Canterbury Tales* and from the anonymous poem *Sir Gawain and the Green Knight*, the choice depended on a range of factors, including the social status and age of the characters, their familiarity with each other but also situational factors like interactional dominance and their power over each other. The use of the more polite *ye* can be described as a deference marker while *thou* is used in situations in which the politeness of deference is not necessary, as for instance when talking to someone of a lower social status or lesser situational power. *Ye* is the normal choice for a wife to her husband if they are both of a higher social class, and sometimes for a husband to his wife. In this usage it clearly differs from the use of its present-day equivalents in languages such as French or German, where the plural pronoun indicates not only deference but also formality and distance, which makes it incompatible with situations of familiarity and intimacy.

The sixteenth century and the Renaissance in England brought a wealth of new influences. Conduct manuals translated from Italian originals became popular and introduced new concepts of polite behaviour, and indeed the first occurrences of the word *polite* in its modern sense are attested in the sixteenth century (*OED*, 3rd ed., polite, *adj.*). As I have argued in Chapter 5, it is at this time that we can perceive the first signs of politeness as a form of surface kindness that hides underlying darker motives. Culpeper (2017) describes how one very influential conduct manual of the sixteenth century, Giovanni della Casa's *Il Galateo*, published in English in 1576 under the title *Galateo ... A treatise of the maners and behauiours, it behoueth a man to vse and eschewe, in his familiar conversation*, gives advice that corresponds somewhat uncannily to Brown and Levinson's (1987) politeness strategies that are used to mitigate face threats. At the end of the sixteenth century, Culpeper argues, Italy had considerable cultural prestige in England:

England was witnessing a consolidation of the middle-ranks and concomitant urbanization ... Hitherto, a concern of politeness was how to demonstrate one's rank through a display of courtly or courteous behaviour. Now, a pressing concern was how to get along with one's new neighbour. Thus, there was a shift from the virtues of courtesy to civility. (2017: 200)

Thus the term *civility* replaces *courtesy* as a key concept. As Gillingham argues:

Ever since the pioneering cultural history of Norbert Elias, the emergence of the words 'civil' and 'civility' in Western European languages, English included, in senses pertaining to refined and polished manners, has been taken to mark a highly significant shift between the Middle Ages and the Renaissance in the styles and tastes of the upper classes, a shift neatly encapsulated in the title of Anna Bryson's book: *From Courtesy to Civility*. It remains generally agreed that the concept of civility developed first in Italy, where its association with 'city' meant a great deal, and that as it spread throughout Europe, so the terms 'civil' and 'civility' changed their meanings, gradually displacing 'courteous' and 'courtesy' as the fashionable terms denoting approved conduct. (Gillingham 2002: 267)

Another term imported from Italian at this time was *sprezzatura*, which can be translated roughly as 'effortless mastery'. It describes the courtier who knows how to behave with cultivated ease, who is well-trained in the arts and sciences, and does everything 'with an air of unhurried and graceful effortlessness' (Cunningham and Reich 2006: 330; see Chapter 5). The analysis in Chapter 5 shows how this description can be applied, for instance, to characters in the plays of Shakespeare. But the polished surface can also be used to hide some unpleasant truths. It may involve a certain amount of deception (see Berger Jr 2002: 297).

In a similar way, Brown and Levinson's (1987) approach describes polite-ness as a discrepancy between a polished surface and underlying motives. Specific linguistic forms are chosen to mitigate face threats, with its two aspects, the threats to the positive face of either the speaker or addressee (i.e. their wish to be liked and approved), and the threats to their negative face (i.e. their wish not to be imposed upon). It is in reference to the plays of Shakespeare that several historical politeness scholars have described the use of negative and positive politeness, that is specific forms that support either the negative or positive face wants of the addressee (e.g. Brown and Gilman 1989; Kopytko 1993, 1995; Bouchara 2009). Kopytko (1995) identified a high rate of positive politeness in his data pertaining to eight plays by Shakespeare. Nevalainen and Raumolin-Brunberg (1995) among others investigated personal letters written in the fifteenth century, and focused on the gradual shift from negative polite-ness of elaborate terms of address, such as *Right honourable and worshipful sir* to the positive politeness of nicknames and terms of endearment. In Chapter 5, I argue that the negative politeness of deference can be seen as a continuation of discernment politeness because its forms are chosen in response to the social context of the interaction and the role relationship between the writer of the letter and its recipient. They are not used to mitigate face threats in the sense of Brown and Levinson (1987). Thus, in Table 10.1, one important type of politeness in the Early Modern English period is deference, and for the other aspect I suggest the term solidarity rather than positive politeness (see Lakoff 2005; Culpeper and Gillings 2018). This terminology has the advantage that it avoids the misleading suggestion that positive and negative are good and bad, respectively.

10.3   Politeness and Manners

The eighteenth century was particularly important for the development of politeness in England. The country was undergoing major social and cultural change, and politeness became a matter of ideology used to reinforce class boundaries against the emerging social mobility. In Table 10.1, I refer to this century as the period of the compliment culture. The term 'compliment' is here to be understood in its much broader eighteenth-century sense. It does not refer to a speech act praising the addressee for their skill or good looks, for instance, but it refers to a ceremonious speech act of polite and courteous interaction. Chapter 7 provides a broad range of extracts drawn from contemporary newspapers and novels referring to such compliments. In newspapers, they regularly concern acts of diplomacy. Emissaries pay their compliments to the nobility of foreign countries on some official occasion, such as the accession of a new king to the throne, the marriage of a royal couple, the birth of a prince or the death of a king. But extracts from novels show that compliments also describe polite and courteous interactions in a private setting, with compliments of introduction, compliments of salutation and so on. In this way, the term captures something of the ceremonious formality of interaction that seems to have been typical of the eighteenth century.

In Chapter 8, I introduced the distinction between the Spectator mode of politeness and the Shaftesbury mode of politeness (Langford 2002: 312; Fitzmaurice 2010, 2016). The Spectator mode was connected to a natural code of behaviour that was open to a broad segment of the population while the Shaftesbury mode was closely connected to the 'polite society' of the aristocracy. In this latter sense, politeness was a matter of being born into the right social class and a way of keeping out those who were not. It was connected to polished manners that could also be used to hide darker motives. The Spectator mode, on the other hand, was more closely connected to the morality of the new middle class. A large amount of educational literature provided edification for socially aspiring readers. Plays provided not only entertainment, but also examples of good, moral behaviours and warnings against straying from the path of virtue. Epistolary novels often contrasted middle-class virtues with aristocratic immorality, as a warning for their middle-class and mostly female readership. The politeness of morality and virtuous behaviour was contrasted to the shallow superficiality of the politeness that the aristocracy claimed as their birthright.

Sell refers to the same dilemma when he alludes to the more cynical understanding of politeness and quotes *The English Theophrastus: or, the Manners of the Age* of 1702: 'Politeness may be defined as dextrous management of our Words and Actions, whereby we make other people have a better Opinion of us and themselves' (Anon. 1702: 108, quoted in Sell 2000: 213). Terkourafi (2011) identifies the eighteenth century as particularly important in the separation of politeness and morality. The separation itself goes back, according to her, to the time of the transition from the monastic to the courtly spheres between the late Middle Ages and early modernity (Terkourafi 2011: 169). But it was in the context of the far-reaching social changes of the eighteenth century that the separation became more noticeable:

The intimate relationship between morality and politeness described so far can become strained at times of rapid social transformation, when competing interests can pull the two apart relegating them to different spheres. The rise of the middle class, urbanization, the secularization of society, and the emancipation of women played this catalytic role in ancient Egypt, medieval Islam, the European Middle Ages, and eighteenth-century Britain, respectively. Emptied of moral content, politeness becomes 'mere conduct', a faint and potentially treacherous reflection of one's underlying morality. This opens the way for 'politeness [to be] seen as hypocritical or insincere [...]. [T]he speaker's linguistic behaviour is evaluated as "polite", only there are doubts as to whether this outward appearance matches the speaker's actual intentions'. (Terkourafi 2011: 178, quoting Eelen 2001: 41)

Politeness as 'mere conduct' becomes insincere but it is still a form of politeness. Eelen's argument, from which Terkourafi quotes in this passage, concerns the possibility for politeness to refer to negatively evaluated behaviour but even as such it does not become impolite in the evaluation of native speakers but hollow and hypocritical, and as such politeness can become a form of dissimulation.

10.4   Politeness, Dissimulation and Sincerity

Today, politeness often has a bad press. It is seen as insincere and hypocritical. The sociologist Kate Fox has put this particularly clearly:

English rules of politeness are undeniably rather complex, and, in their tortuous attempts to deny or disguise the realities of status differences, clearly hypocritical. But then, surely all politeness is a form of hypocrisy ... Our politenesses are all sham, pretence, dissimulation – an artificial veneer of harmony and parity masking quite different social realities. (2004: 97)

The dissociation of politeness and morality seems to be complete in this view. Politeness is the surface that conceals the unpleasant realities underneath. It is no more than dissimulation, an attempt to mitigate what otherwise would be unpalatable. This is a far cry from the discernment politeness and the politeness of humility and gentleness that I have identified in the sources from the Middle Ages, or from the concerns of the educational writers in the eighteenth century who contrasted true politeness with the superficiality of aristocratic politeness.

Brown and Levinson's (1987) perspective is less disdainful than Fox's, but they have taught generations of politeness scholars to view politeness as a way of mitigating face threats. Politeness is used to lessen the unpleasant impact of an imposition on the addressee, and in this sense it is also a form of dissimulation. Formulations such as *can you*, *could you* or *would you* in requests pretend to give the addressee an option, to ask for their ability or willingness to carry out a certain action. As we have seen in Chapter 9, such elements are relatively recent in the history of English. They made a first noticeable appearance in the nineteenth century (see also Culpeper and Demmen 2011), but their real success story only started after the Second World War.

Not all commentators have a negative view of present-day politeness. Sell, for instance, asks: 'So how, if at all, do people think about politeness today? Perhaps as the velvet glove to hide an iron fist. Or as a social lubricant, cheaper and less nocuous than alcohol, but, like free booze, still useful to the corps diplomatique' (2000: 216). But perhaps it is helpful, or even necessary, to make a careful distinction between two types of sincerity, as Pinto (2011) argues in his investigation into the question, 'are Americans insincere?' He started from the widespread stereotype that sees American politeness as insincere and uses elicitation experiments to obtain native speaker judgements of the sincerity of politeness in service encounters in a grocery store. The participants filled out a questionnaire on their evaluations of the sincerity behind routine politeness formulae in cashiers' salutations and service questions ('Hi, how are you today?' 'Did you find everything you were looking for?' 'Have a good afternoon!'). He found that such routine utterances often receive a positive evaluation despite the fact that they are judged to be insincere, which suggests that a distinction needs to be made between the sincerity that reflects the speaker's true beliefs and feelings and the sincerity that reflects the speaker's concern for rapport with the addressee and for making the addressee feel good and comfortable. Pinto writes:

Distinguishing between these two perspectives of sincerity provides a possible framework for explaining how perceptions of politeness may vary according to individual and cultural preferences. At least in the United States, and perhaps other English-speaking communities, rapport-based sincerity probably accounts for a substantial amount of conventionalized routines where expressing one's true beliefs and feelings is not expected. This is certainly not the case in all cultures, which explains why many foreigners in the United States find American politeness to be superficial. Furthermore, it would be theoretically plausible to simultaneously acknowledge both interpretations of sincerity, leading to perceptions of *sincere insincerity*. A person's speech behavior can be interpreted as sincerely insincere in the following way: sincere if it effectively projects concern for supporting interpersonal relationships and making the interaction run smoothly, and insincere in that, if taken literally, there is a lack of symmetry between the actual words and the person's true mental state. (Pinto 2011: 229–30; emphasis original)

The distinction between truth-based sincerity and rapport-based sincerity helps to diffuse some of the controversy surrounding polite behaviour that is seen as dissimulation. Some forms of politeness, and in particular conventionalised politeness, can be analysed as sincere on the rapport level even if the speaker does not express his or her true beliefs and feelings.

10.5   Conclusion

Politeness remains an elusive concept. It means different things to different people and to different cultures, and if this book shows one thing, it is that politeness also changes over time. Whether we search for first-order conceptualisations of politeness or try to impose a specific second-order definition of politeness on our data, we invariably find that people's perception of how they want or should deal with each other in an amicable and harmonious way shifts and fluctuates over time, and so does the evaluation of such behaviour. Is it appraised positively because it communicates kindness and benevolence, or negatively because it is a form of deception, a 'velvet glove' that hides 'an iron fist' to use Sell's (2000: 216) words?

Despite our everyday impressions, politeness cannot easily be quantified. It appears to be impossible to compare politeness levels across cultures. Culpeper and Gillings (2018) compare the north and south of England in order to explore the widespread stereotypes about friendly northerners, but they are quick to point out that they can only assess the frequency of a select number of politeness-related features, such as ability-oriented polite requests, forms such as *please* or *thanks* or various formal and informal terms of address. But the relative frequency of such elements does not allow any inference about the overall level of politeness.

The journey through the history of English in this book highlights a large range of different aspects at different points along the way without any claim of offering a comprehensive picture at any single point of time or a coherent line of development through the centuries. Politeness should always be seen in the larger context of interpersonal communication including all shades of how people discursively negotiate their relationships to each other with and through language. However, I hope that the selected snapshots have opened up interesting vistas and panoramas that encourage further explorations into as yet unchartered territories in the history of the English language.

References

Data Sources and Corpora

Primary Texts and Translations

A New Academy of Compliments: or, the Lover's Secretary: Being Wit and Mirth Improved, by the Most Elegant Expressions Used in the Art of Courtship. (1784) 17th ed., with additions. London: J. Bew.

Benson, Larry D. (1987) *The Riverside Chaucer*. 3rd ed. Boston: Houghton Mifflin. See also www.courses.fas.harvard.edu/.

Campbell, Gordon (ed.). (1995) *Ben Jonson. Volpone, or the Fox, Epicene, or The Silent Woman, The Alchemist, Bartholomew Fair*. Oxford: Oxford University Press.

Chesterfield, Philip Dormer Stanhope, Earl of. (1778) *The Beauties of Chesterfield: or, Remarks on Politeness, and of Knowing the World: Containing Necessary Instructions to Complete the Gentleman and Man of Fashion*. Edinburgh: Robert Jamieson.

Collier, Jeremy. (2011) *A Short View of the Immorality and Profaneness of the English Stage Together with the Sense of Antiquity Upon this Argument* [1699]. Repr. Charleston: BiblioBazaar.

Davis, Norman (ed.). (1967) *Sir Gawain and the Green Knight*. 2nd ed. Oxford: Clarendon Press.

Doyle, Leonard J. (1948) *Rule For Monasteries by Benedict, Saint Abbot of Monte Cassino*. Collegeville: The Liturgical Press.

Evans, G. Blakemore (ed.). (1974) *The Riverside Shakespeare*. Boston: Houghton Mifflin.

Evans, G. Blakemore (ed.). (2003) *Shakespeare, William. Romeo and Juliet*. Updated ed. Cambridge: Cambridge University Press.

Jonson, Ben. *Bartholomew Fair*. In Gordon Campbell (ed.). (1995) *Ben Jonson: Volpone, or the Fox, Epicene, or The Silent Woman, The Alchemist, Bartholomew Fair*. Oxford: Oxford University Press, 327–433.

Jonson, Ben. *Volpone, or the Fox*. In Gordon Campbell (ed.). (1995) *Ben Jonson: Volpone, or the Fox, Epicene, or The Silent Woman, The Alchemist, Bartholomew Fair*. Oxford: Oxford University Press, 1–117.

King James Bible Online (1611), www.kingjamesbibleonline.org.

Lewis, Matthew. (1796) *The Monk*, http://lion.chadwyck.co.uk/.

Lillo, George. 'The London Merchant, or The History of George Barnwell'. In David W. Lindsay (ed.). (1993) *The Beggar's Opera and Other Eighteenth-Century Plays*. London: J. M. Dent, 259–326.

Lindelöf, Uno Lorenz. (1909–14) *Der Lambeth-Psalter: eine altenglische Interlinearversion des Psalters in der Hs. 427 der erzbischöflichen Lambeth Palace Library*. Helsingfors: Druckerei der Finnischen Litteraturgesellschaft.

The New Academy of Complements, Erected for Ladies, Gentlewomen, Courtiers, Gentlemen, Scholars, Souldiers, Citizens, Country-men, and All Persons of What Degree Soever, of Both Sexes. (1681) London: George Sawbridge.

Nicholson, Lewis E. (ed.). (1991) *The Vercelli Book Homilies: Translations from the Anglo-Saxon*. Lanham: University Press of America.

Schröer, Arnold, and Helmut Gneuss. (1964) *Die angelsächsischen Prosabearbeitungen der Benediktinerregel*. Darmstadt: Wissenschaftliche Buchgesellschaft.

Scragg, Donald. (1992) *The Vercelli Homilies and Related Texts*. EETS 300. Oxford: Boydell & Brewer.

Steele, Richard. (1993) 'The Conscious Lovers'. In David W. Lindsay (ed.), *The Beggar's Opera and Other Eighteenth-Century Plays*. London: J. M. Dent, 65–143.

Tolkien, Christopher (ed.). (2006) *Sir Gawain and the Green Knight, Pearl and Sir Orfeo*. Trans. by J. R. R. Tolkien. London: HarperCollins.

The Wits Academy: or, The Muses Delight. (1677) London and Westminster: n.p.

Dictionaries

Anglo-Saxon Dictionary Online, ed. Thomas Northcote Toller et al., comp. Sean Christ and Ondřej Tichý. Faculty of Arts, Charles University in Prague, www .bosworthtoller.com/.

Historical Thesaurus of the Oxford English Dictionary, www.oed.com/thesaurus.

Oxford English Dictionary, www.oed.com/.

Thesaurus of Old English. (2018) University of Glasgow, http://oldenglishthesaurus .arts.gla.ac.uk.

Corpora

British National Corpus (BYU-BNC), www.english-corpora.org/bnc/.

Corpus of Contemporary American English (COCA), www.english-corpora.org/coca/.

Corpus of Early English Correspondence (CEEC), www.helsinki.fi/en/researchgroups/ varieng/corpus-of-early-english-correspondence.

Corpus of Early Modern Dialogues 1560–1760 (CED), http://ota.ox.ac.uk/desc/2507.

Corpus of Historical American English (COHA), www.english-corpora.org/coca/.

Corpus of Late Modern English Texts (CLMET3.0), https://perswww.kuleuven.be/~u 0044428/clmet3_0.htm.

Dictionary of Old English Web Corpus (2009), https://tapor.library.utoronto.ca/doecor pus/index.html.

Eighteenth Century Collections Online (ECCO), www.gale.com/uk/primary-sources/e ighteenth-century-collections-online.

GoogleBooks Ngram Viewer, https://books.google.com/ngrams/.

Helsinki Corpus, www.helsinki.fi/varieng/CoRD/corpora/HelsinkiCorpus/.

Literature Online (LION), https://literature.proquest.com/marketing/index.jsp.

London-Lund Corpus of Spoken English, http://ota.ox.ac.uk/desc/0168.

Project Gutenberg, www.gutenberg.org.

Spoken British National Corpus 2014, http://corpora.lancs.ac.uk/bnc2014/.
Zurich English Newspaper Corpus (ZEN), www.es.uzh.ch/en/Subsites/Projects/zencor
pus.html.

References

Aiden, Erez, and Jean-Baptiste Michel. (2013) *Uncharted: Big Data as a Lens on Human Culture*. New York: Riverhead Books.

Aijmer, Karin. (1996) *Conversational Routines in English: Convention and Creativity*. London: Longman.

Alexander, Michael. (2007) *A History of English Literature*. Basingstoke: Macmillan Palgrave.

Algeo, John. (2001) *The Cambridge History of the English Language*. Vol. 6: *English in North America*. Cambridge: Cambridge University Press.

Bargiela-Chiappini, Francesca, and Sandra Harris. (2006) 'Politeness at work: Issues and challenges'. *Journal of Politeness Research* 2, 7–33.

Baugh, Albert C., and Thomas Cable. (2002) *A History of the English Language*. 5th ed. London: Routledge.

Beetz, Manfred. (1990) *Frühmoderne Höflichkeit. Komplimentierkunst und Gesellschaftsrituale im altdeutschen Sprachraum*. Stuttgart: J. B. Metzlersche Verlagsbuchhandlung.

Beetz, Manfred. (1999) 'The polite answer in pre-modern German conversation culture'. In Andreas H. Jucker, Gerd Fritz and Franz Lebsanft (eds.), *Historical Dialogue Analysis*. Pragmatics & Beyond New Series 66. Amsterdam: John Benjamins, 139–66.

Benson, Larry D. (1987) *The Riverside Chaucer*. 3rd ed. Boston: Houghton Mifflin.

Berger Jr, Harry. (2002) '*Sprezzatura* and the absence of grace'. In Daniel Javitch (ed.), *Baldesar Castiglione: The Book of the Courtier. The Singleton Translation. An Authoritative Text, Criticism*. New York: Norton, 295–307.

Biber, Douglas, Stig Johansson, Geoffrey Leech, Susan Conrad and Edward Finegan. (1999) *Longman Grammar of Spoken and Written English*. London: Longman.

Blake, Norman F. (ed.). (1992) *The Cambridge History of the English Language. Volume 2: 1066–1476*. Cambridge: Cambridge University Press.

Blum-Kulka, Shoshana. (1992) 'The metapragmatics of politeness in Israeli society'. In Richard J. Watts, Sachiko Ide and Konrad Ehlich (eds.), *Politeness in Language: Studies in its History, Theory and Practice*. Berlin: Mouton de Gruyter, 255–80.

Blum-Kulka, Shoshana, and Juliane House. (1989) 'Cross-cultural and situational variation in requesting behavior'. In Shoshana Blum-Kulka, Juliane House and Gabriele Kasper (eds.), *Cross-Cultural Pragmatics: Requests and Apologies*. Norwood: Ablex, 123–54.

Bouchara, Abdelaziz. (2009) *Politeness in Shakespeare: Applying Brown and Levinson's Politeness Theory to Shakespeare's Comedies*. Hamburg: Diplomica.

Bousfield, Derek. (2008) *Impoliteness in Interaction*. Pragmatics & Beyond New Series 167. Amsterdam: John Benjamins.

Bousfield, Derek, and Miriam Locher (eds.). (2008) *Impoliteness in Language: Studies on Its Interplay with Power in Theory and Practice*. Language, Power and Social Process 21. Berlin: Mouton de Gruyter.

Breuer, Anja, and Ronald Geluykens. (2007) 'Variation in British and American English requests: A contrastive study'. In Bettina Kraft and Ronald Geluykens (eds.), *Cross-Cultural Pragmatics and Interlanguage English*. München: Lincom, 107–25.

Brinton, Laurel J. (2007) 'The development of *I mean*: Implications for the study of historical pragmatics'. In Susan M. Fitzmaurice and Irma Taavitsainen (eds.), *Methodological Issues in Historical Pragmatics*. Berlin: Mouton de Gruyter, 37–79.

Brown, Roger, and Albert Gilman. (1960) 'The pronouns of power and solidarity'. In Thomas A. Sebeok (ed.), *Style in Language*. Cambridge, MA: MIT Press, 253–76.

Brown, Roger, and Albert Gilman. (1989) 'Politeness theory and Shakespeare's four major tragedies'. *Language in Society* 18.2, 159–212.

Brown, Penelope, and Stephen C. Levinson. (1978) 'Universals in language usage: Politeness phenomena'. In Esther Goody (ed.), *Questions and Politeness: Strategies in Social Interaction*. Cambridge: Cambridge University Press, 56–310.

Brown, Penelope, and Stephen C. Levinson. (1987) *Politeness: Some Universals in Language Usage*. Studies in Interactional Sociolinguistics 4. Cambridge: Cambridge University Press.

Bryson, Anna. (1998) 'From courtesy to civility'. In *Changing Codes of Conduct in Early Modern England*. Oxford: Clarendon Press.

Burchfield, Robert (ed.). (1994) *The Cambridge History of the English Language. Volume 5: English in Britain and Overseas: Origins and Development*. Cambridge: Cambridge University Press.

Burke, Peter. (2002) 'The courtier abroad: Or, the uses of Italy'. In Daniel Javitch (ed.), *Baldesar Castiglione: The Book of the Courtier. The Singleton Translation. An Authoritative Text, Criticism*. New York: Norton, 388–400. Originally published in Georg Kauffmann (ed.). (1991) *Die Renaissance im Blick der Nationen Europas*. Wiesbaden: Otto Harrassowitz, 1–14.

Burlin, Robert B. (1995) 'Middle English romance: The structure of the genre'. *The Chaucer Review* 30.1, 1–14.

Burnley, David. (1983) *A Guide to Chaucer's Language*. London: Macmillan.

Burnley, David. (2003) 'The T/V pronouns in later Middle English literature'. In Irma Taavitsainen and Andreas H. Jucker (eds.), *Diachronic Perspectives on Address Term Systems*. Pragmatics & Beyond New Series 107. Amsterdam/ Philadelphia: John Benjamins, 27–45.

Busse, Beatrix. (2006) *Vocative Constructions in the Language of Shakespeare*. Pragmatics & Beyond New Series 150. Amsterdam/Philadelphia: John Benjamins.

Busse, Ulrich. (1998) '"Stand, sir, and throw us that you have about ye": Zur Grammatik und Pragmatik des Anredepronomens "ye" in Shakespeares Dramen'. In Eberhard Klein and Stefan J. Schierholz (eds.), *Betrachtungen zum Wort. Lexik im Spannungsfeld von Syntax, Semantik und Pragmatik*. Tübingen: Stauffenburg Verlag, 85–115.

Busse, Ulrich. (2002a) *Linguistic Variation in the Shakespeare Corpus. Morpho-Syntactic Variability of Second Person Pronouns*. Pragmatics & Beyond New Series 106. Amsterdam/Philadelphia: John Benjamins.

Busse, Ulrich. (2002b) 'Changing politeness strategies in English requests: A diachronic investigation'. In Jacek Fisiak (ed.), *Studies in English Historical Linguistics and Philology: A Festschrift for Akio Oizumi*. Frankfurt/Main: Peter Lang, 17–35.

Busse, Ulrich. (2003) 'The co-occurrence of nominal and pronominal address forms in the Shakespeare Corpus: Who says thou or you to whom?' In Irma Taavitsainen and Andreas H. Jucker (eds.), *Diachronic Perspectives on Address Term Systems*. Pragmatics & Beyond New Series 107. Amsterdam/Philadelphia: John Benjamins, 193–221.

Busse, Ulrich. (2008) 'An inventory of directives in Shakespeare's King Lear'. In Andreas H. Jucker and Irma Taavitsainen (eds.), *Speech Acts in the History of English*. Pragmatics & Beyond New Series 176. Amsterdam/Philadelphia: John Benjamins, 85–114.

Busse, Ulrich, and Beatrix Busse. (2010) 'Shakespeare'. In Andreas H. Jucker and Irma Taavitsainen (eds.), *Historical Pragmatics*. Handbooks of Pragmatics 8. Berlin/New York: Mouton de Gruyter, 247–81.

Busse, Ulrich, and Axel Hübler. (2012) 'Introduction'. In Ulrich Busse and Axel Hübler (eds.), *Investigations into the Meta-Communicative Lexicon of English: A Contribution to Historical Pragmatics*. Pragmatics & Beyond New Series 220. Amsterdam/Philadelphia: John Benjamins, 1–16.

Campbell, James. (1991) 'The first Christian kings'. In James Campbell (ed.), *The Anglo-Saxons*. London: Penguin Books, 45–69.

Chapman, Don. (2008) '"You belly-guilty bag": Insulting epithets in Old English'. *Journal of Historical Pragmatics* 9.1, 1–19.

Collins, P. A. W. (1957) 'Restoration comedy'. In Boris Ford (ed.), *From Dryden to Johnson*. The Pelican Guide to English Literature 4. Harmondsworth: Penguin, 156–72.

Cooper, Helen. (1996) *Oxford Guides to Chaucer: The Canterbury Tales*. 2nd ed. Oxford: Oxford University Press.

Crystal, David, and Ben Crystal. (2002) *Shakespeare's Words: A Glossary and Language Companion*. London: Penguin.

Culpeper, Jonathan. (1996) 'Towards an anatomy of impoliteness'. *Journal of Pragmatics* 25, 349–67.

Culpeper, Jonathan. (2009) 'The metalanguage of impoliteness: Using sketch engine to explore the Oxford English Corpus'. In Paul Baker (ed.), *Contemporary Corpus Linguistics*. Contemporary Studies in Linguistics. London: Continuum, 64–86.

Culpeper, Jonathan. (2010) 'Conventionalised impoliteness formulae'. *Journal of Pragmatics* 42, 3232–45.

Culpeper, Jonathan. (2011a) *Impoliteness: Using Language to Cause Offence*. Cambridge: Cambridge University Press.

Culpeper, Jonathan. (2011b) 'Politeness and impoliteness'. In Gisle Andersen and Karin Aijmer (eds.), *Pragmatics of Society*. Handbooks of Pragmatics 5. Berlin: de Gruyter, 393–438.

Culpeper, Jonathan. (2017) 'The influence of Italian manners on politeness in England, 1550–1620'. *Journal of Historical Pragmatics* 18.2, 195–213.

Culpeper, Jonathan, and Dawn Archer. (2008) 'Requests and directness in Early Modern English trial proceedings and play texts, 1640–1760'. In Andreas H. Jucker and Irma Taavitsainen (eds.), *Speech Acts in the History of English*. Pragmatics & Beyond New Series 176. Amsterdam/Philadelphia: John Benjamins, 45–84.

Culpeper, Jonathan, and Jane Demmen. (2011) 'Nineteenth-century English politeness: Negative politeness, conventional indirect requests and the rise of the individual self'. *Journal of Historical Pragmatics* 12.1–2, 49–81.

Culpeper, Jonathan, and Mathew Gillings. (2018) 'Politeness variation in England: A north-south divide?' In Vaclav Brezina, Robbie Love and Karin Aijmer (eds.), *Corpus Approaches to Contemporary British Speech. Sociolinguistic Studies of the Spoken BNC2014*. New York: Routledge, 33–59.

Culpeper, Jonathan, and Claire Hardaker. (2017) 'Impoliteness'. In Jonathan Culpeper, Michael Haugh and Dániel Kádár (eds.), *The Palgrave Handbook of Linguistic (Im)Politeness*. London: Palgrave, 199–225.

Culpeper, Jonathan, Michael Haugh and Dániel Z. Kádár (eds.). (2017) *The Palgrave Handbook of Linguistic (Im)politeness*. London: Palgrave Macmillan.

Culpeper, Jonathan, and Merja Kytö. (2000) 'Data in historical pragmatics: Spoken discourse (re)cast as writing'. *Journal of Historical Pragmatics* 1.2, 175–99.

Culpeper, Jonathan, and Marina Terkourafi. (2017) 'Pragmatic approaches to (im) politeness'. In Jonathan Culpeper, Michael Haugh and Dániel Kádár (eds.), *The Palgrave Handbook of Linguistic (im)Politeness*. London: Palgrave, 11–39.

Cunningham, Lawrence S., and John J. Reich. (2006) *Cultures and Values: A Survey of Humanities*. Belmont, CA: Thomson Wadsworth.

Davis, Norman (ed.). (1967) *Sir Gawain and the Green Knight*. Edited by J. R. R. Tolkien and E. V. Gordon, 2nd ed. edited by Norman Davis. Oxford: Clarendon Press.

De Roo, Harvey. (1997) 'What's in a name? Power dynamics in "Sir Gawain and the Green Knight"'. *The Chaucer Review* 31.3, 232–55.

Del Lungo Camiciotti, Gabriella. (2008) 'Two polite speech acts from a diachronic perspective: Aspects of the realisation of requesting and undertaking commitments in the nineteenth-century commercial community'. In Andreas H. Jucker and Irma Taavitsainen (eds.), *Speech Acts in the History of English*. Pragmatics & Beyond New Series 176. Amsterdam/Philadelphia: John Benjamins, 115–31.

Diller Hans-Jürgen, Hendrik de Smet and Jukka Tyrkkö. (2010) 'A European database of descriptors of English electronic texts'. *The European English Messenger* 19.2, 29–35.

Eelen, Gino. (2001) *A Critique of Politeness Theories*. Encounters 1. Manchester: St. Jerome.

Evans, William W. (1967) 'Dramatic use of the second-person singular pronoun in *Sir Gawain and the Green Knight*'. *Studia Neophilologica* 39.1, 38–45.

Evans, G. Blakemore (ed.). (2003) *Romeo and Juliet*. Updated edition. Cambridge: Cambridge University Press.

Fennell, Barbara A. (2001) *A History of English: A Sociolinguistic Approach*. Oxford: Blackwell.

Finkenstaedt, Thomas. (1963) *'You' and 'Thou': Studien zur Anrede im Englischen*. Berlin: Walter de Gruyter.

Fitzmaurice, Susan. (2010) 'Changes in the meaning of politeness in eighteenth-century England: Discourse analysis and historical evidence'. In Jonathan Culpeper and Daniel Z. Kadar (eds.), *Historical (Im)politeness*. Bern: Peter Lang, 87–115.

Fitzmaurice, Susan. (2016) 'Sincerity and the moral reanalysis of politeness in late modern English: Semantic change and contingent polysemy'. In Don Chapman, Colette Moore and Miranda Wilcox (eds.), *Generalizing vs. Particularizing Methodologies in Historical Linguistic Analysis*. TiEL 94. Berlin: Mouton de Gruyter, 173–201.

Ford, Martyn, and Peter Legon. (2003) *The How to Be British Collection*. Brighton: Lee Gone Publications.

Fox, Kate. (2004) *Watching the English: The Hidden Rules of English Behaviour.* London: Hodder & Stoughton.

Fries, Udo. (1985) *Einführung in die Sprache Chaucers: Phonologie, Metrik und Morphologie.* Anglistische Arbeitshefte 20. Tübingen: Niemeyer.

Fries, Udo. (1999) '"His name with laud and with dew honour rayse": A text- and pragmalinguistic study of Thomas Morley's "Introduction to Practicall Musicke" (1597)'. In Wolfgang Falkner and Hans-Jörg Schmid (eds.), *Words, Lexemes, Concepts: Approaches to the Lexicon.* Tübingen: Gunter Narr, 235–46.

Fries, Udo, and Peter Schneider. (2000) 'ZEN: Preparing the Zurich English Newspaper Corpus'. In Friedrich Ungerer (ed.), *English Media Texts Past and Present.* Pragmatics & Beyond New Series 80. Amsterdam/Philadelphia: John Benjamins, 3–24.

Gillingham, John. (2002) 'From *civilitas* to civility: Codes of manners in medieval and early modern England'. *Transactions of the Royal Historical Society* 12, 267–89.

Gossett, Suzanne. (2000) *Ben Jonson: Bartholomew Fair.* Revels Student Editions. Manchester: Manchester University Press.

Grainger, Karen. (2011) '"First order" and "second order" politeness: Institutional and intercultural contexts'. In Linguistic Politeness Research Group (eds.), *Discursive Approaches to Politeness.* Mouton Series in Pragmatics 8. Berlin: De Gruyter Mouton, 167–88.

Grainger, Karen, Zainab Kerkam, Fathia Mansor and Sara Mills. (2015) 'Offering and hospitality in Arabic and English'. *Journal of Politeness Research* 11.1, 41–70.

Grainger, Karen, and Sara Mills. (2016) *Directness and Indirectness across Cultures.* Basingstoke: Palgrave Macmillan.

Hanson, Elizabeth. (2011) 'Fellow students: Hamlet, Horatio and the Early Modern University'. *Shakespeare Quarterly* 62.2, 205–29.

Haugh, Michael, and Wei-Lin Melody Chang. (2019) '"The apology seemed (in) sincere": Variability in perceptions of (im)politeness'. *Journal of Pragmatics* 142, 207–22, https://doi.org/10.1016/j.pragma.2018.11.022.

Hogg, Richard M. (ed.). (1992) *The Cambridge History of the English Language. Volume 1: The Beginnings to 1066.* Cambridge: Cambridge University Press.

Holmes, Janet. (1984) 'Modifying illocutionary force'. *Journal of Pragmatics* 8, 345–65.

Holmes, Janet. (1988) 'Paying compliments: A sex preferential politeness strategy'. *Journal of Pragmatics* 12.4, 445–65.

Holmes, Janet. (1993) 'New Zealand women are good to talk to: An analysis of politeness strategies in interaction'. *Journal of Pragmatics* 20.2, 91–116.

Holmes, Janet. (1995) *Women, Men and Politeness.* London: Longman.

Honegger, Thomas. (2003) '"And if ye wol nat so, my lady sweete, thanne preye I thee, [...]." Forms of address in Chaucer's Knight's Tale'. In Irma Taavitsainen and Andreas H. Jucker (eds.), *Diachronic Perspectives on Address Term Systems.* Pragmatics & Beyond New Series 107. Amsterdam/Philadelphia: John Benjamins, 61–84.

Honegger, Thomas. (2004) 'Nominal forms of address in Middle English: Pet names and terms of endearment between lovers'. In Christoph Bode, Sebastian Domsch and Hans Sauer (eds.), *Anglistentag 2003. Proceedings.* Trier: Wissenschaftlicher Verlag, 39–55.

Honegger, Thomas. (2005) '"Wyʒe welcum iwys to this place" – and never mind the alliteration: An inquiry into the use of forms of address in two alliterative ME romances'. In Nikolaus Ritt and Herbert Schendl (eds.), *Rethinking Middle English: Linguistic and Literary Approaches.* Frankfurt: Peter Lang, 169–78.

Hope, Jonathan. (1994) 'The use of thou and you in Early Modern spoken English: Evidence from depositions in the Durham ecclesiastical court records'. In Dieter Kastovsky (ed.), *Studies in Early Modern English*. Berlin: Mouton de Gruyter, 141–52.

Hope, Jonathan. (2003) *Shakespeare's Grammar*. London: The Arden Shakespeare.

Hughes, Geoffrey. (1991) *Swearing: A Social History of Foul Language, Oaths and Profanity in English*. Oxford: Blackwell.

Hynes, Peter. (2004) 'Richard Steele and the genealogy of sentimental drama: A reading of *The Conscious Lovers*'. *Papers on Language and Literature* 40.2, 142–67.

Ide, Sachiko. (1989) 'Formal forms and discernment: Two neglected aspects of linguistic politeness'. *Multilingua* 8.2–3, 223–48.

Irvine, Susan. (2006) 'Beginnings and transitions: Old English'. In Lynda Mugglestone (ed.), *The Oxford History of English*. Oxford: Oxford University Press, 32–60.

Itakura, Hiroko. (2001) 'Describing conversational dominance'. *Journal of Pragmatics* 33, 1859–80.

Jacobsson, Mattias. (2002) '"Thank you" and "thanks" in Early Modern English'. *ICAME Journal* 26, 63–80.

Janicki, Karol. (1989) 'A rebuttal of essentialist sociolinguistics'. *International Journal of the Sociology of Language* 78, 93–105.

Janicki, Karol. (1990) *Toward Non-Essentialist Sociolinguistics*. Berlin: Mouton de Gruyter.

Jucker, Andreas H. (2000a) '"Thou" in the history of English: A case for historical semantics or pragmatics?' In Christiane Dalton-Puffer and Nikolaus Ritt (eds.), *Words: Structure, Meaning, Function. A Festschrift for Dieter Kastovsky*. Berlin: Mouton de Gruyter, 153–63.

Jucker, Andreas H. (2000b) 'English historical pragmatics: Problems of data and methodology'. In Gabriella di Martino and Maria Lima (eds.), *English Diachronic Pragmatics*. Naples: CUEN, 17–55.

Jucker, Andreas H. (2006a) '"Thou art so loothly and so oold also": The use of ye and thou in Chaucer's *Canterbury Tales*'. *Anglistik* 17.2, 57–72.

Jucker, Andreas H. (2006b) '"but 'tis believed that . . . ": Speech and thought presentation in early English newspapers'. In Nicholas Brownlees (ed.), *News Discourse in Early Modern Britain. Selected Papers of CHINED 2004*. Bern: Peter Lang, 105–25.

Jucker, Andreas H. (2008) 'Politeness in the history of English'. In Richard Dury, Maurizio Gotti and Marina Dossena (eds.), *English Historical Linguistics 2006. Volume II: Lexical and Semantic Change. Selected Papers from the Fourteenth International Conference on English Historical Linguistics (ICEHL 14), Bergamo, 21–25 August 2006*. Amsterdam/Philadelphia: John Benjamins, 3–29.

Jucker, Andreas H. (2010) '"In curteisie was set ful muchel hir lest": Politeness in Middle English'. In Jonathan Culpeper and Dániel Z. Kádár (eds.), *Historical (Im) politeness*. Linguistic Insights 65. Frankfurt: Peter Lang, 175–200.

Jucker, Andreas H. (2011a) 'Positive and negative face as descriptive categories in the history of English'. *Journal of Historical Pragmatics* 12.1–2, 178–97.

Jucker, Andreas H. (2011b) 'Chauser-no *The Canterbury Tales* niokeru koshou' [Terms of address in Geoffrey Chaucer's *Canterbury Tales*: A case study], translated into Japanese by Yuko Higashiizumi. In Hiroyuki Takada, Michi Shiina and Noriko Onodera (eds.), *Rekishigoyouron nyuumon: Kakono komyunikieeshonwo fukugensuru*. Tokyo: Taishukan: 130–42.

Jucker, Andreas H. (2012a) 'Changes in politeness cultures'. In Terttu Nevalainen and Elizabeth Traugott (eds.), *The Oxford Handbook of the History of English*. New York: Oxford University Press, 422–33.

Jucker, Andreas H. (2012b) '"These imputations are too common, sir": Politeness in Early Modern English dialogues: The case of Ben Jonson's *Volpone, or The Fox*'. In Gabriella Mazzon and Luisanna Fodde (eds.), *Historical Perspectives on Forms of English Dialogue*. Metodi e Prospettive. Milan: FrancoAngeli, 40–58.

Jucker, Andreas H. (2012c) '"What's in a name?": Names and terms of address in Shakespeare's *Romeo and Juliet*'. In Sarah Chevalier and Thomas Honegger (eds.), *Words, Words, Words: Philology and Beyond. Festschrift for Andreas Fischer on the Occasion of his 65th Birthday*. Tübingen: Narr Francke Attempto, 77–97.

Jucker, Andreas H. (2014) 'Courtesy and politeness in *Sir Gawain and the Green Knight*'. *Studia Anglica Posnaniensia* 49.3, 5–28.

Jucker, Andreas H. (2015) 'Höflichkeit im Theater der englischen Renaissance: Ben Jonson's *Bartholomew Fair*'. *Wolfenbütteler Renaissance-Mitteilungen* 36.2, 77–88.

Jucker, Andreas H. (2016) 'Politeness in eighteenth-century drama: A discursive approach'. *Journal of Politeness Research* 12.1, 95–115.

Jucker, Andreas H., and Joanna Kopaczyk. (2017) 'Historical (im)politeness'. In Jonathan Culpeper, Michael Haugh and Dániel Kádár (eds.), *The Palgrave Handbook of Linguistic (Im)politeness*. London: Palgrave, 433–59.

Jucker, Andreas H., and Daniela Landert. (2015) 'Historical pragmatics and early speech recordings: Diachronic developments in turn-taking and narrative structure in radio talk shows'. *Journal of Pragmatics* 79, 22–39.

Jucker, Andreas H., and Miriam A. Locher. (2017) 'Introducing *Pragmatics of Fiction*: Approaches, trends and developments'. In Miriam A. Locher and Andreas H. Jucker (eds.), *Pragmatics of Fiction*. Handbooks of Pragmatics 12. Berlin: de Gruyter, 1–21.

Jucker, Andreas H., and Larssyn Staley. (2017) '(Im)politeness and developments in methodology'. In Jonathan Culpeper, Michael Haugh and Dániel Kádár (eds.), *The Palgrave Handbook of Linguistic (im)Politeness*. London: Palgrave, 403–29.

Jucker, Andreas H., and Irma Taavitsainen. (2000) 'Diachronic speech act analysis: Insults from flyting to flaming'. *Journal of Historical Pragmatics* 1.1, 67–95.

Jucker, Andreas H., and Irma Taavitsainen. (2003) 'Diachronic perspectives on address term systems: Introduction'. In Irma Taavitsainen and Andreas H. Jucker (eds.), *Diachronic Perspectives on Address Term Systems*. Pragmatics & Beyond New Series 107. Amsterdam/Philadelphia: John Benjamins, 1–25.

Jucker, Andreas H., and Irma Taavitsainen. (2013) *English Historical Pragmatics*. Edinburgh Textbooks on the English Language. Edinburgh: Edinburgh University Press.

Jucker, Andreas H., and Irma Taavitsainen. (2014) 'Complimenting in the history of American English: A metacommunicative expression analysis'. In Irma Taavitsainen, Andreas H. Jucker and Jukka Tuominen (eds.), *Diachronic Corpus Pragmatics*. Pragmatics & Beyond New Series 243. Amsterdam: John Benjamins, 257–76.

Jucker, Andreas H., Irma Taavitsainen and Gerold Schneider. (2012) 'Semantic corpus trawling: Expressions of "courtesy" and "politeness" in the Helsinki Corpus'. In Carla Suhr and Irma Taavitsainen (eds.), *Developing Corpus Methodology for*

Historical Pragmatics. Studies in Variation, Contacts and Change in English 11. Helsinki: Research Unit for Variation, Contacts and Change in English. Available online at www.helsinki.fi/varieng/series/volumes/11/jucker_taavitsainen_schnei der/.

Kampf, Zohar, and Roni Danziger. (2018) '"You dribble faster than Messi and jump higher than Jordan": The art of complimenting and praising in political discourse'. *Journal of Politeness Research* 15.1, https://doi.org/10.1515/pr-2016-0044.

Kasper, Gabriele. (2003) 'Politeness'. In Jef Verschueren, Jan-Ola Östman, Jan Blommaert and Chris Bulcaen (eds.), *Handbook of Pragmatics*. Amsterdam: Benjamins, 1–20.

Klein, Lawrence. (1994a) *Shaftsbury and the Culture of Politeness: Moral Discourse and Cultural Politics in Early Eighteenth-Century England*. Cambridge: Cambridge University Press.

Klein, Lawrence. (1994b) '"Politeness" as linguistic ideology in late seventeenth- and eighteenth-century England'. In Dieter Stein and Ingrid Tieken-Boon van Ostade (eds.), *Towards a Standard English 1600–1800*. Topics in English Linguistics 12. Berlin: Mouton de Gruyter, 31–50.

Kleinke, Sonja, and Birte Bös. (2015) 'Intergroup rudeness and the metapragmatics of its negotiation in online discussion fora'. *Pragmatics* 25.1, 47–71.

Knappe, Gabriele, and Michael Schümann. (2006) 'Thou and ye: A collocational-phraseological approach to pronoun change in Chaucer's *Canterbury Tales*'. *Studia Anglica Posnaniensia* 42, 213–38.

Kohnen, Thomas. (2008a) 'Directives in Old English: Beyond politeness?' In Andreas H. Jucker and Irma Taavitsainen (eds.), *Speech Acts in the History of English*. Pragmatics & Beyond New Series 176. Amsterdam/Philadelphia: John Benjamins, 27–44.

Kohnen, Thomas. (2008b) 'Linguistic politeness in Anglo-Saxon England? A study of Old English address terms'. *Journal of Historical Pragmatics* 9.1, 140–58.

Kohnen, Thomas. (2011) 'Understanding Anglo-Saxon "politeness": Directive con-structions with ic wille / ic wolde'. *Journal of Historical Pragmatics* 12.1–2, 230–54.

Kohnen, Thomas. (2012) 'Performative and non-performative uses of speech-act verbs in the history of English'. In Ulrich Busse and Axel Hübler (eds.), *Investigations into the Meta-Communicative Lexicon of English: A Contribution to Historical Pragmatics*. Pragmatics & Beyond New Series 220. Amsterdam/Philadelphia: John Benjamins, 207–21.

Kohnen, Thomas. (2017) 'Non-canonical speech acts in the history of English'. *Zeitschrift für Anglistik und Amerikanistik* 65.3, 303–18.

Kong, Kenneth C. C. (1998) 'Politeness of service encounters in Hong Kong'. *Pragmatics* 8.4, 555–75.

Kopytko, Roman. (1993) *Polite Discourse in Shakespeare's English*. Poznan: Wydawnictwo Naukowe Uniwersytetu im. Adam Mickiewicza w Poznaniu.

Kopytko, Roman. (1995) 'Linguistic politeness strategies in Shakespeare's plays'. In Andreas H. Jucker (ed.), *Historical Pragmatics: Pragmatic Developments in the History of English*. Pragmatics & Beyond New Series 35. Amsterdam/ Philadelphia: John Benjamins, 515–40.

Kytö, Merja. (2010) 'Data in historical pragmatics'. In Andreas H. Jucker and Irma Taavitsainen (eds.), *Historical Pragmatics*. Handbooks of Pragmatics 8. Berlin/New York: De Gruyter Mouton, 33–67.

Lakoff, Robin. (1973) 'Language and woman's place'. *Language in Society* 2, 45–80.

Lakoff, Robin. (1975) *Language and Woman's Place*. New York: Harper & Row.

Lakoff, Robin T. (2005) 'Civility and its discontents: Or, getting in your face'. In Robin T. Lakoff and Sachiko Ide (eds.), *Broadening the Horizon of Linguistic Politeness*. Pragmatics & Beyond New Series 139. Amsterdam/Philadelphia: John Benjamins, 23–43.

Langford, Paul. (1989) *A Polite and Commercial People: England 1727–1783*. Oxford: Clarendon Press.

Langford, Paul. (2002) 'The uses of eighteenth-century politeness'. *Transactions of the Royal Historical Society* 12, 311–31.

Lass, Roger (ed.). (1999) *The Cambridge History of the English Language. Volume 3: 1476–1776*. Cambridge: Cambridge University Press.

Leech, Geoffrey N. (1983) *Principles of Pragmatics*. London: Longman.

Lehmann, Hans Martin, Caren auf dem Keller and Beni Ruef. (2006) 'ZEN Corpus 1.0'. In Roberta Facchinetti and Matti Rissanen (eds.), *Corpus-based Studies of Diachronic English*. Bern: Peter Lang, 135–55.

Leitner, Magdalena. (2013) 'Thou and you in Late Middle Scottish and Early Modern Northern English witness depositions'. *Journal of Historical Pragmatics* 14.1, 100–29.

Leitner, Magdalena, and Andreas H. Jucker. (forthcoming) 'Historical sociopragmatics'. In Michael Haugh, Dániel Z. Kádár and Marina Terkourafi (eds.), *Handbook of Sociopragmatics*. Cambridge: Cambridge University Press.

Lindsay, David W. (ed.). (1993) *The Beggar's Opera and Other Eighteenth-century Plays*. London: J. M. Dent.

Locher, Miriam. (2008) 'The rise of prescriptive grammars on English in the 18th century'. In Miriam Locher and Jürg Strässler (eds.), *Standards and Norms in the English Language*. Contributions to the Sociology of Language. Berlin: Mouton de Gruyter, 127–47.

Locher, Miriam A., and Sage L. Graham (eds.). (2010) *Interpersonal Pragmatics*. Handbooks of Pragmatics 6. Berlin/New York: De Gruyter Mouton.

Locher, Miriam A., and Richard J. Watts. (2005) 'Politeness theory and relational work'. *Journal of Politeness Research* 1, 9–33.

Lutzky, Ursula, and Jane Demmen. (2013) '*Pray* in Early Modern English drama'. *Journal of Historical Pragmatics* 14.2, 263–84.

Marks, Sylvia Kasey. (1986) '*Clarissa* as conduct book'. *South Atlantic Review* 51.4, 3–16.

Mazzon, Gabriella. (2000) 'Social relations and forms of address in the *Canterbury Tales*'. In Dieter Kastovsky and Arthur Mettinger (eds.), *The History of English in a Social Context: A Contribution to Historical Sociolinguistics*. Berlin: Mouton de Gruyter, 135–68.

Mazzon, Gabriella. (2003) 'Pronouns and nominal address in Shakespearean English: A socio-affective marking system in transition'. In Irma Taavitsainen and Andreas H. Jucker (eds.), *Diachronic Perspectives on Address Term Systems*. Pragmatics & Beyond New Series 107. Amsterdam/Philadelphia: John Benjamins, 223–49.

Mazzon, Gabriella. (2010) 'Terms of address'. In Andreas H. Jucker and Irma Taavitsainen (eds.), *Historical Pragmatics*. Handbooks of Pragmatics 8. Berlin/New York: De Gruyter Mouton, 351–76.

Meier, Andrea J. (1995) 'Passages of politeness'. *Journal of Pragmatics* 24, 381–92.

Michael, Ian. (1987) *The Teaching of English, from the Sixteenth Century to 1870*. Cambridge: Cambridge University Press.

Michel, Jean-Baptiste, Yuan Kui Shen, Aviva Presser Aiden, Adrian Veres, Matthew K. Gray, The Google Books Team, Joseph P. Pickett, Dale Hoiberg, Dan Clancy, Peter Norvig, Jon Orwant, Steven Pinker, Martin A. Nowak and Erez Lieberman Aiden. (2010) 'Quantitative analysis of culture using millions of digitized books'. *Science* 331.6014, 176–82.

Mills, Sara. (2011) 'Discursive approaches to politeness and impoliteness'. In Linguistic Politeness Research Group (eds.), *Discursive Approaches to Politeness*. Mouton Series in Pragmatics 8. Berlin: De Gruyter Mouton, 19–56.

Mills, Sara. (2017) *English Politeness and Class*. Cambridge: Cambridge University Press.

Mitchell, Bruce. (1995) *An Invitation to Old English and Anglo-Saxon England*. Oxford: Blackwell.

Mugglestone, Lynda (ed.). (2006) *The Oxford History of English*. Oxford: Oxford University Press.

Murphy, M. Lynne, and Rachele De Felice. (2018) 'Routine politeness in American and British English requests: Use and non-use of please'. *Journal of Politeness Research* 15.1, 77–100.

Mustanoja, Tauno F. (1960) *A Middle English Syntax. Part I. Parts of Speech*. Mémoires de la Société Néophilologique de Helsinki 23. Helsinki: Société Néophilologique.

Nathan, N. (1956) 'Pronouns of address in the Friar's Tale'. *Modern Language Quarterly* 17, 39–42.

Nathan, N. (1959) 'Pronouns of address in the *Canterbury Tales*'. *Mediaeval Studies* xxi, 193–201.

Neumann, Birgitt. (2011) 'Domestic tragedy: George Lillo's *The London Merchant, or The History of George Barnwell*'. In Sibylle Baumbach, Birgit Neumann and Ansgar Nünning (eds.), *A History of British Drama: Genres – Developments – Model Interpretations*. Trier: WVT Wissenschaftlicher Verlag Trier, 158–75.

Nevala, Minna. (2003) 'Family first: Address and subscription formulae in English family correspondence from the fifteenth to the seventeenth century'. In Irma Taavitsainen and Andreas H. Jucker (eds.), *Diachronic Perspectives on Address Term Systems*. Pragmatics & Beyond New Series 107. Amsterdam/ Philadelphia: John Benjamins, 147–76.

Nevala, Minna, and Anni Sairio. (2017) 'Discord in eighteenth-century genteel correspondence'. In Tanja Säily, Arja Nurmi, Minna Palander-Collin and Anita Auer (eds.), *Exploring Future Paths for Historical Sociolinguistics*. Advances in Historical Sociolinguistics 7. Amsterdam: John Benjamins, 109–27.

Nevalainen, Terttu, and Helena Raumolin-Brunberg. (1995) 'Constraints on politeness: The pragmatics of address formulae in Early English correspondence'. In Andreas H. Jucker (ed.), *Historical Pragmatics. Pragmatic Developments in the History of English*. Pragmatics & Beyond New Series 35. Amsterdam/Philadelphia: John Benjamins, 541–601.

Nevalainen, Terttu, and Heli Tissari. (2010) 'Contextualising eighteenth-century polite-ness: Social distinction and metaphorical levelling'. In Raymond Hickey (ed.), *Eighteenth-Century English: Ideology and Change*. Studies in English Language. Cambridge: Cambridge University Press, 133–58.

Newton, Sarah Emily. (1990) 'Wise and foolish virgins: "Usable fiction" and the early American conduit tradition'. *Early American Literature* 25.2, 139–67.

Nicholls, Jonathan. (1985) *The Matter of Courtesy: Medieval Courtesy Books and the Gawain-Poet*. Woodbridge: D. S. Brewer.

Novak, Maximillian E. (1979) 'The sentimentality of "The Conscious Lovers" revisited and reasserted'. *Modern Language Studies* 9.3, 48–59.

Nünning, Vera, and Ansgar Nünning. (1998) *Englische Literatur des 18. Jahrhunderts*. Uni-Wissen Anglistik, Amerikanistik. Stuttgart: Klett.

Ozoux, Mireille. (2002) 'Lecture de The Conscious Lovers de Richard Steele (1728): sémantique et éthique-le concept de "gentility" repris et revisité'. *Etudes Epistémè* 2, 159–99.

Pike, Kenneth. (1954) *Language in Relation to a Unified Theory of the Structure of Human Behavior, Part 1*. Glendale: Summer Institute of Linguistics.

Pinto, Derrin. (2011) 'Are Americans insincere? Interactional style and politeness in everyday America'. *Journal of Politeness Research* 7, 215–38.

Placencia, María Elena. (2008) 'Requests in corner shop transactions in Ecuadorian Andean and Coastal Spanish'. In Klaus P. Schneider and Anne Barron (eds.), *Variational Pragmatics: A Focus on Regional Varieties in Pluricentric Languages*. Pragmatics & Beyond New Series 178. Amsterdam/Philadelphia: John Benjamins, 307–32.

Quirk, Randolph, Sidney Greenbaum, Geoffrey Leech and Jan Svartvik. (1985) *A Comprehensive Grammar of the English Language*. London: Longman.

Raumolin-Brunberg, Helena. (1996) 'Forms of address in early English correspondence'. In Terttu Nevalainen and Helena Raumolin-Brunberg (eds.), *Sociolinguistics and Language History: Studies Based on the Corpus of Early English Correspondence*. Amsterdam: Rodopi, 167–81.

Reber, Elisabeth. (2018) Quoting in Parliamentary Question Time. A Short-term Diachronic Study of an Evidential Practice. Unpublished Habilitation thesis, University of Potsdam.

Ridealgh, Kim, and Andreas H. Jucker. (2019) 'Late Egyptian, Old English and the re-evaluation of discernment politeness in remote cultures'. *Journal of Pragmatics* 144, 56–66.

Robinson, F. N. (ed.). (1933) *The Complete Works of Geoffrey Chaucer*. Boston: Houghton Mifflin.

Romaine, Suzanne (ed.). (1998) *The Cambridge History of the English Language. Volume 4: 1776–1997*. Cambridge: Cambridge University Press.

Sato, Shie. (2008) 'Use of "please" in American and New Zealand English'. *Journal of Pragmatics* 40, 1249–78.

Searle, John R. (1969) *Speech Acts: An Essay in the Philosophy of Language*. Cambridge: Cambridge University Press.

Searle, John R. (1979) *Expression and Meaning: Studies in the Theory of Speech Acts*. Cambridge: Cambridge University Press.

Sell, Roger D. (1985) 'Tellability and politeness in "The Miller's Tale": First steps in literary pragmatics. English Studies'. *A Journal of English Language and Literature* 66.6, 496–512.

Sell, Roger D. (1991) 'The politeness of literary texts'. In Roger D. Sell (ed.), *Literary Pragmatics*. London: Routledge, 208–24.

Sell, Roger D. (2000) *Literature as Communication*. Pragmatics & Beyond New Series 78. Amsterdam/Philadelphia: John Benjamins.

Shvanyukova, Polina. (2019) 'Promoting negative politeness in nineteenth-century England: The case of letter-writing manuals'. In Annick Paternoster and Susan Fitzmaurice (eds.), *Politeness in Nineteenth-Century Europe*. Pragmatics & Beyond New Series 299. Amsterdam/Philadelphia: John Benjamins, 171–95.

Singman, Jeffrey L., and Will McLean. (1995) *Daily Life in Chaucer's England*. Westport: Greenwood.

Skeat, W. W. (ed.). (1894) *Complete Works of Geoffrey Chaucer*. Oxford.

Spencer-Oatey, Helen. (2011) 'Conceptualising "the relational" in pragmatics: Insights from metapragmatic emotion and (im)politeness comments'. *Journal of Pragmatics* 43, 3565–78.

Spencer-Oatey, Helen, and Peter Franklin. (2009) *Intercultural Interaction: A Multidisciplinary Approach to Intercultural Communication*. Research and Practice in Applied Linguistics. Houndmills, Basingstoke: Palgrave.

Sperber, Dan, and Deidre Wilson. (1981) 'Irony and the use-mention distinction'. In Peter Cole (ed.), *Radical Pragmatics*. New York: Academic Press, 295–318.

Stein, Dieter. (2003) 'Pronominal usage in Shakespeare: Between sociolinguistics and conversational analysis'. In Irma Taavitsainen and Andreas H. Jucker (eds.), *Diachronic Perspectives on Address Term Systems*. Pragmatics & Beyond New Series 107. Amsterdam/Philadelphia: John Benjamins, 251–307.

Stewart, Miranda. (2005) 'Politeness in Britain: "It's only a suggestion ... "'. In Leo Hickey and Miranda Stewart (eds.), *Politeness in Europe*. Clevedon: Multilingual Matters, 116–29.

Studer, Patrick. (2008) *Historical Corpus Stylistics: Media, Technology and Change*. London: Continuum.

Taavitsainen, Irma, and Andreas H. Jucker. (2007) 'Speech act verbs and speech acts in the history of English'. In Susan M. Fitzmaurice and Irma Taavitsainen (eds.), *Methods in Historical Pragmatics*. Berlin: Mouton de Gruyter, 107–38.

Taavitsainen, Irma, and Andreas H. Jucker. (2008) '"Methinks you seem more beautiful than ever": Compliments and gender in the history of English'. In Andreas H. Jucker and Irma Taavitsainen (eds.), *Speech Acts in the History of English*. Pragmatics & Beyond New Series 176. Amsterdam/Philadelphia: John Benjamins, 195–228.

Taavitsainen, Irma, and Andreas H. Jucker. (2010) 'Expressive speech acts and politeness in eighteenth-century English'. In Raymond Hickey (ed.), *Eighteenth-Century English: Ideology and Change*. Studies in English Language. Cambridge: Cambridge University Press, 159–81.

Taavitsainen, Irma, and Andreas H. Jucker. (2015) 'Twenty years of historical pragmatics: Origins, developments and changing thought styles'. *Journal of Historical Pragmatics* 16.1, 1–25.

Taavitsainen, Irma, and Andreas H. Jucker. (2016) 'Forms of address'. In Carole Hough (ed.). *Oxford Handbook of Names and Naming*. Oxford: Oxford University Press, 427–37.

Terkourafi, Marina. (2011) 'From Politeness1 to Politeness2: Tracking norms of im/politeness across time and space'. *Journal of Politeness Research* 7, 159–85.

Thomas, Keith. (2018) *In Pursuit of Civility: Manners and Civilization in Early Modern England*. New Haven: Yale University Press.

Tieken-Boon van Ostade, Ingrid. (2014) 'Eighteenth-century English normative grammars and their readers'. In Gijsbert Rutten, Rik Vosters and Wim Vandenbussche (eds.), *Norms and Usage in Language History, 1600–1900: A Sociolinguistic and Comparative Perspective*. Advances in Historical Sociolinguistics 3. Amsterdam: John Benjamins, 129–50.

Triandis, Harry C. (1994) *Culture and Social Behavior*. New York: McGraw Hill.

van Gelderen, Elly. (2014) *A History of the English Language*. Rev. ed. Amsterdam/ Philadelphia: John Benjamins.

van Kemenade, Ans, and Bettelou Los (eds.). (2006) *The Handbook of The History of English*. Oxford: Blackwell.

Walker, Terry. (2003) 'You and thou in Early Modern English dialogues: Patterns of usage'. In Irma Taavitsainen and Andreas H. Jucker (eds.), *Diachronic Perspectives on Address Term Systems*. Pragmatics & Beyond New Series 107. Amsterdam/Philadelphia: John Benjamins, 309–42.

Walker, Terry. (2007) *'Thou' and 'You' in Early Modern English Dialogues: Trials, Depositions, and Drama Comedy*. Pragmatics & Beyond New Series 158. Amsterdam/Philadelphia: John Benjamins.

Wallace, David. (1992) 'Bourgeois tragedy or sentimental melodrama? The significance of George Lillo's *The London Merchant*'. *Eighteenth-Century Studies* 25.2, 123–43.

Watts, Richard J. (1989) 'Relevance and relational work: Linguistic politeness as politic behavior'. *Multilingua* 8.2–3, 131–66.

Watts, Richard J. (1991) *Power in Family Discourse*. Berlin: Mouton de Gruyter.

Watts, Richard J. (1992) 'Linguistic politeness and politic verbal behaviour: Reconsidering claims for universality'. In Richard J. Watts, Sachiko Ide and Konrad Ehlich (eds.), *Politeness in Language: Studies in its History, Theory and Practice*. Berlin: Mouton de Gruyter, 43–70.

Watts, Richard J. (1999) 'Language and politeness in early eighteenth century Britain'. *Pragmatics* 9.1 Special issue 'Ideologies of Politeness', ed. Manfred Kienpointer, 5–20.

Watts, Richard J. (2000) 'Mythical strands in the ideology of prescriptivism'. In Laura Wright (ed.), *The Development of Standard English 1300–1800: Theories, Descriptions, Conflicts*. Cambridge: Cambridge University Press, 29–48.

Watts, Richard. (2002) 'From polite language to educated language: The re-emergence of an ideology'. In Richard Watts and Peter Trudgill (eds.), *Alternative Histories of English*. London and New York: Routledge, 155–72.

Watts, Richard J. (2003) *Politeness*. Key Topics in Sociolinguistics. Cambridge: Cambridge University Press.

Watts, Richard J. (2005) 'Linguistic politeness research: Quo vadis?' In Richard J. Watts, Sachiko Ide and Konrad Ehlich (eds.), *Politeness in Language: Studies in Its History, Theory and Practice*. 2nd ed. Berlin: Mouton de Gruyter, xi–xlvii.

Watts, Richard J. (2011) 'A socio-cognitive approach to historical politeness'. *Journal of Historical Pragmatics* 12.1–2, 104–32.

Watts, Richard J., Sachiko Ide and Konrad Ehlich. (1992) 'Introduction'. In Richard J. Watts, Sachiko Ide and Konrad Ehlich (eds.), *Politeness in Language: Studies in Its History, Theory and Practice*. Berlin: Mouton de Gruyter, 1–17.

Wierzbicka, Anna. (2006) 'Anglo scripts against "putting pressure" on other people and their linguistic manifestations'. In Cliff Goddard (ed.), *Ethnopragmatics: Understanding Discourse in Cultural Context*. Berlin: Mouton de Gruyter, 31–64.

Wilcockson, Colin. (1980) '"Thou" and "ye" in Chaucer's "Clerk's Tale"'. *The Use of English* 31.3, 37–43.

Young, Shirley. (2010) 'Natural manners: Etiquette, ethics, and sincerity in American conduct manuals'. In Michael Lambek (ed.), *Ordinary Ethics: Anthropology, Language and Action*. New York: Fordham University Press, 235–48.

Youths Behaviour, or Decency in Conversation amongst Men. (1663) London: W. Lee.

Index